GOLDEN STONE

GOLDEN STONE

THE UNTOLD LIFE AND TRAGIC DEATH OF BRIAN JONES

LAURA JACKSON

St. Martin's Press
New York

Library of Congress Cataloging-in-Publication Data

Jackson, Laura.
Golden Stone : the untold life and tragic death of Brian Jones /
Laura Jackson.
p.   cm.
ISBN 0-312-09820-0
1. Jones, Brian, d. 1969.   2. Rock musicians—England—Biography.
I. Title.
ML420.J754J2   1993
782.42166′092—dc20   [B]   93-5861   CIP   MN

First published in Great Britain by SMITH GRYPHON LIMITED.

First U.S. Edition: December 1993
10 9 8 7 6 5 4 3 2 1

This book is dedicated to my beloved
husband, David Jackson, whose love, support and unwavering
belief in me have made this all possible

CONTENTS

ACKNOWLEDGEMENTS

Grateful appreciation to all those I interviewed who spoke openly and movingly of Brian, many of whom expressed strongly the need for this biography. My thanks for all contributions to: Ian Anderson; Julian Mark Andrews; Pat Andrews; Raie Appleby; Bachir El Attar; Mick Avory; Ginger Baker; Chris Barber, OBE; Alan Barton; Dr Arthur Bell; Pete Boswell; Les Chaplin; Helen (Spittal) Cobby; Jonny Couvreur; Ray Davies; Keith Fordyce; Mary Hallett; Ken Hannis; Gordon Harper; Father John Heidt; David Jacobs; Alastair Johns; Glyn Johns; Julian Brian Jones; Robin Jones; Phil Kent; Violet Lawrence; Linda Lawrence Leitch; Donovan Leitch; Fred Lloyd; Gered Mankowitz; John Mansfield; Det. Chief Insp. Robert Marshall; Mick Martin; Phil May; Ronni Money; P. G. Newcombe; Bill Nile; Cherie Nutting; Harold Pendleton; Janie Perrin; Stephanie Perrin; Jill Price; Noel Redding; Robert Sandall; Sir James Savile OBE, KCSG, LLD; Volker Schlöndorff; Don Short; Dick Taverne; Bernard Taylor; Dick Taylor; David B. Thomson.

Special thanks for their co-operation and invaluable advice to: HM Coroner David Wadman; the Home Office; the Crown Prosecution Service; the Sussex Police; and Dr M. G. Henderson. Grateful thanks to my publisher, Robert Smith for his confidence and encouragement and to my skilful editor, Helen Armitage. Also to BBC TV; Channel 4 TV; LWT; Melvyn Bragg; Mark Paytress/*Record Collector*; Denis Richardson/Konk Studios; Billy Sloan/*Daily Record*; Jason Ashworth/*Gloucestershire Echo*; *Windsor Express*; Mirror Group of Newspapers; *New Musical Express*; Performing Rights Society; Derek Briggs; National Sound Archive; British Newspapers Libraries; National Union of Journalists and Mark Chambers, Bissett & Taylor for keeping me from throwing my typewriter out of the window.

PREFACE

To the world at large Brian Jones has been represented in a rigidly one-dimensional way, and it seemed that everything available on him had for too long been wrapped in an enormous cloak of sensationalism. It is true that all of us see only what we want to see, but we need to look with clearer eyes at Brian. Time moves on and there is no longer the need helplessly to cling on to the wild and wanton tales of the past. Looked at closely and calmly, Brian was a multi-talented man – a man with a profoundly complex nature. From the start he was a restless boy, on fire for life. Excess within control made him a memorable man. No one who knew him could forget his tremendous personal impact. When his excess grew out of control, it only served to enhance the mystique. Arguably Brian Jones was the most exciting man of one of the most exciting decades in living memory – the sixties.

To catch up with Brian requires the mental agility of a roller-skater, not to mention enormous resolve and resilience – for there was nothing remotely safe or predictable about him or the path of his amazing life. He brought intense pleasure to millions, while chasing fulfilment himself. He was also used and hurt deeply by many and, in turn, used and hurt others. His twenty-seven short years are a chessboard of complex moves, aided by complex players. A natural chameleon, Brian was easily the sixties most enigmatic figure. As he sprinted through life, he could have associated closely with the words of a Bob Dylan song:

I had so much left to do.
I had so little time to fail.

Brian cannot speak for himself and so far to date no one has properly spoken for him. Through my countless interviews with family, former lovers, friends and enemies alike I have tried to rectify this now.

LAURA JACKSON
SPRING 1992

xi

PROLOGUE

The concerts were rowdy affairs, trouble erupting often within the first few numbers. The very atmosphere oozed menace. Back in the clubs, Brian had caused the most aggro. Nothing had changed. He was still the most aggressive one in performance, even by his provocative stillness. Undoubtedly Mick went on to become the world's best front man, but he learned his craft by watching and copying Brian.

And Brian was unique on stage. Now he pushed an audience. His sense of recklessness communicated openly as a tangible thing, as vibrantly as the rapacious sexuality he generated so effortlessly; he would aggravate the boys to a state of fevered hatred they could not control. To say simply that Brian was incredibly exciting to watch would be to deny him his due. His tantalizing body language whipped girlish screams into howling hysteria. His playing was a lethal fusion of sensuality and aggression; his sinuous, blatantly suggestive gestures a natural extension of him which made Mick's new-found fad of tossing about his untidy clump of hair look very tame. The effect was dynamite which often exploded right in Brian's face.

Boys watching him on stage found their hands clenched in fists of rage until, driven too far, they would scramble madly over the parapet

1

determined to pulverize him. With the first over the top, more would follow and the Stones would have to stop playing and start trading punches with their guitars still slung about them. It wasn't uncommon for Keith, brawling on the left, to glance across and see Brian taking on three fans at a time. Though not tall, and with a build as slim as a reed, Brian had a compact frame with powerful shoulders and legs, and he was incredibly – deceptively – strong. Even so, he finished many a gig by pressing an ice pack to a very sore face.

ONE

SAX, SEX AND SOLITUDE

B rian Jones didn't enjoy defiance. He was driven not by a desire to hurt those close to him, but by the powerful urges within himself to explore and release his talents. The repercussions of his mutiny left him isolated throughout his life – not alone, but incredibly lonely.

He was born Lewis Brian Hopkin-Jones on 28 February 1942, the eldest of three children, one of whom, Pamela, died tragically young at the age of two. His second sister Barbara was just four years his junior. As a child Brian was exquisitely beautiful, with a shock of startling blond hair inherited from his mother Louise, a local piano teacher, and captivating aquamarine eyes. Born in the middle of the Second World War, he was too young to recall huddling with Louise in air-raid shelters as German bomber planes droned over Cheltenham on their way to the vital British wartime base at Bristol. Instead, his earliest recollections were of playing with his sister, and – the centre of his world – his pet tabby cat Rollader. Why he chose that name for her, no one knows, but he was a child who had a special affinity with animals; utterly devoted to each other, he and Rollader went everywhere together.

Boisterous and energetic he soon became his own person. According to his mother, even from early on he had never liked to act like everyone else. This was a trait that would grow stronger throughout his life and lead him, at one of his lowest points ever – in 1967 – to confide to a psychiatrist that uniformity in males frightened him: different was Brian's stamp. Initially it is probably true to say that his individuality was thrust upon him through conditions beyond his control: poor health as a child. When he was four he developed croup, which left him prone to bronchitis, and asthma, the latter a chronic affliction which certainly plagued him as a boy, but when adult seemed to develop into a more nervous asthma, induced at moments of high stress.

Home was Ravenswood, 335 Hatherley Road in Cheltenham, Gloucestershire, a traditional provincial house with white-washed walls, single bay window downstairs and up, and red lozenge brickwork framing the front door. In front of the house there was an island of grass and trees, perfect for kids to congregate and play. Yet there were times, particularly in summer or after a family trip to the beach, which invariably sent him to bed wheezing and coughing. He would have difficulty breathing, so badly sometimes he was afraid he wasn't going to get his breath back at all. Then he would have to go and sit quite separate from his friends with his back to a tree and just watch the fun carrying on without him while he slowly recovered. According to Louise, this enforced isolation turned him into a dreamer.

Perhaps it did start then, but Brian was rapidly beginning to show that his was a highly fertile mind. Creatively he was always on the boil and in his early days it didn't take much to stimulate him. He loved train exhibitions, adored being overawed by the enormous locomotives and, once home, would spend hours duplicating their design in remarkable detail, his photographic memory pushing his hand over page and page of his drawing books. It was this interest in transport which would give him his initial link years later with one of his early mentors, John Appleby, who became his lifelong friend. It also prompted his father Lewis, an aeronautical engineer with one of Cheltenham's biggest employers Dowty & Co., to make him the toy wooden bus which he loved to push about the carpet even later, as a young man, on his trips home.

4

Despite his blond angelic looks, Brian was something of a rogue. There lurked in him an inveterate daredevil and his play wasn't always conventional: he enjoyed reconstructing mock crashes. In itself this is hardly unique – young boys revel in this kind of play – but Brian wouldn't stop there. He would want the resulting fiery explosion too. Phil Kent, himself a musician who later went into recording, remembers the playmate who was daring enough literally to play with fire. He explains how,

> *Risking his dad catching him, Brian would take a baking tray, heap on whatever came to hand – usually Airfix models – and create the crash. Then with some pinched matches, he'd set it alight. For just those few illicit seconds as the flames blazed, there was this little drama going on before our eyes.*

For a boy who donned a surplice of a Sunday and masqueraded as a choir boy, such behaviour was something of an eye opener.

When Brian was six, Louise started him off on his first piano lessons with the school's music teacher, Grace Stone, and a more natural pupil would have been hard to find. He was inherently musical and though his mother taught him to read music, deep down it was recognized that Brian's aptitude was exceptional. Instinctively, he bypassed the conventional routes and found his own variations and short cuts. From the piano, it was an easy transition to the recorder and beyond that the clarinet. Brian went on to master all the reed instruments by ear and intuition, sometimes stumbling upon melodies which surprised even himself. There wasn't a music teacher who could keep up with him and so pronounced was his talent that at one stage his father thought he might be destined for a career as a classical musician. But the writing on the wall spoke of a different language, though if Brian had set his sights thus, there is no doubt that today he would rank among the best of them, for it was becoming clear that whatever he decided to do, he invariably achieved, for good or ill.

By 1947 he had started school, enrolled as a fee-paying pupil at Dean Close Junior in Cheltenham, where it didn't take long for his personality to make an imprint on his teachers. Throughout his school years he deeply detested the regulation of wearing school uniform and 'though we'd row him for it,' says his mother, 'he would still hide his shorts and blazer so that I literally couldn't dress him.' In fact Brian was just discovering that growing up was full of pitfalls. Never a gawky boy, at nine though he went through that painfully self-conscious stage, that afflicts all children, when he suddenly hated the way he looked. This wasn't helped by the advent of the dreaded specs, big round rimless ones. Like the uniform, if he could have got away without wearing them, he would have, but he needed them for his school work and, alerted by his parents, his teachers made sure they stayed on his face.

The second master of Dean Close Junior then was Gordon Harper and he remembers the young Jones very well.

Brian was a wiry little boy with very fair hair and large round glasses, like the Milky Bar Kid. It was before the days of universal christian names, and he was known to me and the other masters as Jones LBH. We needed the initials to distinguish him from another Jones in the same form. Brian, though, was a far stronger, more independent character who had, however, quite an amount of cheeky charm which he used most effectively on the female members of staff. My wife was matron at Dean Close, and Brian would always help her distribute the buns at morning break, his reward being all the currants left at the bottom of the tray.

I taught him English and considered him outstanding in composition; an opinion I shared with his previous teacher in the preparatory department who remarked on his ability even from as early an age as seven.

Brian stayed at Dean Close until he was eleven when he sat the eleven-plus examination then used to assess the intellectual capacity of a child and which apparently separated the sheep from the goats. But Brian had no worries about passing and sailed through with flying colours, earning himself entry to the classy Pates Grammar School down in the exclusive promenade district of town, an achievement guaranteed to please his parents very much. The headmaster of Pates Grammar in 1953 was Dr Arthur Bell, who described Brian as the first boy he knew who deserved the term 'intelligent rebel'. 'Brian was a very clever boy,' he stresses, 'but introverted, withdrawn, with a pasty face and with his father on his back all the time. He wasn't a bad lad.'

For all that, Brian's stay there was to prove the school's most controversial. As he charged through his adolescent years and galloped into maturity, his character growth kept apace. From its seed of individuality, his rebellious streak had flourished and was daily finding new ways to express itself; ways which led to him constantly cooling his heels outside Dr Bell's study door. It seemed he just couldn't help himself; he bucked the system every chance he got.

Scholastically, Brian was brilliant. His capacity to absorb and store knowledge was phenomenal, and even though, according to his headmaster, they had great difficulty in getting him to knuckle down in class, he could do so if forced. His IQ was an impressive 135, but he was still very much a square peg in a round hole. When summing Brian up later, his hometown friend Richard Hattrell recalls, 'He was a rebel without a cause, but when it came to examinations he was brilliant!'

But, of course, anarchy could not be tolerated. Grammar-school life was an extremely strict regime with no scope for disorder, certainly not on the scale of which Brian presented it. Such potent chaos had to be stamped out and the school did their best to do so. Twice they imposed sanctions on him – once admonishing him for campaigning against the school rule of wearing straw boaters in the summer and mortar-boards in the winter (Brian's unforgivable sin being to use his mortar-board as a boomerang until, as planned, it fell to bits), then suspending him, this time for leading a revolt against the prefects. The week's suspension was supposed to be a salutory lesson to Jones LBH. In fact, it only made things worse, as Brian had a whale of a time, swimming daily at the Cheltenham Lido, and returned to the school turf a hero.

Brian's parents were mortified at his suspension. Lewis felt the school had gone about disciplining his son in the wrong way, but then Lewis's rapport with Dr Bell could hardly be considered agreeable. Dr Bell reveals that 'Brian's father was forever turning up in my study, usually unannounced, with complaints. Once he demanded that I get his boy to get his hair cut, which of course had nothing to do with me. But it was always that sort of thing.'

At home his parents would sit down with Brian and ask him sternly why they were forever receiving complaints about him, to which Brian would reply coolly: 'They are only teachers. They've never done anything.' He would be so calm and logical in his response that it was hard for Lewis to know how to combat it.

If others found him difficult, for Brian himself, it was a very confusing time. He was extremely conscious of the barrier which by now existed between him and his parents, and communication had been dwindling steadily for some time. Although he was intelligent enough to work out where he was going wrong in his parents' eyes, he also knew that to conform to being the boy they envisaged meant denying his own impulses and needs. This dilemma was expressed as defiant mischief, yet his awareness that he was causing ructions not only for himself but also for the family did not cheer him.

In BBC Radio 4's *A Story of our Time* which profiled Brian, Lewis had this to say about his son:

Up to a certain point Brian was a perfectly normal, contented little boy, who was well behaved and was well liked. Well liked, I suppose, because he was well behaved. He did his studies and he was quite a model school boy. Then there came this peculiar change in his early teens. At the time, I suppose he began to become a man, where he began to get some resentment of authority. It's something we hear an awful lot about now – less about then. But it was becoming apparent in him.

He seemed to have firstly a mild rebellion against authority, which unfortunately became stronger as he grew older. It was a rebellion against parental authority, and it was certainly a rebellion against school authority. He often used to ask, Why should he do something he was told, just because the person who was telling him was older?

This was a sentiment unlikely to warm any parental heart. But the trouble with Brian by no means began and ended here. His fractious rejection of blind obedience was but a symptom, and more fundamental differences at home were creating and widening the chasm between him and his parents – and others in authority – all the time. At the core of this strife lay one thing: Brian's determined departure from the kind of music of which his parents approved and had trained him to play and appreciate, to jazz which, in his father's words, 'became an absolute religion with him, always coming first'.

Here, there was no give and take. For Lewis and Louise, this new direction was something to be blocked at every turn. For Brian, though, already a brilliant guitarist at twelve, it was time to take a stand. With an outright flouting of parental orders, he stopped practising classical pieces on the piano and clarinet altogether in favour of listening to the kind of music his parents not only loathed, but vociferously made it known so. Brian dug in his heels and matters escalated badly when two years later, having initiated himself into the music of Charlie 'Bird' Parker, who could make a saxophone sing, he sold the clarinet his folks had given him and bought a second-hand alto saxophone. In the teeth of furious opposition he would disappear into his bedroom, to play it behind closed doors. Of a summer's night his aghast neighbours heard the first shaky but determined strains of the sax wafting towards them over their regimentally clipped hedges. They were soon to realize the direction in which the teenage Jones was heading.

.   .   .

If his time at home on the sax was a battle, outside life was different as Brian had found an outlet for his breakaway music by playing with a local skiffle group. Among other things he played washboard, assuming he hadn't lost his vital thimble; but at that point it didn't matter in any case as all the kids were just messing about. Later though Brian tightened up his act when he became good enough to play sax with local bands belting out the trad jazz of Chris Barber and Humphrey Lyttleton.

Meanwhile, back in class, Brian's outrageousness was getting out of hand and proving disruptive to his fellow pupils, who alarmingly were drawing inspiration from his antics. One of his classmates Peter Watson once recalls the time Brian turned up in class wearing football boots, maintaining they were comfier than shoes and remembering how 'Brian said it was boring to drink regulation milk at break, so he started the fashion of drinking brown ale instead. It became a whole fashion to drink brown ale at break instead of milk.' Another classmate Colin Drew remembers the time he and Brian were each given half a crown (12½p) by their teacher to go into town instantly and get their shocking shoulder-length hair cut. They both came back with ten Woodbines instead.

These antics hardly endeared Brian to his masters. In today's world, hot on child psychology, he would be diagnosed as hyperactive, put on special diets and given some space to breathe. In those days he was seen as a flat-out troublemaker, with a capital T, who revelled in being insubordinate for the pure hell of it. Perhaps in part they were right. Dr Bell did say that, 'As far as his masters were concerned? Well, they were his natural enemies, full stop!' But again, it was more complicated than that.

At home, time was no healer. The older his sister Barbara became, and the more conventional and placid she proved, the wilder Brian appeared and the more estranged he felt, hurt by his need to compete with his sibling and bewildered by trying to establish his identity. Indubitably stirred into this cauldron was also his great sense of restlessness, his need to spice up life and find ways to let off steam. The obvious and socially legitimate place for him to have done this would have been on the sports field, but Brian hated sport – although he excelled at a wide range of activities from table-tennis to judo, and swimming, being a very strong swimmer and an even better diver. 'It wasn't the swimming as such,' explains his mother, 'it was the mad dash up the slippery rungs of the ladder to the diving board that grabbed his attention.' But unlike most children who tend to like what they are good at, Brian rejected sport as a waste of energy. He said once:

> I just couldn't take to games, don't really know why. Except that all that running around for no real reason seemed a waste of time. I skived off whenever it was possible, and my regrets were that I simply had to turn up and play on some occasions. But the funny thing was, that almost despite my own attitude I wasn't bad at badminton. At least there was a bit of action at that sport. Mostly though, it was just that I couldn't stand being bored.

The one thing that Brian had no time to be now, or at any time in the future, was bored. For, as if life weren't complicated enough already, badminton by now was not the only exercise he was getting. Immediately adjacent to Pates Grammar stood the very exclusive Girls' Grammar School. Come mid-morning break the swing doors would part and out would run the sweet and sheltered Cheltenham fillies, frolicking and frisking on the grass, beneath the watchful eyes of the senior boys across the way.

During their own break, having stampeded for prime position at the window to ogle the forest of firm thighs, fervently praying for a helpful breeze to inch a passing gymslip just a shade higher, the boys were teased and tantalized to fever pitch; their young sexual taste buds invoking fantasy upon fantasy, the boasts bandied about grew more outlandish as each boy tried hard to up his standing in the eyes of his mates. But what the other boys were content to brag about, Brian was already doing.

Every boy in his grade knew that of the select few who had actually got beyond the grope-'n'-grapple stage, Brian Jones was among them. Further more, it was even whispered that he scorned the contraceptives which any senior worth his salt insisted on flashing in his wallet. If Brian was tackled about it, he would rap back, 'Bareback's the best!' His mates didn't know whether to believe his wickedly lascivious yet impishly innocent smile, and even when he did – as all boys do at that unkind age – boast ungallantly of a conquest or two, still he had the knack of masking his confession by drawing back at the last second behind an intriguing air of mystery which left them guessing. Common sense said he was bluffing, but then with Jones you could never tell.

In fact Brian with his who-dares-wins motto, really was raiding those maidenly preserves in all-too-handy proximity. By this time he was a promiscuously good-looking guy. From the cheeky charm which had so easily won over matron at Dean Close, he had perfected his precocious appeal into a lethal art. And more. He had discovered just how potent this natural asset was: like Lord Byron he was mad, bad and dangerous to know and from time immemorial women have found this an irresistible allure.

For most girls of course it was one thing to dream of dicing with danger but another actually to go the distance. It was definitely more fun to flirt. Meeting Brian in secret, against school rules, he was considered highly desirable, but at the same time most girls were scared to death of his volatile directness and appeal to their baser instincts. Some, though, proved undaunted and in time, inevitably, things came unstuck. It was, after all, mere reckless folly carried out with the blinkered vision of one young and wayward boy and an equally wayward girl. Every sense in Brian was overdeveloped for his

11

age, be it intellectual, musical or physical. Sexually he was already highly sensual and curious just to find his way. His girlfriend, just as curious was determined, like him to know no better.

The news when it broke – that a fourteen-year-old pupil of the select Girls' Grammar was pregnant and Brian Jones named as father – hit harder than a ten-ton bomb. The fact that his mates now knew beyond doubt that he hadn't been fooling them was of little moment. They were shocked. As indeed was the whole of Cheltenham: scandal like this was unknown then and at once everyone began to consider how it might redound on them, and on to whom they might deflect it and attach most blame. For Lewis and Louise it was a catastrophe, as it was for the shattered parents of the girl. In utter disgrace Brian had no option but to drop out of school and try to ride the storm. His first thought was for his girlfriend to have an abortion, but that was not to be. The girl, by now his ex, refused to have anything more to do with him and insisted on having her baby – a son, who was later adopted. But the ripples of alienation were strong and not likely to die down overnight.

Brian felt utterly exposed. His school friends were sufficiently sobered by the incident to be frightened of associating with him. They backed off, condemnation writ large in their eyes. At home his position was completely untenable: there could be no support or sympathy for what he had done and everyone, from his next-door neighbour out-wards – in a pulsating spiral choking the whole of Cheltenham – was speaking about him. It was a very big deal and Brian could hardly bear its weight.

Having quit school he now faced the daunting prospect of trying to find a job in this unhealthy atmosphere. Academically he was extremely well qualified, having attained nine GCE O-Levels, and Advance Level passes in both chemistry and physics; he could have walked into university with ease. But, at the same time, and of considerably more interest to him, he was already an exceptionally fine guitarist, pianist and saxophonist. In time he would play sax semi-professionally with a local Duane Eddy-style combo the Ramrods, and jazz would move over for a new love – the raw and raunchy rhythm and blues.

For now, though, he was the local pariah, shunned and pilloried from all sides, and it is not hard to understand why he associated so closely with the mournful wailing sounds of a music which to him precisely mirrored his mounting frustration. Already his only love, music, was his only friend.

TWO

YOUNG, GIFTED AND STUCK

Realistically Brian was finished in Cheltenham – at least for a while. Secret arrangements had been made hastily between the two sets of parents, as his girlfriend conveniently melted from the scene. As the unscrupulous seducer, all eyes were focused on him. What was he to do? The solution was severe: he was encouraged to leave town, even the country, a wish echoed by his family. Brian realized he had no choice in the matter when suddenly his girlfriend's father took seriously ill and the pressure on him to leave town, already enormous, intensified. Virtually no one would speak to him. More than ever his girlfriend refused to see him and he was told he would never be allowed to see the baby he had fathered. With some money, clothes and his precious £3.00 guitar – recently purchased – he left home, ostensibly to see the world, in truth to hitch-hike through Scandinavia and Germany, scratching a bare living.

This episode in his life scared the hell out of him and possibly the only person to come close to guessing just how frightened he felt was the girl with whom he would soon fall in love: Pat Andrews. As Pat says:

It was very hard on Brian. He was too young for something like that. He told me harrowing stories of things that'd happened in Germany and, though he wouldn't say it, I sensed his unhappiness. I mean he couldn't speak any of the languages, he'd never been away from home before and here he was thrust out on his own. It's not that Brian wouldn't have been open to an experience like that. But it was the circumstances. It just wasn't right!

Right or wrong, Brian was stuck with an itinerant lifestyle for a while. Fighting back a natural desire to panic, and eking out his small cash reserve, he started to sing and play in bars and bistros, night after night brassing his case in den after den, facing up to the less salubrious side of life, his wits of necessity sharpening as the weeks passed.

When he judged enough weeks had gone by to allow tempers to cool he made his way back home, but the months of roughing it had wrought some changes. He was still good-looking – perhaps more so for the worldly glint in his eyes – and appeared extremely laid back in jeans, open-neck shirt and sweater, his luxuriant blond hair at this point still cut conventionally short, very much typifying the new youth of the day. It was inwardly, however, where he was really different and, if he had been independently strong-minded before, he was an even freer agent now. Having stood on his own two feet, he knew he could hack it alone, and with the excessive liberalism he had encountered abroad his contempt for the Cheltonian breed had deepened.

Back in town though there had been some changes too. As the new coffee bar craze had swept westward from London in the mid-fifties, by 1960 Cheltenham was brimful of in-places to hang out. Places like the Patio, the Aztec, the El Flam and, most popular of all, the Barbeque/Waikiki in Queen's Circus. To the older generation they were looked on as seedy joints, run by socially depraved misfits. Yet, to the teenagers, in the words of one of Brian's friends Pete Boswell, 'The Barbeque/Waikiki was the place used by all the people who mattered in Cheltenham at that time.' In style it was the typical coffee bar, complete with juke box and fruit machine, partitioned tables with high fixed cushioned seats and no leg room down one side, and a long narrow shelf table with stools down the other. Here Brian would hang out with his crowd, scoffing burgers and cokes and generally killing time by

15

talking music, surveying the skirts and finding out what was on at Filby's that night.

Filby was Mrs N.E. Filby whose address at 38 Priory Street would become synonymous with uproarious parties, and the place to which all jazz bands gravitated after their gigs, despite perhaps having to travel miles to get there – big names like Lonny Donegan, Terry Lightfoot, Acker Bilk, the Temperance Seven and Tommy Steele. It was quite unique. As John Appleby has written in his excellent book, *38 Priory Street and All That Jazz:* 'It's my belief that Mrs Filby did as much as, if not more than, any individual organization in town to launch Cheltenham's younger generation on the sea of life, simply by throwing open her door to hundreds of young people.'

Priory Street was an elegant tree-lined residential backwater off London Road and Number 38 was the last house but one of the terraced three-storey buildings, with its distinctive primrose-yellow front door. All the action took place in the large oak-panelled basement, made more roomy once the billiard table got the heave in favour of an upright piano, a microphone and a tiny tape recorder, and as a kind of co-operative youth-club-cum-basement-jazz club Brian was hardly away from the place. With its garlic-laced cheese dip, free-flowing fruity punch and trad jazz belting out full blast, it had a carnival atmosphere which appealed to him greatly, especially since it also allowed him to dodge the growing hassle at home.

It wasn't that Brian didn't appreciate his parents' concern that he wouldn't settle down, but the mere thought of becoming a nine-to-fiver spooked him beyond belief and despite their incessant nagging he avoided the word job like the plague. With no regular wage coming in, he depended largely on his folks' forking out to let him exist, although by 1960 he began playing with a local jazz band the Cheltone Six for a small fee and was more than happy to channel all his energies into that. That and, of course, the ladies. Rather more experienced by now Brian had been picking up the girls with consummate ease, though at the same time careful, after his schooltime romance, to steer clear of anything steady. That was until he met Pat Andrews, a bright outgoing and extremely attractive sixteen year old.

Pat herself, although born in Cheltenham, was part of an evacuee family of Londoner parents and hadn't had it easy in town. 'Well, there we were,' she explains, 'working class, but brought up in a snob part of town. We felt stuck in no man's land most of the time.' Although clever, Pat like so many others at that time didn't have the money to go on to college and in her own words she was as a result 'starved of education'. But she was resilient. 'I looked to others to learn from,' she confesses. 'I'd look for intelligence in the people I went around with.'

It was Brian's brain rather than his body which first attracted Pat to him, although she wasn't totally impervious to the magnetic drag of his steel blue eyes.

Yeah, I thought he was nice looking even though he was short. Well he wasn't short-short. He was taller than me. But he wasn't a hulking six-footer. But he was intelligent, really clever. He also listened. You see that was the beauty about Brian. He wouldn't just spout off. He wanted a feedback – to listen to other people.

Brian, though not a fan of blind dates, reluctantly had agreed with a friend to chance this one, unaware that he'd been built up to his date as something of a challenge. Pat remembers how:

It was some mutual mates who did it. They described Brian to me as a 'bit of a loner, an oddball, with a shady reputation'. And I thought, oh, yes? This could be interesting! Blimey, when I got my first glimpse of him I thought no way!! God, he was wearing a Harris tweed suit like my dad would wear, looking dead out of place in the coffee bar.

An inauspicious first impression, but one which rapidly evaporated as soon as Brian got talking to her. The topic of conversation was always music in those days and on this Brian was in a class of his own. Pat continues:

I couldn't believe it. He was like a sheet without starch before, then suddenly he was full of starch! A 40-watt bulb had just suddenly glowed to 140-watt! It was amazing. The energy Brian radiated had to be experienced first hand even to half begin to grasp. He had an incredible feel for music and an even more incredible burning desire to play it. It was something totally unique to Brian. Music came first and foremost and everything else was very much a poor second.

Perhaps – but something clicked that first date. Coming up to Christmas 1960, their romance would grow to span the most formative years of Brian's career and their affair would prove to be a volatile one. Today Pat readily admits he was not the easiest of men to understand.

17

He was so up and down. Seventy-five per cent of the time Brian was
miserable because he was so thwarted musically at home. He felt
deeply that he got no encouragement and it was so frustrating for him
because music just ate away inside him.

.   .   .

The hassle at home let up when, also just before Christmas, Brian did
the decent thing at last and got a job – although it was hardly the kind of
which his parents approved. He worked as a coalman, lugging heavy
sacks of coal on his broad back round to people's houses, ending up at
the end of the day with black dust coating his clothes and hair,
streaking his handsome young face. As an ex-grammar school boy from
Hatherley, this was not something to be advertised to the neighbours,
and Brian had to wash and change in a friend's house before making his
way home, supposedly from the office. This elaborate charade to keep
up appearances, though he hated it, lasted as long as he worked the
lorry.

His next stint at earning a living was in a factory. He had to wait
each morning at a pick-up point for his lift with the other men in the
works' van, and it was then, because of an incident early one morning
when his van was involved in an accident, that Pat met his parents for
the first time. In the smash, Brian was thrown about and nastily shaken
up, lucky to escape with a banged knee and a bashed-out front tooth.
En route to the dentist to have his tooth screwed back in, bruised and
bedraggled he called into Boots the chemist, where Pat worked, to ask
her to come to his house that night as he was too shaken to pick her up.
So far to date Brian had never taken Pat home to meet his parents; from
past experience of taking mates home he knew she would fail the acid
test. No one ever seemed to be good enough, and he had wanted to
spare her any hurt. That night, however, he felt too lousy to cope,
something he must have regretted the instant he introduced Pat to his
parents who received her with a politeness born of formality. As he
knew she would, Pat, coming from a madcap loving family herself,
found his set up at home most peculiar, in particular, the fastidious way
his mother acted:

It was – sterile, you might say, – I mean all very proper. But no
feeling. She showed me in saying she'd done Brian and I a tea. The

18

*room was spotless with a buffet formally laid out under starched
cloths. I didn't know what to think. All I could think of was, here was
Brian feeling like death with an aching blooded mouth, and somehow
the performance of 'taking tea' still had to go on – cucumber
sandwiches, the lot.*

*They didn't like me. I knew that right away, even before they
asked where I worked. When I said Boots, I felt the physical chill. No
one said it, but it was clear. Forget it, honey, not good enough. His
mother went on about his previous girlfriend and all that, but I didn't
take it to heart. All I cared about was that Brian was standing
watching all this – weighing it up. I felt for him.*

No amount of disapproval, however, could dissuade Brian from
Pat. Their relationship was by now an intimate one, and Pat was very
much part of his life. She took a keen interest in his music, not just to
please him but because she believed in him and was also keen on music
herself. Her open, eager mind fascinated him and, when he could, he
taught her a lot. In turn, Brian learned from Pat: there was no pretence
in her, she called a spade, a spade, and though her equally strong
personality caused them spectacular rows, there was a quality in her
capable of reining him in, to which part of him responded.

Musically he was going from strength to strength. He had left the
Cheltone Six and was playing alto sax now with a new group called the
Ramrods, which was good enough to be attracting some local fame.
They rehearsed at 38 Priory Street and Brian would take Pat along with
him to watch. By then an acknowledged authority on music, he was
often the centre of lively debates on the various merits of one musician
and style or another. His uncanny perception, not to mention tolerance, was widely respected and already his vision, which would forever
stretch his insatiably inquisitive mind continually to break new
ground, was starting to show. At this point he was heavily into Johnny
Cash, Ray Charles and his favourite Julian 'Cannonball' Adderley. He
played breathtaking guitar, increasingly forming his own style, and if
he wasn't playing music, he was talking it. Even at work he would be
thinking it, always scheming his way towards pushing it along. As Pat
says:

*Brian without music would be like a man without arms. When he was
low on money, I'd give him some and it was always for things like*

19

guitar strings. Because of that, people have said that he used me. But it was nothing like that. I wanted to help him and he let me. Where's the crime in that? To understand Brian you had to grasp the depth of his drive. Simple as that.

Life never seemed simple to Brian. Problems at home were worsening again, as he felt continually under one pressure or another and he was becoming prone to dark moods. Though he confided in Pat as much as he allowed himself, by nature he was very private and kept his feelings locked up. Consequently he could be very unpredictable. He also had a temper, although when he tried to throw his weight about he didn't have it always all his own way:

We rowed a lot. We parted a lot too. I can't count the times I walked out on him and it was always Brian who came to me to patch it up. I'm not saying I wouldn't have gone to him the next day, but I didn't get the chance to. He always came to me within hours of our falling out to say sorry. Brian knew I wouldn't pull a fast one on him. He knew he'd get the truth from me, even if he didn't like it.

At the root of most of their arguments were other boys. Brian was desperately insecure of himself; he didn't see himself as being anything special and lived in fear that Pat would fancy someone else. This would spill out as fiendish jealousy over the slightest thing and on occasions he would vent it physically: 'Oh, when he lost his temper, you had to look out,' Pat confesses. 'He never lifted a hand to me, but boy he could be violent. We both could. We'd chuck things at each other, literally anything that came to hand including our shoes.'

Yet, Brian didn't help to assuage any jealousy Pat might have felt entitled to express when their roles were reversed. To his surprise, the Ramrods were going down a storm, and he found himself their main attraction as he stepped off stage to a growing clutch of eye-batting admirers who would immediately form a circle around him. Even if Pat were there, or perversely at times because Pat was there, he wasn't averse to casting an experienced and appreciative eye over them. Not surprisingly, he would have to face the music from Pat on the way home.

By now Brian had changed jobs again, this time to something more suited to his intellect – the architects' department of Gloucestershire County Council where he had a post as a junior assistant. His parents were pleased and, so, on paper, were his bosses. But from first setting foot inside the place, Brian detested the work. He knew by now there just wasn't a job on earth he was ever going to like and his attitude betrayed him at every turn.

He worked alongside P. G. Newcombe, according to whom it would be a gross misrepresentation to say that Brian actually worked there: 'He was very often late, or sometimes just didn't arrive at all.' But the beef went deeper than that. His lack of commitment spread itself thick when once Brian persuaded a council colleague to stand as guarantor for a new overcoat from the menswear chain of Burtons. Being totally untrammelled with any sense of responsibility to the man, the small matter of making regular repayments fast went to the wall and inevitably Brian defaulted. The colleague ended up feeling conned as finally he found himself stumping up for the full cost of the coat, about £30 which in 1961 was a fortune. This, again, came down to Brian's total single-mindedness: he allowed no room – felt no responsibility – for anything now but his music and whatever trappings it required. The man Brian skinned is still waiting to this day for his £30: 'It made no difference when he was famous,' complains Newcombe. 'The colleague wrote to him but never got so much as an acknowledgement.' He continues in another vein about how Brian 'tried to get into the Cheltenham School of Architecture but was unsuccessful, and I do not think it was because of his academic background.'

His school chum, Pete Boswell, however, was more direct than Newcombe: 'It was rumoured,' he reveals, 'that the reason Brian was refused was on the grounds of his reputation with women.'

Still, despite hating every second of it, Brian was giving the regular life its shot. He knew his folks desired this of him and, trying to live up to their expectations, he hung on in there at work. Something he found impossible to do any more at home.

His relationship with Barbara, from being close and solid as children, had become brittle as they had grown older. Partly because Brian was seen as a negative influence on his younger sister, his parents had decided they should protect her from him, though partly this crisis of confidence stemmed from within Brian himself. He had felt an outsider at home for many years now, never willing to conform, and with the path his life had already taken, there was slim chance that he ever would. His family spoke a different language from his own and he did not know how to translate. Short of a turnabout on their part, to accept him for himself, the relationship was never going to work. Finally accepting this, he left home and was never to return on any permanent basis.

Brian, however, could not divorce himself completely from his family. No matter how tense relations were, he would never have wanted that, and his mother and father, though having failed to accept their radical son's individuality, in their own way did not want that either. The three of them were to orbit some form of fragile negotiation for the rest of Brian's life; sadly, it seems, only making some real inroads when it was almost too late. Years after Brian's death, Lewis talking of their entrenched resistance conceded:

> *But then, of course, in time he proved us wrong, and I will always say to his credit that he never once came home and said, 'I told you so.' He only said with a rather wry smile, 'Well, I haven't done so bad, Dad, have I?'*

Unfortunately, the many crucial times Brian had yearned for that warm tolerance, it hadn't been there.

.   .   .

Initially Brian took a room with Pat's married sister, but the nine months he stayed with the Taylors turned out to be turbulent, eventually producing acrimony on both sides only worsened when he fell four weeks behind with the rent. At this point, Mr Taylor kicked him out to find his own place: a flat in Selkirk Street. He needed a flatmate and Pete Boswell almost moved in with him, until a friend's sister, sent to inspect it, knocked that idea on the head by declaring it unsuitable. In the end Brian shared with an architectural student called Graham Ride who, like him, was an alto-saxophonist. Pleased to have the company of a kindred spirit, especially since Graham's allegiances, like his own, had jumped from trad jazz to the rawer, less disciplined music called rhythm and blues, Brian was in his element.

His new passion was all eclipsing. He would sit for hours, enraptured by black artists such as Muddy Waters, Bo Diddley and Jimmy Reed, and soon discovered he had a feel, a real feel, for the music. It was forever to remain the corner-stone of his life and destined later to stamp its seal all over the Rolling Stones' most memorable recordings. It was through listening to this music that Brian taught himself the blues.

How to play pure blues was a closely guarded secret. On stage musicians, particularly white blues artists, were even known to turn their hands away to hide their fingers. To master blues from records was a considerable feat, but Brian's zest was unflagging and by now he had added Howlin' Wolf and Elmore James to his growing list of heroes. His latest wish became a burning desire to emulate James by playing slide guitar.

Stumped at first, he thought hard, his quick brain racing ahead of him, until one night he slammed out of the apartment and tore round to Pat's house. 'He arrived like a bleedin' tornado,' Pat recalls. 'He grabbed my hand and yanked me out and down the road before I knew what was happening.' What Brian was after was something to use as a bar to play slide guitar. He had tried using the broken-off neck of a bottle, but kept cutting his finger, when it dawned on him that the best place to find what he wanted, free, was a plumber's yard. Pat laughs as she remembers how:

> *The great lummox was that excited he'd thought of it. Well, we searched and searched through this filthy scrap-heap for this bloody bit of piping, just something he could cut to size. Finally in a garage tip we found it. About two inches long and it fitted Brian's finger perfectly. He was happy.*

Now he could also play slide guitar – a rare and outstanding achievement. In an interview years later for Radio One, Bill Wyman spoke of Brian's genius, 'He was a brilliant slide guitar player and the first slide guitar player in England that ever was.'

There was little holding Brian now. Steeped in R&B, he enjoyed the freedom of his lodgings, his job though barely tolerable paid for his guitar strings and he was happy with Pat. He had recently gone with her to London to her cousin's wedding and, while there, they did the rounds of the clubs, the highspot being a visit to the Ken Colyer Club to sample one of the famous Sunday lunchtime jazz sessions. Inspired and home again, Brian started toying with the idea of writing songs, although it wasn't actually songs in which he was interested – the words were only tools to which to set chords and, on the floor, with his guitar grafted to his body, it would be music he'd be composing in his head. Looking on, Pat felt content, but was unaware that less happy times were looming.

There was always an element of urgency and restlessness about Brian; nothing ever stayed the same for very long. Soon he moved out of Selkirk Street, this time to 73 Prestbury Road, with a new flatmate Dick Hattrell whom he had met the previous year, and who also enthusiastically shared his passion for R&B. It was 1961 and in their £5.10s (£5.50) a week apartment their lives virtually revolved around music; increasingly, there was less time for anything else.

When Brian discovered that the great blues musician Alexis Korner was coming to Cheltenham Town Hall, he was ecstatic. He and Dick already recorded every scrap they could of Alexis's music from their tinny old radio and listened to the tapes over and over until they literally disintegrated. Brian flipped at the prospect of seeing his hero in the flesh. Unaware that this night would prove to be a major turning point in his life, he rushed out and bought tickets for the three of them – Pat, Dick and himself – for the one-night stand.

Their behaviour up in the balcony during the performance was something few there that evening will ever forget: Brian went completely berserk with enthusiasm during Alexis's set. After the show he discovered that Korner had gone across the road to the Patio wine bar. Propelling Pat and Dick in that direction, he plucked up courage and went straight over to Alexis to introduce himself. Within seconds of that first meeting, a special bond was forged between Alexis and Brian, whose knowledge and evident ability impressed the hell out of Alexis. When Korner did manage to squeeze a word in edgeways all he had to say to Brian was 'For God's sake you have got to come to London! You've just got to!'

When the time came for Pat to be going home, Brian left the Patio and walked with her, talking every step of the way about Alexis. Having seen Pat to her front door, he collected his guitar from his apartment, and charged back to the Patio to pick up the threads again with Alexis. He soon became Brian's firm friend and invited Brian to London to stay with him and his wife Bobbie, although they could only offer him a floor. But, Brian would have slept on a razor blade if it meant he could be in London with Alexis Korner. He was already beside himself with plans, if he could, to hitch there the very next weekend.

Years later, describing Jones that night, Alexis Korner called him:

This pent up ball of obsessive energy, talking away to the dozen in an incredibly intense manner. But that's how people talk when they reminisce about Brian. I vividly recall the first time I met Brian, but I can't for the life of me remember where I first met Mick.

Yet, any impact Brian had on Alexis was overshadowed by the impact Alexis had had on Brian and if his fervour now broke all bounds, his restlessness was worse. From then on he was on the road to London of a Friday night every possible weekend, guitar case in hand, thumbing a lift to the city. Arriving in the early hours of Saturday mornings, he would crawl through the kitchen window of the Korners' Moscow Road flat and quietly curl up on the floor with the family cat. In the hubbub of London's clubs and pubs, brimming with talent and bursting at the seams with opportunity, Brian would accompany Alexis, sometimes just to watch, listen and learn, other times to sit in himself and play, cutting a very noticeable figure among all the beery bluesmen, with his broad-shouldered but slim build, blond hair and blue-eyed intense good looks.

He was getting a taste of real life, of what it would be like if he were in London full time, and he liked it – a lot. Jamming to all hours was great fun, but tiring and so much so that sometimes he didn't make it back to Cheltenham on Sunday night to be in time for work on Monday morning. Inevitably this went against him in the office where he was already unpopular, and it wasn't long before he was out of a job and unemployed again.

With his all consuming passion for music it is quite likely Brian might never have stirred himself to work again, but moves were afoot to ensure he didn't just doss around. John Appleby, with whom Brian had become matey while hanging out at the El Flam, was also friendly with Brian's parents and armed with pleas from Louise, John put pressure on Brian to fix himself up with a new job. Brian liked John very much and regarded him, though only ten years older, like a father.

25

Despite trying initially to worm his way out of looking for yet more dead-end work, eventually Brian was put on the spot when John announced that he had a job interview lined up for him, and was personally going to see that he attended, even if he had to drag him there and push him into the building. Not about to risk calling John's bluff, Brian backed down and agreed to give it a try.

In 1961 there was a chronic staff shortage on public transport, simply because their wages were not competitive with other bigger organizations. The Cheltenham Branch of the Bristol Omnibus Company practically had to kidnap people off the streets to work on the town's red buses, so Brian didn't have to do more than to turn up for the Traffic Superintendent Ken Hannis to take him on board as a conductor, and invite him to start right away. Brian expected to hate the work, but he didn't and in fact found the variety of colleagues and punters – and what they got up to – surprisingly interesting. He even rang John to thank him.

John Appleby had a valuable calming influence on Brian. He and Fred Lloyd, a driver with the same bus company, were founder members of the Tramway Museum at Crich, Derbyshire where, of a weekend, they restored old trams and buses. One Sunday John invited Brian to join them and Brian came to enjoy the many outings that followed. Although he had no real devotion to restoring trams – that wasn't what was important to him – he enjoyed the wonderful feeling of belonging and sharing – that special father-teaching-son relationship which he never tired of with Appleby.

Fred Lloyd wasn't Brian's driver on the buses, but he saw him daily at the depot. He also lived close to Brian. He tells how:

I often met Brian as he walked by my house to town. Obviously I was much older but we were friends and I couldn't help but see he was burning the candle at both ends with work, a girlfriend and lots of late nights playing till dawn.

His boss Ken Hannis knew it too and was keeping a watchful eye on Brian. But, the shit really hit the fan when one night at his apartment Pat innocently turned to Brian and asked him why he thought her periods had stopped. She confesses:

I really was as naïve as that. We'd been sleeping together for some time and within weeks my periods had stopped. But I didn't realize it meant I was pregnant. Even when my skirts got tighter and I began to feel sick in the mornings, I still didn't twig. It was Brian who broke it to me that I was pregnant and even then I told him not to be daft.

But Brian, of course, had been through all this before. He urged Pat to go to her doctor for tests, but she refused to believe him. It wasn't until her sister finally frogmarched her in to see their GP that Pat finally accepted the truth.

Brian's reaction was strange. Inevitably he wondered whether this was going to be a rerun of the last time, with all the high drama, secret agreements and alienation. He worried for Pat, too, but understandably he was wary of what was going to happen. A shotgun wedding held no appeal for him and, as it happened, neither did so for Pat. She admits:

Marriage wasn't something we ever discussed. It wasn't what either of us necessarily felt we had to consider at that time. It was very much a two-way thing. I loved him but I was only sixteen and not hankering for a husband, and Brian wasn't in any way ready to settle down.

Having said this, later Brian stated repeatedly in a letter that Pat was his fiancée whom he intended to marry.

Because the pregnancy had passed for several months undetected, the baby's birth was imminent. Pat entered hospital in late October 1961 and on the 23rd gave birth to a beautiful blond boy, of whom Brian soon became extremely proud. He wanted to show his pleasure by buying Pat an enormous bouquet of flowers, but as usual he was broke. His solution was to pawn the only precious possessions he had: his albums. He parted with four of them, and with the cash went out and bought not only flowers, but also a new skirt and sweater which he knew Pat wanted, before belting off to the hospital, full of joy at their little miracle, and hiding mischievously behind the gigantic spray of flowers.

Pat was speechless, but when she discovered how he had come by the cash, she was overwhelmed. She stresses how

the sacrifice was enormous for Brian. You really had to know him to fully appreciate that. But he really did have a very kind nature and it showed when he'd go and do things like that . . . . Well, that's what would keep me going when times were rough, because I knew then how much he cared.

They named their son Julian Mark, Julian, on Brian's insistence, after Julian 'Cannonball' Adderley, and Mark because its simplicity appealed to Pat.

Meanwhile, back on the buses, Brian had been sailing too close to the wind for comfort. Ken Hannis wasn't without sympathy for the young high-spirited Jones, who on top of everything was now a dad, but he had a depot to run and after six months of their newest and liveliest recruit stretching their nerves to breaking point he had to do something about it. Ken explains that:

To a certain extent the awkward hours suited Brian because when he was on the early duty it left him free in the afternoons and evenings to pursue his music. The trouble was him getting to work in time the following morning after a late-night session, usually miles away.

I must say when he was at work he did his duties well. But his main interest very obviously was always music. In the end his record of late reporting, mainly for those early stints, was as long as your arm and I just had to give him notice to leave. He simply wasn't cut out for bus work.

It would have been difficult to know what work Brian was cut out for. Still with no particular preference in mind, this was the time when he doubled back on his days with the council and made that application to the Cheltenham School of Architecture – an application initially accepted. It is doubtful that Brian cared much about its subsequent withdrawal, but he certainly didn't relish the reasons why. With the month's rent still owing to him, Brian fell foul of Bernie Taylor's smouldering wrath and consequently lost his place at the school. Taylor says:

When I discovered he'd been accepted there I went along to see the principal – this being the manly thing to do – a Mr Abbott. At this stage I'd had enough of Brian, was up to my ears with him after the way he had acted over the months he'd stayed with me. Then when I'd given him his marching orders after I'd broken up a violent fight between him and Pat, he'd buzzed off owing us four weeks' rent. I told Mr Abbot the truth about Brian, his temper and him having about twenty-four jobs in two years . . . even coming home as a coal man! Mr Abbott hauled Brian in and withdrew his offer of a place.

It was a move which months later Brian would complain about bitterly, while fighting a rearguard action to stave of being sued for the £12.00 rent outstanding. In a private letter he told Taylor's solicitor:

I feel you ought to know that your client has already seriously jeopardized my career. I was accepted by the Cheltenham School of Architecture as a full-time student. The principal then received a letter [Brian did not know that it had been a personal visit and not a letter] from your client which caused him to withdraw the place he had offered me. . . . I must explain that my fiancée, who is your client's sister-in-law, was expecting a baby, though we both regretted it very deeply. . . . I have not seen the letter written by your client but it must have been very damaging. This happened at about the same time as he hired you, so he was really out to get me. I think you will agree that this was a very underhand way of wreaking a petty revenge on me.

That debt to Bernie Taylor would take until 1963 to be settled, but for now Brian had got himself a job. As it turned out, his last in Cheltenham, but one at least closer to his great love, music, when he started a brief spell as a store assistant at the record counter of Currys. Now he was working at something to which he could relate, but even there he ran into trouble as Pete Boswell ruefully recalls: 'He'd get me and his other mates to come into the shop to the record booths to listen to the latest R&B discs even though it'd really rile his boss.'

It was becoming increasingly clear that Brian had skates beneath his feet, and that however often he had to swerve to avoid life's obstacles very little had the power to slow him down. He still shared his flat with Dick Hattrell, but Pat and Mark, living with her parents, came round to see him nearly every evening. On Wednesdays, half-day closing at the store, Brian would meet Pat with the pram outside Currys and together they would take Mark to the park. But it was a veneer of domesticity and at night swinging parties were, if anything, more common than ever. Indeed the shindigs at 73 Prestbury Road had become legendary, not least for the jazz giants who had made a habit of casually dropping by. Guests like Sonny Boy Williamson, Muddy Waters, Bo Diddley and the great Howlin' Wolf himself. Invariably the noise leaking from these wild parties sent neighbours screeching down their telephones at the police. Pat remembers how:

*Once a coloured group arrived from London and this tremendous jam
session got up in the kitchen. Brian was on guitar and he played out of
himself that night. He was so carried away in fact his fingers finally
bled and he never even noticed.*

After the cops paid their ritual visit that particular night to break up
the party, Brian more than three-parts pickled ended up leading a
band of merry outlaws down town to break into the Cheltenham Lido
for a swim to sober up.

This was late 1961 and it wasn't long afterwards that Brian finally
made the decision to uproot and go to London. Pat had been sensing
the move. He had always been restless, but with all the dramatic
changes of that year, and what was clearly driving him as she listened to
him talk during their many long walks, more and more she carried the
inner fear that she was losing him. She remembers:

*It wasn't so much losing him physically, as if his moving to London
had to be the end for us. It was that I could feel I was losing him
emotionally. He was slipping away from me, to music. I knew it.*

Brian had known it for a long time. He didn't think less of Pat or
of Mark, but he knew his own determination and had been lying awake
nights, aware of what he really wanted to do and trying hard to equate it
with what everyone else wanted of him. He didn't suddenly vanish
from the scene cowardly without a word, but he talked it through with
Pat for days, in many ways relieved that she knew him well enough to
have foreseen it. They made arrangements to write to each other every
day and Brian promised that when he could, he would send for her and
Mark. But, when he left Cheltenham this time, he left for good.

THREE

THE ROLLIN' STONES

L ondon, 1962, the nerve centre of life – and music – in Britain was exactly what Brian had hankered after for a long time. This was a year in which his survival instincts would be tested to the limit. His most immediate concern was to find lodgings. While the Korners' home had been great for staying over weekends, it was now up to Brian to establish his own base. His thoughts turned naturally to picking up a job and though options were far wider than they had been in Cheltenham, basically there was still nothing which appealed to him, and so anything would have done to fill the gap and his wallet. However, it didn't work out like that.

Though one hundred miles away, the hand of his parents was still at work trying to steer him. Having had to accept Brian's decision to upsticks and move permanently to London, Lewis and Louise were not prepared to accept the thought of him drifting rudderless in the city. After approaching Dr Bell to help him, Lewis travelled to London with a few career ideas to persuade Brian round to his way of thinking. Not yet having found a job and seeing his father's anxiety, Brian caved in under pressure and agreed, despite his hatred of school, to try for entry into the London College of Applied Optics. As Dr Bell explains:

Well he had gotten all his school certificates, you see, and he could really do something for himself. He got into the London College of Optics. It was a very stiff course, too – a three-year course – and we were all very proud of him for gaining it. If he'd stuck it, and he could have, the opportunities were there at that time for TV, communications etc. He had natural ability, you see, but then it was a lonely life for the boy.

That perceptive empathy only told half the story. Certainly, being trapped in class by day, and stranded in dingy lodgings by night playing his guitar or writing his promised letters to Pat was sending Brian up the wall. But his real regret was that, having bowed to pressure and pleased his parents, he knew he would inevitably disappoint them again. The soft option was backfiring and it hung heavy on his mind that once more he had failed them. But there was no way Brian could bear living such a life, and in a very short time he bailed out of it.

It was now he cultivated the nifty knack of avoiding the rent man. Landladies were generally better as they could usually be sweetened nicely to stretch his dubious credit. If not, or in the case of those who got wise to him, he would just disappear at night, leaving unpaid rent piling up behind him. He had no qualms about this. By now his sole concern was finding the best and most effective way of fixing his finger on the pulse of what was happening in the music world. He had already reverted to what he had done to survive as that green seventeen year old on the Continent, and was hustling some gigs, playing in his neighbourhood pubs. He had a plan, which was taking root night after night as he returned late to his lodgings and sat practising relentlessly to get better and even better than he was already.

He tried to tell his parents about his gigs in letters home, at times exaggerating how much he earned to stop them worrying about him, but unhappy at his quitting college, they were not impressed. Not surprised by their stance, Brian bore it, figuring probably everyone back home took a dim view, but he was quite wrong. Dr Bell reflects:

We all thought it was very plucky of him and much to his credit, because it wasn't an easy thing to do by a long chalk. Especially as his personality wasn't geared to that sort of thing. He was an academic and very withdrawn. To go out and sing and play in public took enormous courage. He'd tried college and didn't like it. He liked his music more and so he set himself this aim to form his own band. But then you see, that was Brian and if he set himself a task, guaranteed he'd do it.

Brian set about reconnoitring the pubs and backroom clubs in and around London, travelling about, sitting in with local bands, sussing out the prospective partners he needed. He knew precisely what he wanted. One of his regular haunts was Guildford where he would sit in at the Wooden Bridge Hotel, playing with a scratch band called Rhode Island Red and the Roosters that featured a pale and apparently mediocre guitarist named Eric Clapton. Then in time Brian ran across someone he considered a real find.

He was an Oxford English undergraduate named Paul Pond who led a blues band with the untidy title of Thunder Odin's Big Secret. Paul Pond would later change his name to Paul Jones and become lead singer with Manfred Mann, but then he was just another singer into the blues. Paul's first impression of Brian was of someone extremely well dressed in his Italian box jacket, winkle-picker shoes, with never a hair out of place. Brian, with his gimlet eye for talent, was weighing up Pond as a potential blues partner. It took him just a few sittings with Odin to come to the conclusion that Paul was his man. They played well together and since he stayed with Paul every time he passed through Oxford, he also knew they got on well together, talking about their plans and hopes well into the night until either fell asleep.

This was early 1962. Trad jazz still had its mantrap grip on the music scene, but a British blues revival was on its way, the avid passionate pockets of R&B disciples were sure of it. A vague but persistent sense was gathering that times were a-changing and that this was not at all welcome. Chris Barber led one of the biggest Dixieland trad jazz bands in Britain and it had been after seeing Muddy Waters perform in Chicago in the late fifties that he had introduced a blues segment into his repertoire, drafting in Alexis Korner and Cyril Davis to play electric R&B with the band's vocalist Ottilie Paterson. The sets proved alarmingly popular, especially at the Marquee Club in Oxford Street which was run by Chris and Harold Pendleton, and was also the headquarters of the National Jazz Federation.

33

R&B with all its bite and resonance was far too primitive and physical, too sexually insinuating by half and a total anathema to the legions of staunch traddies. Hostility was quick to mushroom against this new and threatening faction in their midst. At least, it seemed that way to Brian and many like him. Reality was something less intense. Chris Barber explains:

> I'd been into blues since '49. Ten years later it was Alexis and me who were responsible for creating the blues in this country. I mean I saw Muddy Waters in southside Chicago and was knocked out. When I brought him over, I had to do it out of my own pocket. My Robert Johnson record collection was even bigger than Alexis's. I loved blues, but I wasn't prepared to play it all night.
>
> I play trombone and to play blues on trombone is very restrictive. It has to be done correct, and that's limiting. I was all behind R&B, but not all night. I felt it was a waste of our talents. Alexis now? He felt different. He decided he wanted to play nothing but blues and so he left and formed his own blues band.

Generally it wasn't seen like that. When Alexis and Cyril broke away from Chris Barber, after playing the blues break for over a year, to form Blues Incorporated – the very first white blues band – they took on the mantle of crusaders, partisans with a determinedly revolutionary aura which appealed to young enthusiasts. Blues Incorporated's line-up was a curious one. Alexis was of exotic Turkish-Greek and Austrian decent with curly hair and moustache, and in a pristine white shirt and tie he would play acoustic guitar with electric pick-up, sitting on a stool. Next to him stood Cyril Davis, a solid fifteen-stone panel beater from South Harrow, a gifted blues harmonica player. On sax there was the aloof and unapproachable Dick Heckstall-Smith. On double bass was Jack Bruce, who later went on to become the bass guitar maestro with Cream. And the drummer, when Alexis could persuade him, was a doleful-looking guy called Charlie Watts.

Alexis always had planned to start up his own club, as Ken Colyer had done, but as it turned out he felt forced into it when, as R&B's tide continued to swell at a rapid rate, it became patently obvious to him that it would be necessary to do so in order to protect the music and its musicians from the prejudicial resentment that they generated as Chicago blues' exponents. Pop promoters, too, wouldn't touch R&B

with a barge pole. There seemed to be a concerted effort to crush it altogether. Tired of doing battle, therefore, Alexis advertised a new blues club, opening in his own patch, the West London suburb of Ealing. The venue was a tiny room under the ABC Bakery Teashop just across the road from Ealing Broadway Station. The first session took place on St Patrick's Day 1962 and was announced by a small display ad in the *New Musical Express* which read:

ALEXIS KORNER'S BLUES INCORPORATED

The Most Exciting Event of the Year

G Club

Ealing Broadway Station.
Turn left, cross at Zebra and go down steps
between ABC Teashop and Jewellers.

Saturday at 7.30 p.m.

The club was like a gigantic magnet to iron filings. The day the ad appeared it caused excited shockwaves to ripple through all the isolated pockets of R&B fanatics who had all previously assumed they were alone in the world. Fanatics like two members of a small local band called Little Boy Blue and the Blue Boys, twenty miles away in Kent: Mick Jagger and his neighbourhood sidekick Keith Richards.

Mick, christened Michael Philip, born 26 July 1943, was the son of a physical education teacher and had grown up sheltered middle class in the more distant London suburb of Dartford. Having left Dartford Grammar School he had newly graduated to the London School of Economics where for a while he had latched on to left wing politics. Keith born on 18 December of the same year had grown up just a block away. Rather a loner as a boy and close to his mother, he found a strong mutual bond with Mick which, though broken when his folks moved house and sent him to a different school from Mick, struck up again when they had met again by chance as two skinny eighteen year olds.

Quite separately both had been ploughing a frantic furrow towards R&B. It was at a time when Elvis Presley had already induced a collective coronary with his groin-thrusting, strutting arrogance and the majority of British kids were feverishly trying to foster a fetish for Presley substitutes in the less convincing, wholesome Cliff Richard and Billy Fury. But for Mick and Keith their leanings were heavily towards the far more meaty sounds of the black Chicago blues artists Chuck Berry, Bo Diddley and Muddy Waters.

To buy Muddy Waters LPs was scandalously expensive in Britain in the early sixties, providing you could first find them. The resourceful young Jagger solved his dilemma by importing them privately direct from Chess Records, Chicago. He had been carrying some of these gold-dust albums under his arm when he'd boarded a busy train and fatefully bumped into his old Roy Rogers playmate Keith Richards, minus hat and holster but with a sparkling beady eye right then fastening on to the treasure trove wedged under Mick's arm as he greeted his old buddy.

Little Boy Blue and the Blue Boys had been the inspiration of another Dartford guy Dick Taylor, later founder member of the Pretty Things, and to date their only public appearance had been in the back garden of a Bexleyheath council house. Despite this, when they saw Alexis's ad for the new blues club, they quickly made a tape and rushed it off to Alexis. Alexis almost immediately misplaced that small spool tape, but remembered frankly that it was terrible. Mick had asked for Korner's professional opinion of the three songs they had performed with more haste than grace, but bags of heart, and though Alexis's feelings weren't quite what they had hoped for, it did serve a very useful purpose by providing the crucial first link for an introduction to the big hearted Alexis Korner himself.

From the moment its doors opened the Ealing club went down a storm. Alexis was thrilled. Not only was he thoroughly vindicated in his prediction of a blues revival but, sweeter still, his poky club was packin' 'em in, poaching business at a crippling rate from the Soho cellar jazz clubs which he'd felt had given him such a hard time. Blues Incorporated at that time had no regular vocalist, but each Saturday night there was no shortage of young men eager to volunteer. Anyone who wanted to sing or play with Blues Inc was welcome to give it a go, but, not surprisingly, the results were often truly painful. Within two weeks of receiving Mick's awful tape, Alexis with his legendary kindness to musical beginners invited him up to blow, as it was called, on the bandstand with Blues Inc.

That Saturday a very young and gauche Mick Jagger mustered up all his courage to step on to the tiny stage covered in serviceable tarpaulin and sing in public for the first time. He looked entirely the LSE student in his linen shirt, lassoed tie and chunky cardigan as behind him the blues dignitaries began to vamp the near offensive for them, simple chords of Chuck Berry's 'Around and Around'. Though Blues Inc had only newly acquired an excellent singer, the staggeringly tall 'Long' John Baldry, after Mick's creditable performance he was taken on as their second-string vocalist for a fee of £1.00 plus beer. Whenever Baldry couldn't make it, Jagger got his shot.

Brian, meanwhile all this time enmeshed with Alexis, had already been sitting in with the band on a regular basis. The established musicians were hot, but Jones knew he was good enough to hold his own in their company. They knew it too and he was a popular player. At that time anyone who ever went on later to become anyone in R&B orbited each other. Every possible combination imaginable played together. Even so, at this point, though Mick occasionally sang and Brian sat in and played, the two never actually met until the first week in April. Brian as excited as Alexis about the Ealing club had also made a tape with Paul Pond, presenting it to his friend for a hearing. This time Korner was so impressed he instantly offered Brian the job as interval band.

On 7 April 1962 Brian made his first guest appearance with Paul Pond. He had prepared long for this. In a new Italian suit with the fashionable tab-collar shirt and clasping a brand new shiny Gibson by its pearl-inlaid neck – the money for which had been half earned, half stolen – he stepped up and utterly floored his audience by performing with stunning brilliance the Elmore James' classic 'Dust My Blues', playing breathtaking bar slide guitar. That night he had adopted the stage name of Elmo Lewis which was a derivation of his own name and his idol's, and it was as he was about to fret his Gibson with a metal slide, producing with startling precision that ruthless yet sensitive speechlike Delta whine, that Mick Jagger, Keith Richards and Dick Taylor walked in and got their first glimpse of Brian Jones.

On Keith the effect was one of instant hero worship. Working himself into a lather, with his propensity to muddle up names he kept elbowing the others whispering, 'It's Elmore James! It is man! It's fuckin' Elmore James!' Dick, though no less knocked out, remembers rather more:

I first saw Brian when he and Paul Jones were announced on stage by Alexis that night at Ealing. Brian sat down and began playing slide guitar extremely well. I mean real riveting stuff. Both of them were wearing shades. Blues musicians, sort of thing. And Brian, he was doing a 'Robert Johnson', like he would turn his back on the audience and all that. Real calm, you know. Oh, yeah, we were dead impressed!

In fact the impression Brian had given Dick of being a seasoned campaigner had been a convincing façade. Inside, he had been a bag of nerves and, though exhilarated, he was also relieved to step down. The moment he did so, three very tentative wide-eyed Dartford guys approached him gazing at him with that kind of shameless reverence usually reserved for God. 'We're just amateurs, man,' they breathed at Brian, 'but we dig to play!'

On stage, Brian had appeared nothing short of a musical Messiah. Now that he was standing before them, he didn't look like the kind of guy to mess with either. He was also the most raffish figure they had ever come across. Unlike them, all still living with mum, he was worldly. Just how worldly became abundantly clear when their jaws jointly clunked off the floor to learn that though only a year their senior, he was already the father of a baby. Grabbing themselves half pints, they hotly pursued Jones to a corner and grouped round his table, determined to befriend him.

Tearing into the blues for the rest of that night, Brian was delighted to find three new enthusiasts and eagerly exchanged views, listening intently to what Keith told him about Chuck Berry, whom Brian, whose interest was primarily based in jazz-influenced blues, had not yet discovered. What was clear to Brian though as they talked was that his own ambitions were a great deal higher and more focused than any of those there.

·   ·   ·

The team of Elmo Lewis and Paul Pond lasted only that one night. Paul wanted to return to Oxford, to his studies. Brian pleaded with him to stay and help him start a band, but Paul replied, 'Look, you're wasting your time, Brian. Nobody's going to listen to our music. You can forget that. It's nice to play occasionally but quite frankly you're being wildly optimistic.' One of life's perennial pessimists in practically all else, probably 'wildly optimistic' at that point really would have best described Brian to someone who fancied himself as an intellectual with singing as a hobby. Brian, however, was convinced he was right and refused to be disillusioned. He placed an ad in Soho's club information sheet *Jazz News*, inviting prospective players to audition with him in the backroom of the Bricklayers Arms in Berwick Street, which he had hired for 5 shillings an hour. Prowling about the bare boards, listening to his blaring Howlin' Wolf LP, he waited.

First to roll up was Ian Stewart or Stu, as he was known, a blues pianist from Scotland. Thickset with a lantern jaw, dressed in leather shorts and munching a cold pork pie, he didn't inspire confidence in Brian. But reservations fled after Stu bashed out 'Bye Bye Blackbird' on the old nicotine-stained keys. He had been playing boogie piano in jazz clubs part-time and before he had finished his brash rendition, he was in. The two were never easy friends. Later Stu seemed to acquire a deep-rooted resentment of Brian, but right then they agreed to become business partners in blues. The second hopeful quickly on Stu's heels was a guitarist named Geoff Bradford. Others followed suit. Then a day or so later the three from the Ealing club turned up.

Dick Taylor recalls how:

Mick sang for Brian, and Brian invited him in. Mick said he would only join if Keith came with the deal. When Keith joined, the others all promptly left. He was too much for them . . . I effectively left my band and joined Brian's.

When Dick spoke of Keith scaring off the others he was referring to the hostility which Keith, being an ardent Chuck Berry acolyte, elicited from Geoff Bradford in particular. As a pure blues guitarist Bradford refused to tolerate Keith. Brian tried to handle the hot dispute, but eventually resigned himself to the futility and ejected Bradford. Such snobbery wasn't confined to the fledgling band either; Brian came under serious fire at the Ealing club too where the bluesmen around Alexis found it impossible to understand why one of their most gifted members would willingly choose to hang out with rock 'n' roll freaks.

They hassled Brian so much, in the end he turned on them: 'Fuck you,' he blasted, 'I'm gonna get it together with these cats!'

He set about booking practice sessions at the Bricklayers three times a week. As yet the group had no name, no drummer and more to the point no prospect of a booking, but Brian was working on that. They played of course at Ealing, but at this early stage more often than not Brian had his work well cut out for him. Ginger Baker, arguably rock's greatest drummer, explains why:

> I'd just met Brian at the club. He'd just got together with Mick Jagger and they were going to play the interval. Alexis asked Jack Bruce, Johnny Parker and myself if we could help them out. I didn't like Mick Jagger, but we agreed to play. It was really quite amusing. Jack and I got into some pretty complicated time patterns with the evil intent of throwing Jagger. And it worked! Then to my surprise, Brian went over and stood beside Mick and shouted, 'One, two, three, four' showing Mick where the beat was!

Brian earned Ginger's instant respect that night and from then on the pair got on very well together.

As Brian was fast twisting the reins of his new life, however, the days of living his old life by remote control were fast fading. Lying on his lumpy bed by a peaky bulb, he was most eloquent in his passionate love letters to Pat about how much he missed her and Mark and was staying faithful to her. Brian had a rare capacity for making people believe exactly what he wanted them to. But he overlooked one vital thing: Pat knew him.

'I knew what the crafty bugger was up to,' she says. 'I didn't need people to tell me he was seeing other women in London.' Restive and barely bearing up anyway at home, this was the last straw. Already missing him badly, when the waiting stretched into April Pat took what she described herself as the 'brave but, on hindsight, foolishly ignorant' step to uproot and go to London. Waiting until her mum and dad had gone to the pub that Saturday evening, Pat bundled up Mark and dashed to the house of a friend who was in on her plan. At 3 a.m. she boarded the London-bound bus. She arrived at the capital's Victoria Station at 8.30 a.m. on Easter Sunday with practically no money left and miles to travel. Pat remembers:

I was about skint. I asked one driver how far he could take me on what was in my palm. I'll never forget his kindness. He put me, Mark and the pram on board, pushed my shillings back into my pocket and let me travel free.

At that journey's end she still hadn't reached Brian's flat. Fishing out his address, trying not to wilt with a bulging case, a pram and one tired and hungry youngster, she was preparing to walk the rest of the way when a chance meeting with a Samaritan couple in a car saved her. Eventually she arrived at the gates of the drive to the huge rambling old house in which Brian had a room.

Brian wasn't entirely caught napping. Phones all over the south of England had been ringing red hot all through the night, trying to reach Brian to whom Mr and Mrs Andrews had had to resign themselves Pat had fled. They wanted to reassure themselves that she had arrived safely. Not an hour since Brian had been told that Pat was on her way and he was sitting outside the house on the wide stone doorstep bathed in watery Easter sunshine, waiting for her and his six-month-old son.

There then followed a very difficult couple of months. They shunted their way through a series of temporary, pretty awful apartments; Brian having to argue and cajole at every one to let them stay more than just overnight. The problem was that one landlord after another refused to allow a baby in the room. It got so bad that Brian and Pat were backed into a corner. They had no choice: Mark had to be placed in foster care until they could get a suitable place that they could hold on to. 'Brian hated being forced to give Mark up to the foster mother,' Pat remembers, 'absolutely hated it! He vowed as we left Mill Hill, both of us upset, that he would quickly get his son back.'

With responsibilities now Brian went out and got himself a job. Pat worked too so that they could pool their resources. Eventually they found a room in Finchley Road, Hendon. It was spartan with only the hotplate not shared, but it had the attraction of being near Mill Hill, which meant they could see Mark every day. Still it wasn't satisfactory. Brian was working at a Civil Service clothing store and when he finished work he would tramp the streets looking at ads in shop windows for places to rent. Pat was on the look-out too and at nights and weekends they would pound together. 'Brian was so tired right then,' Pat recalls. 'He was even rising at the crack of dawn to go looking before starting work in the mornings too.'

Someone who watched this keenly was Alexis. He had met Pat in Cheltenham but though he and Bobbie had been Brian's surrogate London parents they knew little of his private life. It had come as a surprise to Alexis after seeing Brian with innumerable tight mini-skirted beauties at the club, to discover his young friend had a family to worry about. Seeing Brian take Pat around the endless accommodation boards, with steely determination to get his boy back, showed him another side of him. Alexis was also fully aware that three nights a week after this ritual he would leave Pat and head to his rehearsal at the Bricklayers Arms.

How Brian managed to turn up sharp and enthusiastic is quite remarkable. Especially since because he kept his private pressures strictly to himself, none of the lads knew he had good reason sometimes to be late. Stu often sniped that after having set rehearsal time for 7 p.m. Brian himself then wouldn't appear. 'The one you could never depend on,' he complains 'was Brian. He'd disappear, then turn up again and want to get another rehearsal going.' For this reason Stu felt he could never trust Brian.

Dick who was gradually getting to know Brian saw things differently. 'Brian was always quite withdrawn. Sometimes at my house my mum would worry about him. I couldn't tell her what was troubling him because I didn't know myself, although he was beginning to open up a bit to me.'

At rehearsals Brian was a hard taskmaster, something they all responded to well. Dick agrees, saying:

Oh, yeah, we had to concentrate! But then that's what we were there for and, I mean, the only way we could be there at all was because Jones made it possible. He was embezzling his boss blind. He didn't go mad like. He just took what he needed to book us rehearsal rooms.

Having said that, we had some terrific laughs too. Especially when Brian was in one of his ebullient moods. Because he wasn't always serious, by a long way.

What particularly sprang to Dick's mind about those fun times was something which happened around summer 1962 and became a standing joke for years. One night when rehearsal was over they'd packed up and straggled out into the pub itself for a beer. Dick continues the story:

> *Well, this guy walks up and says, 'I'm Keith Norris, Artistes Representative, Cockfosters. You could do well with your country and western music.' You should've clocked Brian's face at that! 'Yeah,' says Norris, 'I'll get you suits and you could play on the American bases, you know. Here's my card.' Well! We all fell about laughing! And Brian? He's this great impersonater, you see, and for ages after he'd just suddenly burst into a room and say, 'I'm Keith Norris, Artistes Representative, Cockfosters . . .' and all that! And he'd have it off to an absolute T! God! What a laugh the guy was!*

Life for Brian was roundabouts and swings, but what kept him going were recent developments in his beloved R&B. Real ground had been broken just recently when Alexis was invited to take Blues Incorporated into the Marquee for a regular Thursday night booking. R&B fanatics took it to be proof that jazz was finally confessing that it was being fast greased on to the skids. But really that was hardly fair. Harold Pendleton explains:

> *Chris and I ran the Marquee. We set aside twenty minutes for the R&B set, but when I saw how popular they were I said to Chris we ought to give it a night of its own. Thursdays were free, so we made it a Thursday night. We welcomed it. The very first R&B LP, 'R&B at the Marquee', was done by Alexis there with Chris's drummer.*

Whatever the politics of it, Brian was thinking hard. His fledgling band was showing tremendous possibilities, though it wasn't easy either. Indeed were it not for the adhesion Brian brought to it, no band would have ever emerged at all. Dick condenses the problem:

> *Stylistically, you see, there were a lot of differences in the band. Keith was heavily into Chuck Berry, whereas Stu was a Jimmy Witherspoon buff and so on. Brian was the bridge. He was really exceptional. Musically he was razor sharp, which I've got great admiration for, but even more than that he would find common ground for everyone to relate to and move towards. He always had a great sense of style and I guess it was because he had such a good musical background which encompassed all forms of music that he was able to understand all*

43

forms, could tolerate them and therefore knew how to mediate. Whatever it was, it was Brian who found a way to merge the various influences.

Brian's plan was clever. Reviewing his band he knew, as well as being short of a drummer, they were top heavy with guitars, but he had devised an ingenious way to take advantage of that. He envisaged an interaction between himself on his Gibson and Keith on his Hofner. With hard practice Brian felt they could play not as lead and subordinate rhythm, but in time as a merging duet, matching one another solo for solo and blending in a natural two-amp harmony, one zigzagging down the bass notes, while the other climbed into treble register. He knew it would take slog, but the emergence of a two-guitar band would, he believed, be a classic feature of a unique band.

He talked to Pat about it. Many a time it was the only thing that kept their spirits up as their fruitless search went on. A breakthrough was all they needed, he would tell her. That breakthrough was just around the corner.

Blues Incorporated were offered their first nationwide broadcast on the BBC Light Programme's *Jazz Club* on 12 July 1962. It was a Thursday, which clashed with Alexis's regular Marquee spot. Jagger should have gone with Blues Incorporated as singer, but the Beeb, frugal to the end, were counting the pennies and refused to splash out for more than five musicians, so he was dropped. In the interests of bringing R&B to a national audience finer feelings were axed and Mick unselfishly wasn't unduly put out. It was agreed, therefore, between Alexis and Harold Pendleton to offer the Marquee date to the group which had been doggedly rehearsing at the Bricklayers Arms.

As soon as Brian got wind of their Marquee gig, he at last named the band. In honour of his long-time idol Muddy Waters he lifted the title of a Water's song 'Rollin' Stone'. Though Stu balked at the choice, it was generally agreed that Brian could call his own band whatever he liked. Next on his agenda was finding a drummer for the all important gig. 'Mick Avory drummed with us occasionally,' says Dick, 'but he hardly ever came to practise. He was always going to Liverpool or somewhere.' Mick Avory's relationship with Brian was remote. Avory explains:

'Brian had a kind of sarcastic humour and to me wasn't very sociable.' Having said that, Mick Avory, later drummer with the Kinks, agreed to help out.

Time passed in a blur as the 12th approached: the day before, *Jazz News* announced their Marquee début; the night itself, their playing order was scribbled on a page torn from Stu's pocket diary. Then they were on: Brian on lead guitar; Mick vocals; Keith rhythm guitar; Dick on bass; Stu piano; and Mick Avory on drums. The six Rollin' Stones facing their very first audience together. Perhaps it was confidence from seeing his band build, but unlike the butterflies he'd contained at Ealing with Paul, this time Brian was not intimidated. Dick remembers:

No, he was all right. We were all pleased it went down well. We got a good enough reception, which was doing not bad considering we were so raw and trying our damnedest to look nonchalant. Underneath we were all rather nervous. Except Brian. He was quite happy.

He would have been happier if he'd been able to read the thoughts of a man standing watching them, newly arrived in the Marquee. Blues Inc had wound up at the BBC earlier than expected and Charlie Watts, already known to them all, had come down to see the band who'd been depping for them. Standing quietly he studied Brian, Keith and Mick performing together on stage for the first time. He was impressed.

.   .   .

July really was a major turning-point for Brian for many reasons: not only did he carry away from that gig new fuel to the fire, but this coincided with an upturn in his domestic fortunes. Finally he and Pat managed to secure a suitable home in Powis Square, North Kensington, which meant, at last, that he was able personally to go and take back Mark from the foster mother.

Life as a dad was certainly strange to Brian, but he adjusted. More than that he coped remarkably well. A bundle of energy himself, he clowned about for hours with Mark who, by now, was at the crawling-madly-all-over-the-place stage and getting into everything he shouldn't. Pat says:

Brian was good with Mark. He only once got angry with him, and that was when Mark suddenly took off and started twiddling knobs galore on his amplifier which he'd left on the floor. Brian didn't do anything of course. He just made one almighty dive for Mark and, hoisting him clean away from it, ended up holding Mark at arm's length above his head. Between his dad's broad hands Mark giggled happily down at him and Brian's scowl just melted clean away.

Between Brian and Pat, however, scowls were becoming less easy to dissolve. It was tough on them both. Now it wasn't easy for Pat to go with Brian to Ealing to hear him play, although as often as he could Brian fixed up a babysitter. For Brian his attention was being nailed more and more to the swelling crowds they were attracting at the club. It was they – the Rollin' Stones – who were now packing them in, with fans hitching to see his band just as he'd hitched to see Alexis. In response, his drive was unrelenting. By the time the Flamingo Club in Wardour Street recognized the upsurge and started their own R&B night, the Stones's following had soared into treble figures and Brian's vision was taking shape more and more.

At this point Mick was still at the LSE, swithering. Keith was on the verge of being kicked out of Sidcup Art School and Brian was still at the Civil Service store, still robbing them blind. If he'd ever had any compunction before, he had none now. Money, as it had always been, functioned purely as a means to provide his musical needs, which now included rehearsal rooms. With two mouths to feed too, and the necessity of keeping their Powis Square flat, not only resources were spread thin.

Pat had been with him when the dream had first seeded back in Cheltenham. He knew she understood. Now that it was starting to show real growth, it didn't stop their relationship, however, from feeling the first strain. Pat doesn't blame Brian:

He pushed himself so much you'd never believe it. He would literally starve himself if it meant saving money that he could put towards the Stones. He'd see I had food and Mark, but would do without himself. He was really the Van Gogh of music for his time.

Pat was tough. The spell apart when she had waited for Brian to send for her had put her through trials Brian never found out about, but it helped her to work together with him through these lean times. Still, the pressure was telling and neverending.

Brian was the only family man among them. The others were foot loose and fancy free. Pat though not married to him was considered Brian's 'old lady'. Brian, still incurably possessive of her would at times catch himself eyeing Mick suspiciously. Overworked and overtired, he would tend to misread perfectly innocent situations. Pat remembers:

There was the time Mick made a pass at me. Brian and I were in bed one morning when there was this helluva banging on the flat door. It must've been about 4 a.m. It was a Saturday. Brian got up and answered the door. It was Mick and he was drunk. He said he'd been at a Rothschild do with Alexis and couldn't get back to Dartford. He'd walked from his party to our flat, hoping to crash with us. Brian pushed Mick on to the settee and came back to bed, annoyed that he couldn't get back to sleep. He'd to work. In those days shops closed at 1 p.m. on Saturdays, and he was working half day.

When it came time to get up, I was seeing to Mark, and Brian, in bad cut anyway, seemed to be lurking about. Eventually it dawned on me he wasn't happy at going off to work leaving Mick, who was still hungover, in the flat. I don't know whether it was that he knew he couldn't be trusted in like circumstances, or if he didn't trust Mick or me. Anyway, scowling he went off. It'd only been hours since Mick had arrived and he was still woozy. I made him coffee and sat on the end of the settee to give him the mug. Mick swung up grinning. He put his arm around me and made a pass. I wasn't interested. Brian was a very jealous man, but I had never been unfaithful to him and I wasn't about to start with Mick. I loved Brian.

Pat says herself that it is doubtful if Mick remembered much about it. She recalls how, 'It was a blurry botched pass anyway, and rejection didn't seem to bother him.' He certainly had no qualms, once he had freshened up, in announcing that to pay Brian back for putting him up he would buy in supper and cook it. When Brian came out of the store at 1 p.m., he found Pat, Mark and Mick laden with shopping, waiting for him. He would beat himself up over his suspicious mind, but he could also tell when he had been wrong: kissing Pat, he knew he'd been wrong.

Mick cooked that meal, and when it emerged that they had no babysitter to enable Pat to come to Ealing that night, as she'd been known to do before, it was Mick who roped one in. 'That was the night I first met Keith,' Pat says. 'We walked to a Wimpey Bar to meet him. I never liked Keith. He was lazy, slovenly . . . I dunno. Used to Brian, Keith had no class.'

That mini crisis survived, however, a parting was always on the cards. To get it together as a family man Brian would have had to relinquish his dreams for the Stones. He wasn't able to do that and Pat didn't ask it of him:

We were just too young. Too much was in the offing. One day late in September when Brian was at work I packed, took Mark and left. It was the only thing to do. I didn't tell Brian. I bottled out and left a note.

It was all change again then for Brian. About the same time as his split with Pat, he swapped his job at the Civil Service clothing store for one in the electrical department of Whiteleys in London's Bayswater, where he immediately started dipping into their cash register. He also now moved out of Powis Square and into a flat with Mick and Keith so that they could concentrate twenty-four hours a day on the band. It was a two-roomed apartment on the middle floor of a three-storey slum in Edith Grove, near the unfashionable end of Chelsea's King's Road; in many ways all Brian had done was to swap the responsibilities of one family for another. At least initially he had a job, the only one of the three ever to work, but that only lasted a few weeks. His bosses at Whiteleys were more up to the mark than his previous ones and soon cottoned on to him. He was summarily sacked and extremely lucky he wasn't prosecuted, but by now Brian was a dab hand at wrangling out of trouble. As he'd done before, and would do again, he spun his bosses a right sob story, managing with a combination of his intelligently sensitive eyes and soft well-mannered voice to con them into believing he'd been on the emotional rack since his wife had deserted him, persuading them not to call in the cops.

No job, however, meant no money. Mick's contribution was the little he could spare from his £7.00 a week grant and Keith had absolutely no income. His mother Doris Richards would send him food parcels and once a week collected his laundry which helped, as did the odd luncheon voucher Stu picked up cheap from dieting girls at ICI's typing pool. But it was still down to Brian to keep body and soul together, physically, mentally and musically. Cushy middle class may have been his pedigree, but Brian was a survivor and thoroughly streetwise. There was no way he was prepared to let them sink. In the months ahead Brian was the single linchpin of their sheer existence. To keep a roof over their heads and food in their bellies, he stole. If he had a job he stole money, on the streets it was food – the grocer shops around the Fulham Road were his favourite haunts. As a last resort he stole from adjoining houses, creeping in and gathering bottles after a party to trade the empties for cash. Still, there were times when he couldn't cope. When that happened, they starved.

To ease the despair so easy to feel in the damp-ridden, rat-infested house with peeling wallpaper and tattered cobwebs slung across grime-encrusted windows, Brian would act the fool, challenging Keith to face-pulling competitions for a laugh. He would draw crazy murals on the walls too in defiance of the fungus growing there. And, moreover, he kept a tiny trickle of money coming in from the gigs he would manage to arrange in outer-London venues. These were mainly weekend dances in church halls, where the fee was seldom more than a couple of quid, which Brian would receive and then share among the other five. The others didn't know, since Brian didn't tell them, that he invariably kept a little extra back for himself as their manager and booking agent.

Against the odds, his determination only strengthened. Despite their successful booking at the Marquee they still felt under siege from the established clique and Brian would hit out with blisteringly erudite letters to *Jazz News*, complaining of the pseudo-intellectual snobbery:

> *It must be apparent that rock 'n' roll has a far greater affinity for R&B, than the latter has for jazz insofar that rock 'n' roll is a direct corruption of rhythm & blues, whereas jazz is Negro music on a different plane, intellectually higher, but emotionally less intense.*

Meanwhile, at home, he worked harder than ever, relentlessly slaving to figure out how Bo Diddley rhythms worked. Brian was the only one who ever cracked the Diddley sound without sounding a mere imitator. He spoke the native tongue, and practised endlessly, encouraging Keith, even at his laziest, to slog too. The result was that they became really tight, not just on guitar, but as mates. In many ways the necessity for the two of them to work so closely, while the third hovered on the sidelines for his turn to be involved was the start of feelings of neglect. Then it was Mick who felt out of place, just as later, when the songwriting team struck up, Brian was to be the spare cog in the wheel.

Practising together until their fingers felt like dropping off, they closed in rapidly on Brian's unusual and powerful two-guitar innovation. If Keith felt like chucking it, the inspiration he needed was sat across the floor from him, often so exhausted he would be literally slumped forward, fast asleep over his guitar. Says Keith:

Brian was just about making enough to keep us from being chucked out of this place and it's winter, like the worst winter ever. Brian and me sitting around this gas fire wondering where to get the next shilling to put in to keep the fire going. Mick was still at school. I was sort of half-way looking for a job. I went out one morning and came back in the evening and Brian was blowin' harp, man. He'd got it together. He's standin' at the top of the stairs yellin', 'Listen to this!' All these blues notes comin' out. He'd figured it out. One day, man!

As a band in performance they had improved so much that Brian decided to experiment. He booked them into the tiny North London studio, Curly Clayton Sound. Of this, Dick says:

God, yeah, I remember that! Little studio, with one microphone and we walked in thinkin' this's gotta to be a bit dodgy! But we'd never seen inside a studio before. Anyway, we did a few hours and out popped the tape. One of the tracks was 'Soon Forgotten' with Brian on brilliant slide, but it was never released.

Armed with that acetate, a metal disc with a lacquered coating, Brian went round all the major music publishers including EMI, who all kicked him out as a long-haired lout with no talent. For a while Brian was depressed. The guy who has that acetate today says: 'Sure Brian's head went down, but he was still determined. But in those days they were desperate and in the end, Brian swapped the acetate literally for the shirt off my back.'

It was a testing time. Because of the winter, most bookings were cancelled and those who held good were to drastically reduced attendances, which made the managers highly reluctant to part with the agreed fee. They travelled to bookings on buses, carrying all their gear and neatly avoiding paying the fares as Brian would shamelessly chat up the clippies. At home a fourth tenant had joined them: Jimmy Phelge. An utter maniac, as Dick dubbed him, who thought nothing of walking about the perishing flat completely naked with his underpants on his head, spitting as he went. Mick to top it all was, for some incomprehensible reason, going through his first camp period and while Phelge was blithely baring all, he would be floating dizzily about in a ladies housecoat, limp wrist hoist high. It was an antic for which Brian and Keith both, as Dick puts it, 'took the piss out of him severely!'

Come December Brian was facing serious problems with the band's line-up. Already perennially short of a drummer, now Dick, whom Brian considered to be a great bass player, had decided to quit – 'I dunno. It was a combination of a few things,' Dick explains. 'I was trying to get into the Royal College of Art and I was kinda disgruntled with bass anyway. I fancied lead, but I lacked the confidence and so on. Anyway, I left.'

Once again Brian advertised, this time in *Melody Maker* for an enthusiastic bass player for an established R&B group. Responding to that ad was Bill Wyman, born William George Perks on 24 October 1936. Ex-RAF, he was working for an engineering firm in Streatham, South London, married with a son. Bill had been playing semi-professionally with the Cliftons, mainly in youth clubs, and despite an audition at which neither side seemed particularly taken with the other, he became Dick's replacement. 'They didn't like me,' Bill will admit. 'They liked my amplifier.'

The Rollin' Stone's drummer problem was still not resolved. Tony Chapman would sometimes drum, as would Carlo Little, but it was an unsatisfactory arrangement. One night at Ealing Brian spotted Ginger Baker arriving just in time to hear their last number. Afterwards he went up to Ginger and asked him what he thought of the band. 'I told Brian that they needed a drummer, that the one they had was pretty awful,' said Ginger. 'I suggested that they get Charlie Watts.'

Ginger had just confirmed what Brian was already thinking and Brian had had his eye on Charlie for a while. Equally, though, he knew he was in no position to poach him from Blues Incorporated. Watts had a real feel for R&B. Despite his penchant for jazz and his po-faced style, he would always deliver. But wooing him proved an arduous task. Charlie held out for some time and it wasn't until he had consulted Alexis on what he should do that he made the decision to join the scruffy rabble, all of whom were a little in awe of him. But he did join, and so the Harrow Art School graduate reluctantly became a Rollin' Stone.

Just as Brian with his new line-up was raring to go, a certain agent, among the many who spawned about the clubs on the look-out for talent, was in town to grab a piece of the action: John Mansfield. Part owner of the Ricky Tick Club in Windsor, John normally booked trad jazz bands, but he had heard well of Alexis and decided to go along to Ealing to see for himself. He was so impressed with Blues Incorporated that he booked them for the second Friday of December. 'I wanted them back the next week,' John says, 'but Alexis couldn't do it. "Who you should get," Alexis told me, "is a group called the Rollin' Stones".'

John had read something somewhere about the Rollin' Stones and taking Alexis's advice he phoned Stu at ICI. With Stu having the only access to a phone, this meant he was in a position to be the contact for the bookings. John continues:

They were booked for the third Friday in December. For that booking it was the real line-up: Brian, Keith, Mick, Charlie and Bill with Ian Stewart on piano. They got £12.00 for the gig, that's £2.00 each and they went down every bit as big a storm as Alexis had done the week before. The second they struck up, everyone knew they had it.

Brian didn't have to approach John that night. Mansfield got to him first, desperate to book them again for the next week. But, the Stones were booked elsewhere and in the end the slot went to a group calling themselves the Paramounts, who later became known as Procol Harum. John, however, wasn't about to let the Rollin' Stones slip through his fingers, and with Brian he booked them into the club for every second week, thereby sparking off a phase of which Windsor had never before seen the like.

The Ricky Tick Club took place in a huge old fifty-four roomed mansion, owned originally by the diamond millionaire Oppenheimer. After going through various uses, it lapsed into disrepair. John, with an eye for an opportunity, took it over for the rent of £16.00 a week, using only a small part for the club. One huge room with leaded windows and an enormous carved fireplace served as a coffee bar, while it was in the ballroom itself that the bands played. The decor was ingenious. Rolls of black paper, courtesy of a local firm, covered the walls, packing cases and parts from old Volkswagen cars were covered in felt and provided benches, and the lights were Walls ice-cream cartons with cut-out tops and coloured light bulbs. The final touch were fish nets looped from the ceiling which later on would prove an irresistible temptation to the more intrepid girls.

The Stones were to attach a tremendous following there. That first Friday night the poster which billed the R&B group had caused quite a stir among the local trad-jazz fiends, who had hitherto never had R&B inflicted on them. Some were resentful, others curious. Of the curious ones who made up the audience that night was a shy slim dark-haired beatnik girl named Linda Lawrence, the daughter of a local builder. She would become the next love of Brian's life. Noticing the grave eyes steadily studying him on stage that night, Brian went over to speak to her when they had finished. He was shy and so was she. Tentatively Brian suggested she might like to come back to see them the next time they played there. Linda agreed.

The year 1962 went out not with a bang, but a decided whimper as they played an absolutely atrocious Boxing Day booking at the Piccadilly Club, run by a colourful character who would also feature heavily in the year ahead: Giorgio Gomelsky. For the remaining five days they were condemned with the memory of that flop to spend every minute huddling frozen stiff in their dingy flat. To stave off hypothermia, Brian kept playing his guitar. Hunger and boredom made for tetchy moods, which even pulling faces couldn't cure anymore. For some peculiar reason the fact that Brian refused to let his personal hygiene slide because of their derelict existence niggled the other two no end.

Keith and Mick never failed to whine about Brian washing his heavy hair every day, taking care to dry it properly. Always luxuriantly thick, it was growing long now and though some months away from becoming his famous heavy pageboy style, it needed handling and even then was eyecatching. Perhaps it was a form of inverted jealousy,

53

or suspicious envy that Brian could always produce a precious shilling for the meter, that began their subjecting him to petty name calling, their favourite being Mr Shampoo. In time, the tenor of that nickname would alter, but for now Brian let it bounce off his broad back. He was looking ahead.

The year had seen the emergence of a Liverpool group the Beatles, whose first chart single 'Love Me Do' had reached number seventeen after having been rejected at their audition by Decca. Parlophone, a record label in trouble, had picked them up and these four scouse lads were set to be the biggest thing to hit Britain since the bubonic plague. Brian's first reaction had been one of depressing gloom, but then again, that Piccadilly flop aside, they were looking good. The feeling he had nursed that it would happen grew stronger. The only problem was – he was in a hurry.

FOUR

COME ON, COME ON!

B rian was up and running – from the first day of 1963 through the following twelve months all crucial moves with the Stones were down to him. From the start the year augured well when they were brought in as Alexis Korner's regular support band for his Thursday night sessions at the Marquee. R&B had the music world by the throat, and there were no better exponents of it than the Rollin' Stones. Unquestionably the credit for this lies with Brian: his manically assertive personality rammed home the message that theirs was a new brand of R&B, a particularly harsh and vibrant variety which attracted a following outstripping anyone's expectations. Where Alexis had been pulling crowds of between 200 and 300, the Stones were topping one thousand. Brian was delighted, though his glee was shortlived as only four weeks later they were out. Chris Barber recalls:

We brought in the Stones as support group to Alexis, but after a few weeks we sacked them. They weren't authentic enough. Even then there was this element of them being too commercial to be real blues. They were into Bo Diddley and Chuck Berry and we had this, I admit, high and mighty attitude that that was tacky and so we sacked them. If I remember right, Alexis lurked somewhere behind the decision too.

Definitely not behind the decision was Chris's partner Harold Pendleton, who explains:

I didn't even know who they were then. In those days bands did two or three sets which was hard work, and of course we needed interval bands. Alexis took in this band, the Rollin' Stones. But I never saw them. You see I went with the main band to the pub during the break and returned when the interval band was finished. So I never actually saw them perform.

After about a month, I was leaving one night with a friend and I saw this band loading up their gear. I shouted, 'Goodnight, lads!' They shouted back, 'Fuck off!' I said to my mate, 'Oh? What's gotten up their backs, then?' He said, 'Cyril [Davis] sacked them tonight, said they were no good – awful in fact.' Cyril didn't like them.

Although a prestigious gig and a bad one to lose, their Marquee stint had greatly boosted morale. Forming their own itinerant club, they set out to cover all the outer London boroughs of Sutton, Richmond, Putney, Twickenham, Eel Pie, Ealing and of course Windsor. Saturdays and Sundays, they bombed about in Stu's beat-up transit van, sticking up illegal posters advising that 'Rhythm & Blues with the Rollin' Stones. Admission 4s' had come to their neighbourhood; their following was blossoming by the night. Their army of fans pursued them from venue to venue until poky clubs burst at the seams and snaking queues filled dark alleys ten deep of cuban-heeled boys and bare-kneed mini-skirted girls, all pushing and jostling to get in before the doors closed.

Their style was inimitably unique. Dressed in whatever they could afford or felt comfy, they initially arrived with stools nicked from various pubs and would sit down to play, a beer at their feet, lighting up a cigarette between numbers. The punters had never seen the like, and would stop dancing to flock around the stage, gaping at them. The stools were soon to go.

On his feet, free and flexible, Brian's star shone brightest from the start. Undoubtedly the most talented member of the band, musically it was his guitar which agitated, injecting the airless claustrophobic club atmospheres with a seething malevolent energy that was all his own. Visually, too, even this early it was he who was the arresting one. As many boys were homing in on his powerful pull, there were as many girls already fantasizing about his disturbingly seductive eyes. He had a magnetic stage presence, as Ray Davies, later lead singer with the Kinks, freely concurs: 'Brian was probably the most conceited-looking person I have ever met. But he was also one of the most compelling musicians ever on stage.'

Alexis took it further:

In terms of feeling, Brian was vitally important to the Stones because he had more edge to him than any of the others. And he was the nasty one. I mean the whole nasty image of the Stones really started with Brian, not Mick. Because Brian was a bitch! You know, if you were talking of winning over audiences. That wasn't Brian's attitude. You broke an audience. Or an audience broke you. That was Brian's attitude. And he went out to needle people, to get them up, to really arouse them, so they really responded. He could be really evil on stage, Brian. You'd see him dancing forward with a tambourine and snapping it in your face and sticking his tongue out at you. In a nasty way. Not a schoolboyish way. And then he'd move back before you actually took a punch at him.

Brian did enjoy performing. He thrived on the physical interaction with an audience, so volatile and raw. And he was entirely unpredictable. Ginger Baker recalls:

Brian invited me and Jack [Bruce] to the first gig that the Stones played at the Cy Laurie Club in Windmill Street [London's Soho] and we went. Mick was just standing stationary at the microphone singing. But Brian was leaping all about the stage, playing laying on his back and even jumping into the audience while he was playing. It was Brian, not Mick who was the showman in the band.

Off stage Brian's adrenalin flowed, if anything, even higher. His ambitions were climbing; he wanted yet bigger crowds, more clubs to play. He began campaigning passionately for attention for his band from the musical press, setting out to cultivate the right friends and contacts. He wheeled, cajoled and downright pestered journalists and agents alike to take notice of them. He also began writing to the BBC, chancing his luck at getting them on to the popular radio programme, *Jazz Club*. He was hard to shake off.

Towards the end of January, the Stones played the Red Lion in Sutton. The pub's owner Glyn Johns was senior engineer with IBC Recording Studios in Portland Place, west London and after seeing them perform he was impressed enough to offer them the chance of cutting a few tracks. To date their only experience had been at Curly Clayton and naturally Brian leapt at the chance. Glyn explains how:

> *IBC Studios were owned by two guys, George Clouston and Eric Robinson. They were approaching middle age at the time and not particularly clued up about the pop scene. As senior engineer I had an arrangement with them that I could bring in any musician/band I liked in my free time to record. The stipulation being that the tapes would remain their property.*

Of Brian specifically, Glyn says:

> *At this point Brian appeared to be very much the leader of the band. Musically, he was extraordinary and very inventive, extremely instrumental to their sound. At my instigation they cut about four tracks, which turned out really good. The Stones were the first group I'd brought in to record. Clouston and Robinson took the tapes round the record companies, but they took them to all the wrong people . . . even the classical guy at Decca. As a result, quite obviously, they'd no luck.*

Disgusted, Glyn began leaving *New Musical Express* and *Melody Maker* music papers strewn about their desks in the hope of educating them into the pop business.

Meanwhile, Brian had his ear to the ground. He had discovered that Giorgio Gomelsky had newly opened a club in Richmond and despite their embarrassing Boxing Day flop at the Piccadilly Club, he wanted in. Giorgio was a flamboyant 29-year-old Russian *émigré*. Exiled to Switzerland and educated in Italy and Germany, he had once worked as a courier, escorting American blues singers to continental dates. His first blues club was the Piccadilly, but now he had started a new club in the substantial back room of the Station Hotel, Kew Road, Richmond. Already close mates with Chris Barber and Harold Pendleton, when Harold discovered what his irrepressible friend was up to, he was aghast. He laughed, 'Giorgio got his own club going and came round the Marquee, if you please, passing out leaflets. I told him,

"Get out of here with your poxy leaflets! God, with friends like you who needs enemies!"' But they were good friends and into this useful web Brian had already wangled his way. He became the bane of Giorgio's life, pressing him to book the Rollin' Stones, blending a mixture of urgency with a pleadingly infectious appeal that Giorgio found hard to resist.

The club was called the Crawdaddy, after the Bo Diddley song 'Do the Crawdaddy' and it all happened on Sunday nights between the then licensing hours of 7 p.m. and 10.30 p.m. Giorgio, not holding the Boxing Day disaster against them, had seen them perform since in the Red Lion and was greatly impressed with their progress, but he was in a tight spot. He already had a resident band, the Dave Hunt Group, featuring Ray Davies, and could hardly dump them, no matter how stringently Brian pleaded. But, then fate took over. Subjected to frozen pipes and blocked toilets at Edith Grove, Brian had cursed the worst winter for one hundred years a million times, until the snowbound roads stopped the Dave Hunt Group from making their Crawdaddy gig early in February. Then the magic words came to his ears, 'You're on next Sunday.'

At the Marquee their fee had been £15.00. At the Crawdaddy the arrangement was different: Giorgio divided the door receipts equally with Brian. Gomelsky guaranteed them 30 shillings (£1.50) each and since there were six of them, he needed to rake in £18 before he could break even. That first week it was a great deal less than that; attendance was dismal and Giorgio had to lure customers in from the main pub with a 'buy one ticket, take a friend free' incentive.

Richmond had been a sedate borough until that first snowy Sunday in February. Then bang went the neighbourhood. As had become automatic, within weeks attendances leapt as Stones's fans discovered their new haunt. In electric atmospheres, girls would have to agree to sit on their boyfriends' shoulders to get in. Then one night Giorgio's assistant Hamish Grimes got so carried away with the beat, he jumped on to a table and began cavorting about. The rest promptly followed and instantly the Crawdaddy Dance was born. The Stones ended every session with a Bo Diddley number and left their audiences sweaty, exhausted but curiously elated.

.　　.　　.

There was nothing curious about Brian's elation. Wherever they went now, it was the same story. With other bands boys would get up and jam with them. Nobody dared jam with the Stones, even people like Eric Clapton watched. Hysteria was becoming an accepted extension of their performance. In Mansfield's Ricky Tick, Windsor, the girls in particular had flipped. Somehow they would manage to get up into the fish nets hanging from the ceiling to crawl their way over the heads to the Stones. Once Chrissie Shrimpton, sister of *Vogue* model Jean Shrimpton, who would soon become Mick's first serious relationship, came a cropper and fell out while climbing across to the band, nearly landing right on top of Brian.

'They were hot, Brian especially,' John Mansfield enthused. 'He played all the harmonica solos. In fact all the solos full stop. He and Mick were slap out front. You know, their two microphones at pole position.' Often, afterwards, John would treat the ravenous six to a meal in a local swish restaurant, ignoring the huffed outrage of the other clientele. John's most lucid memory of Brian in 1963 were the times he would invite the Stones out to his home with its big garden sweeping down to the river.

They used to come to relax. The garden was enormous, with knee-high grass. Jokingly someone suggested that I get a goat to keep it down. The next week, when they turned up, there she was grazing happily away.

Larking about, one of them grabbed the goat's hind legs and walked it forward to 'mow the lawn'. Brian was not amused! Nobody had meant the goat any harm, but Brian was having none of it. The bleedin' goat saw Brian as its saviour that day. From then on she stuck to him like glue. Straight up. If you couldn't find Brian in the garden, you only had to look for the goat because she wouldn't be far behind him. Brian fell in love with her. In the end I'd no option. I had to give him it. I mean the goat just pined for him when he wasn't there anyway! Crazy beast!

Of all the Stones, John's favourite was Jones:

He was . . . well, I guess you'd say, earthy and real. You could get a good conversation going with him. A sensitive bloke too. If he was

60

alive today he'd be heavily into Green Peace and ecology. That sort of thing.

By now Brian's attachment to Windsor far transcended the Ricky Tick. As he had suggested, Linda had come back to see Brian play again and again and, attracted to her quite refinement, Brian and she had begun dating. It had even come to the stage when he had actually met her parents. Linda says:

Dad was a building contractor. He and mum were just ordinary people. They were amazed when they first met Brian. They'd only seen him performing before and expected him to be a long-haired hippy. But that first night, he finished playing and rushed backstage to wash quickly and change into a clean shirt before coming out front. The first thing he said to them when they shook hands was, 'Please forgive my appearance. I'm supposed to look like this.'

That same evening my parents invited him back to our home to introduce him to the rest of the family. Everybody liked him immediately, and he liked us. He was happy sitting in the garden chatting to mam and dad about everyday things, or discussing poetry and art with my sister Carole.

Linda was as dark as Brian was blond, and together they made a very striking couple. He saw her whenever he could, but by now his schedule was pretty hectic. They were still rehearsing three times a week in the cheapest back rooms of local pubs. They had no money to speak of, and what they earned went on either equipment or records. Times were still tough, but now they were thrilling. For Brian the best kick of all was finally seeing that trad-jazz days were over. Keith Richards has claimed that: 'Singlehandedly we discovered we'd stabbed Dixieland jazz to death. It really collapsed all because of us. Brian was so pleased to see the last jazz band disband, and us taking over the clubs. It was his happiest, proudest moment.'

Brian had reason to be proud. His concept of two guitars dueting was now perfected to the point that many felt it was like two guitarists playing as one. It certainly packed power into their performance, already unique for its delivery and the aggression Brian generated was now bordering on lunacy. According to Stu he could have been killed many times. He certainly confused his audience: one moment he would look incredibly randy, exciting the girls, inciting the boys, then seconds later he would drop back into tranquil innocence, defusing the time bomb.

But Brian was becoming impatient. Since writing to them in January, he'd had no word from the BBC, so he turned his attentions back to Giorgio, this time pressuring his friend to chivvy up his contacts in the music press. He badgered Gomelsky incessantly to get someone down to see them. He got his wish when on 13 April, the *Richmond and Twickenham Times* ran a whole page on the Crawdaddy and its resident band, crediting the Rollin' Stones with having bumped up membership from fifty to seven hundred in weeks. About the same time, also at Brian's behest, Giorgio had managed to lure *Record Mirror* journalist Peter Jones to listen. One Sunday lunchtime meeting with Brian, and Jones promised to do his best to get them into the *Mirror*.

But a week later Giorgio surpassed himself. The Beatles were not yet famous, but as near as damn it and Giorgio had arranged with them to drop by the Crawdaddy one night, after they had finished recording ITV's *Thank Your Lucky Stars*, to see the Stones. He sprang it on Brian that night, just before they started, and from that second on Brian was edgy all evening. As he played, he glanced continually at Giorgio, but with no sign of the four, his faith diminished. When they still had not arrived by 9 p.m., Brian was convinced they just weren't coming, but Giorgio's reminder that they would need time to travel there from the television studios cranked him up again, and as a result he was as wound up as a watch when John, Paul, George and Ringo finally all filed in quietly at the back. At his edgiest, Brian was also at his most startling best.

On harmonica just at that second, the impact he had on John Lennon in particular was astounding. Lennon classed himself a good harmonica player, but by his own admission Jones was in a different class. With his heavy hair hanging about his face as he stooped slightly to the mike, Brian sucked and coaxed caressingly on the blues harp cradled in his hands, bending the notes to produce his own special whiny sound. By the time he had finished, it was John who was desperate to pounce on him. With unashamed hero worship Lennon cried, 'You really play that harmonica, don't you? I can't really play. I just blow and suck!' That night all ten wound up back at Edith Grove. The Beatles were soon to appear in their first major London concert – a pop prom at the Royal Albert Hall – and excitedly they doled out front-row tickets to their new friends.

The Beatles performance at the Royal Albert Hall was quite an experience for the hungry Stones. Later helping the roadies, Brian was mobbed mistakenly as one of the Beatles. Despite his protests that they'd got it all wrong, the girls climbed all over him pressing scraps of paper and pens into his hands, body and face for his autograph. Signing a few to please them, Brian made his getaway tumbled and breathless. Giorgio found him later standing thoughtfully alone, watching the true Beatles handle their fans. 'That's what I want Giorgio,' he told his friend.

In a step towards this, Brian's persistent badgering of the BBC had finally achieved results: the Stones were to be considered for *Jazz Club*. In his letters he had told them that, 'in view of the vast increase in interest in rhythm & blues in Britain an exceptionally good future has been predicted for us by many people.' The BBC decided to try them out and invited them one Tuesday, 23 April to audition. Later the tape was played to the production panel, who didn't share Brian's belief and wrote to Brian telling him that, 'the performance was not considered suitable for our purposes.' The reason for this, according to Bill, was that only Brian, Mick and Keith went to that audition as he, Charlie and Stu were working.

I think they got the two people from Screamin' Lord Sutch's band who were playing with Cyril Davis, someone called Ricky Fensen, bass player and Carlo Little the drummer. I think they used the rhythm section. So it really wasn't the Rollin' Stones and it wasn't really authentic. They probably played loads of fast Chuck Berry numbers. I dunno.

Days later they presented themselves at yet another recording studio – R.G. Jones in Morden, London. Giorgio had booked them in and Robin Jones remembers that first session very well.

What vividly sticks out in my mind was the sound Brian asked for. In those days we were all striving for the purest sound. Not him. He wanted a distorted sound. That's about as best I can describe it, but he very much knew what he wanted.

His harmonica was this bashed old thing, all taped up and in as bad shape as their torn speakers. And his hair! Well long hair just wasn't on then, and Brian's was long! Yeah, you could say he made an immediate impression.

At R. G. Jones, Giorgio filmed a twenty-minute documentary of the Stones which remains unreleased, just as the tracks the Stones cut privately with Robin have done. 'They did it one Sunday,' he recalls, 'a twelve-track LP it was. It was coming up to my twenty-first birthday and I played the tape to my guests. Nobody knew who they were, but everybody was rockin' to them!'

Exactly one week after the Beatles's Crawdaddy visit, two men turned up specifically to see the Stones do their by now legendary stuff at the club. One was nineteen-year-old Andrew Loog Oldham and the other an older man called Eric Easton. Oldham was the son of a Dutch American airforce officer. Since his days as a private boarding-school pupil in Witney, Oxfordshire he had been something of a movie buff and a dreamer, with delusions of becoming among other things, a pop star, albeit that he could neither sing nor play an instrument. He hung about television stations and numerous London agents, working for a spell as a tea boy for Mary Quant, before inveigling his way into a place with Brian Epstein's company North East Music Stores (NEMS) Whitechapel Enterprises as a publicist. He did not, however, promote the Beatles, but was assigned to another string of the Epstein bow. After fleetingly rubbing shoulders with Phil Spector, suddenly he decided that's who he wanted to be.

By this time he had lost his retainer with Epstein and had been loafing around the *Record Mirror* offices, hoping to pick up tips. By chance he had overheard Peter Jones raving about an unknown blues group who were about to hit the big time. Andrew's decision to get there ahead of the pack was the best move he would ever make. Thinking fast, he knew he would need a partner. He had no money or influence and realized he was in no position to manage a pop group on his own. After Epstein rejected his offer to come in fifty-fifty with the Stones, Oldham turned to Eric Easton, old established London agent used to handling middle-of-the-road artists. A former organist, balding and quiet, he made an odd potential bedfellow for a shaggy haired, aggressive R&B group. None the less, he agreed to go along with Oldham to Richmond that Sunday.

On 28 April 1963 Oldham and Easton watched the Rolling – the g having just recently been added – Stones perform; it wasn't their best performance. There was a subdued air about the place as Giorgio's dad had suddenly died and he had taken off to Switzerland. Still, Oldham knew what he was seeing: in his own words, 'Blues roots, yes. But it was sex with a capital S.'

After that night's performance the teenage Andrew swaggered up to Brian, only to have his wings clipped by just one of Brian's disconcertingly direct stares. As Andrew confessed later, 'Brian had incredible power. He could make you focus on his head and neck.' Eric Easton, meanwhile, placidly brought up the rear. As far as he was concerned, he had winced more than once during the performance, but was experienced in spotting talent. Astutely he recognized it in the Rolling Stones and a lot of fast talking went on that night between Brian and the two would-be managers. At one point Eric insisted that Mick should be dropped for 'someone who could sing.' Frankly, Brian had no particular objection. It wasn't anything personal, for relations were by and large very good, but he hadn't clawed his way this far to be nice about details. If Eric wouldn't budge, Brian would have agreed. Oldham, it appears, interceded and argued that Jagger stay. So it was left.

On Monday the 29th, at Eric's Argyll Street offices in London's West End, Brian signed an exclusive management contract on behalf of all the Stones. Unknown to the others, he also signed an even more exclusive contract with Eric that he would receive £5.00 a week over and above what the others got. The first thing management insisted on were two changes: one minor, in that Keith was encouraged to drop the s from Richards to give him a better pop image; the other, the far from minor decision to drop Ian Stewart. It was Andrew's decision that Stu wasn't part of the mould. He cited excuses, such as him looking too normal and being too ordinary, and that six faces were too many for the fans to memorize. Whatever, he wanted him out. What he wasn't prepared to do was the dirty work. That was swiftly shifted on to Brian. According to Keith,

Brian had known him longer than us and the band was Brian's idea in the first place. Brian had to tell Stu how we'd signed with these people, how they were very image-conscious and how he didn't fit in.

If I'd been Stu I'd have said, 'Fuck it, fuck you.' But he stayed on to be our roadie, which I think is incredible. So big-hearted. Because by now we were star struck, every one of us.

Possibly part of Stu's decision to remain had something to do with the fact that he couldn't face returning to ICI after being involved so deeply with the Stones. But Stu didn't take it big-heartedly and there's no earthly reason why he should have done so. It was a big blow, but just how big then wasn't apparent. The most unfair thing about it, though, was that Stu didn't blame Andrew: he laid this squarely on Brian and resented him bitterly for it ever after.

Regardless of whether Brian, who after all had been prepared callously to jettison Mick if need be, had really cared about Stu being dropped, it had not been his decision. He had been but the hatchet man, and he took no pleasure in it either. He genuinely felt sorry for Stu, but this didn't stop what had been an already uneasy collaboration from turning into a deep-seated hostility on Stu's part, although his best friend Glyn Jones refutes this. He remembers that 'Ian always made time for Brian over the years.' It certainly never appeared that way to Brian.

Put bluntly, Brian's perceived role as victimizer of Stu provided a cop-out for the rest of the band. In times not so distant, Brian's leadership would be continually dragged into the ring for a bashing. In that decision to oust Stu, however, the others were quick enough to acknowledge Brian unanimously as undisputed leader. No one else wanted dirt on their hands. Nevertheless, that done, Brian had no time to debate moralities: there was fast footwork required.

.   .   .

About the same time as Oldham and Easton had signed the Stones, a certain Dick Rowe, head of Decca's A&R, was reading a letter he had received from Giorgio Gomelsky, telling him that a new blues group was raising the roof in Richmond. Rowe was the most unenvied man in the music business right then for his horrendous gaffe the previous year in turning down the Beatles, and he was still looking for a way to redeem himself in the eyes of his bosses at Decca who were livid that it was their longstanding rivals EMI who had mopped up their mistake. Decca's Chairman, Sir Edward Lewis's angular face was a daily reminder of his fermenting wrath. So, when a chance collision with George Harrison in Liverpool casually confirmed that the Rolling Stones were worth watching, Rowe was right on to them. After a hair-raising drive from Liverpool that same night, he arrived at the Crawdaddy, prepared to grab the Stones within the hour. A&R protocol dictated, however, that he approach their manager first and since he couldn't find out that night in the crush who that was, he had to wait till morning to do some phoning around. Eventually he was put on to Eric Easton and the deal went through in days.

Before it could close, however, there was one vital hurdle to jump. They had made that tape with IBC Studios. Although nothing had been done with it, none the less, it could be construed as a prior commitment if IBC were allowed to hold on to it. They had to get it back and subtly, a job for which Brian was cunningly qualified. As Keith puts it:

This recordin' contract, though it's nothin', is still a bindin' contract and so Brian pulls another one of his fantastic get-out schemes. Before this cat Clouston can hear that we're signin' with Decca, Brian goes to see him flashin' a hundred quid that Andrew and Eric had given him and he says, 'Look we're not interested. We're breaking up as a band. We're not going to play anymore. We've given up.'

Brian went on to explain in his quiet, well-modulated voice that they would so like to keep the tape as a souvenir and could they please buy it back? Swallowing every word of Brian's plausible lie, the unsuspecting IBC agreed to sell the ever-so-grateful Brian the tape. Hiding his china-cat smile until he was out of the office, as they were leaving the building, Brian, with the others, smacked straight into Glyn Johns coming in after his lunch. Says Glyn:

I met them coming out and asked them what they'd been doing there. When I discovered that they'd bought back the tape for £90.00, the cost of the studio time, I was quite angry. Obviously it was a blunder of some magnitude on Clouston's part. But I was angry that they hadn't even consulted me, since it had been me who had recorded them.

There was nothing, however, but wide smiles and anticipation on the Stones's faces when on 3 May Eric Easton signed them to Decca. It was a straightforward two-year contract, but generous on Decca's part, since in contrast to the miserly rate at which Epstein had been forced to sign the Beatles to EMI, the Stones, though unknown and untried, were offered the standard record royalty rate of 5 per cent of the retail price for each copy sold. The only hiccup in negotiations arose when Oldham outrageously insisted that the Stones would not be using Decca's studios, and furthermore would not require a producer, since he intended to fill that role. Undoubtedly, Oldham was remembering something he had overheard one day from Spector.

All material taped in a record company's studio automatically attaches the company's copyright. By recording the Stones independently, then leasing the record masters back to Decca for manufacture and distribution, the Stones would retain the copyright and simultaneously rob Decca of control over what was recorded. Such a deal had never been proposed in the whole history of British record music. It is a measure of how desperate Decca were to sign their answer to the Beatles that they caved in. Oldham of course had run his neck into a noose, for in truth he knew no more about being a record producer than he did about the dark side of the moon.

The first flush of euphoria at being signed very swiftly evaporated into a cloud of unease. With the summary sacking of Stu, now that the glares were veiled, no one felt particularly confident or comfortable. John Mansfield reveals how:

> We were on the way back from a gig in Cambridge one night and had stopped at a transport café, and I remember Bill and Ian talking earnestly. Bill was seriously concerned, frightened even, that he was next for the chop because he was too old.

A personality clash, too, was already setting in between Brian and their so-called producer. Not impressed with the bluster, Brian had serious doubts that Andrew knew what he was doing and his scepticism showed when, in accordance with the bold decision to record outwith the capable hands of an established record company, at Oldham's command they trotted in to cut their first all important disc at Olympic Studios, Barnes.

For £5.00 an hour they got a sound engineer tossed in, too, and under the jaundiced eye of Roger Savage they set to work. Which number to choose was tricky. Their best was 'Dust My Blues' with Brian on slide, but it was so widely performed, it would have little impact as a commercial single. In the end they decided on 'Come On', a Chuck Berry number with Willie Dixon's 'I Want to Be Loved' as the number on the B-side. They ate up three hours and fifteen quids' worth of time on a number they didn't like and which lasted barely two minutes.

As Brian had suspected, Oldham's contribution was merely to calculate the money per minutes. He stopped them when he did, not because they were satisfied, but because he was loath to part with another fiver. As Oldham promptly turned to walk out, boggling, Savage asked, 'What about mixing?', indicating that having taped vocals and instrumental on two separate tracks, they now required to be mixed. Without the foggiest idea of what the engineer meant, Oldham snapped, 'You mix it.' The result not surprisingly was a disc produced way below standard, which Decca threw out and, in the end, rerecorded at their West Hampstead studios. The release date was set for 7 June.

Brian was so excited he immediately rang his dad. Lewis says that 'I clearly remember Brian ringing me up almost speechless with excitement that they were to cut a record.' According to Lewis, this was the turning-point in their previously sticky relationship; and that after this they were completely reconciled.

To mark their public launch into the musical world 'Come On' was consolidated by the Stones's début on the television programme *Thank Your Lucky Stars*. Recorded in Birmingham, the artists mimed to their records against pre-recorded girls' screams. Sixteen-year-old Helen Shapiro, all bouffant hair and petticoats, topped the bill that night and judgement devolved on to two DJs, Pete Murray and Jimmy Henney, sandwiching a local girl named Janice Nicholls, whose phrase, 'Oi'll geeve eet foive and oi'll boiy eet' [I'll give it five and I'll buy it] became famous. The presenter was BBC radio *Saturday Club*'s Brian Matthew.

That was the only time the Rolling Stones tried their best to appear conventional. Eric had bought them matching jackets of hound's-tooth check into which Andrew dragooned them. Oldham is fond of crediting himself with giving them their image, but it was he indeed who tried to spruce them up. Though their performance lasted under two minutes the television-station switchboard was jammed with complaints at their unacceptable scruffiness. The controversy had started.

'Come On' was received very lethargically: *NME* charts squeezed it no higher than twenty-six, only one place higher than the Beatles's 'From Me To You', released three months earlier. And, worse, after *Record Mirror* gave it a glowing review, Ind Coope Brewery, hitherto in the dark about the shenanigans on its property, read about the Crawdaddy with outrage. Giorgio was summarily bounced out of the Station Hotel. Undaunted, he promptly moved the venue to the Richmond Athletics Club, but, in spite of their regular slot there, Eric's task was now to get them more gigs.

. . .

True to form, just as life was hotting up on the music front for Brian, his private life capsized. By now he was having an affair with Linda, content in her restful companionship. He enjoyed the long walks he would take with her – and his precious goat – in the Windsor countryside. For Linda's part Brian was her first serious relationship and one which had her family's full approval. But their harmony was abruptly shattered when just over a year after her first arrival in London, Pat returned.

This time there had been no warning and Brian was taken completely unaware. Linda was devastated. Just as she had begun to feel sure of Brian, his longstanding ex-girlfriend had to appear. As the mother of Brian's son too, Pat held a powerful hand and Linda was paralysed with panic. She knew perfectly well how threatened Linda felt, but had little sympathy for the younger girl. She remembers how 'Linda was dazzled by Brian, then of course the pivot of a popular band and one obviously on the rise. And there's nothing more ruthless than a young girl out to get her clutches into someone else's boyfriend!' In fairness, Pat could hardly still class Brian as her boyfriend, since she'd left him some eight months ago, but then her bond with Brian, Mark's father, was very strong and she had needed to see him again.

Caught slam in the middle, Brian was in trouble whichever way he turned. The Sunday Pat arrived, the Stones were playing a gig in Slough. Leaving Edith Grove he took Pat with him to the booking. Linda, as had been prearranged, arrived too. For a while Pat was overwhelmed, totally diverted from her personal problems by seeing for herself just how big the Stones had become. But then reality returned and, as she herself says: 'I still loved Brian and was prepared to fight for him. Having said that, there was a limit. Linda, though, would do anything to keep him.' Pat was referring to the embarrassing scene which developed that day. It was very humid, there had been a summer storm with the rain falling in buckets. It had dried just as quickly, but left patchy glinting puddles everywhere. During the band's break Pat couldn't see Brian and eventually went looking for him. Going out the back of the building she discovered Brian with an hysterical Linda on his hands. Unseen by either of them, Pat stopped.

Linda was actually on her knees in a puddle in front of Brian begging him not to finish with her just because Mark and I had come on the scene. Brian was trying to haul her up, but she kept collapsing clutching at him. He was upset too and telling her that it had to be off between them. Although, I must be honest, I wondered seriously if he really meant it.

Brian must have wondered himself. He hadn't envisaged Pat turning up and understood why Linda had come unglued. He didn't want to hurt either girl, and in the midst of all he was torn too to see his son, now almost two and quite simply himself in miniature. For the next few days he spent his time with Pat and Mark, taking his son on a memorable shopping spree for new clothes. Pat laughs as she remembers:

Oh, Lord, was that a task! Brian was trying hard to get these grey trousers to fit Mark who was having none of it. Mark was so slim, exactly like his father, all shoulders and nothing else. No waist, no bum, short legs. In the end Brian, exhausted, came out of the cubicle with Mark, triumphant . . . the pair of them eyeing each other. They'd called a truce!

The previous year Brian had often taken Mark to the fair at Battersea, sitting with him on the swings. This time when he took him, the Stones were playing an open-air gig, competing with all the other park attractions. After they had finished, Brian swiped Mark and, as promised, took him on the rides. Later, hoisting him up on to his broad shoulders, Brian happily horsed about, running madly all over the place with Mark clinging on to him giggling delightedly. All the while

71

Brian was unaware that Andrew was scowling darkly in his direction. 'Oldham was absolutely livid!' says Pat. 'I heard him telling anyone who would listen that Brian should not be romping about with Mark like a bloody family man.'

Between Brian and Pat feelings had obviously changed. 'I was less emotionally insecure,' she said. 'Brian was more confident and really we were like good mates who just happened to sleep together. It was far healthier.' It wasn't, however, enough. Brian wouldn't take a stand, and it was tricky for both girls, neither prepared to give ground. In the end Pat pulled back and taking Mark, returned to Cheltenham leaving Brian to Linda.

With immaculate timing, just then the Stones were thrust out on to the ballroom circuit with a virtual non-stop round of one-nighters. They usually went down atrociously and felt depressed three-quarters of the time, but the strategy was sound in that Eric wanted them to work, to get out there and get their names and faces known. Eric was busting a gut to lever the Stones on to the path to stardom and it was very much to his credit that, after the unspeakable 'Come On', he managed to staple them on to the tailcoats of a nationwide tour about to begin in late September, headed by the famous American duo the Everly Brothers and including Bo Diddley.

From a purely selfish point of view, dotting about the country-side, albeit playing to hostile audiences, had come as a welcome breather to Brian in his fractured relationship with Linda. Not unnaturally wounded over the recent débâcle, she needed reassurance, which, once recharged, Brian was happy to give. He had just needed a little rope himself first. Soothing and placating Linda brought them dramatically closer together than ever, to the point that Linda's parents then invited him to come and stay with them.

Doubtless tucked away in there somewhere was a shrewd attempt seriously to minimize the risk of another episode with Pat ever happening again. However, having slummed it for long enough, Brian was grateful for the offer. His departure from Edith Grove effectively split up the household, as Mick and Keith promptly moved out too and into a flat with Andrew in Willesden, North London. For Mick and Keith it was a good move as they liked Andrew very much. Whereas Brian, who didn't find it at all funny that their so-called producer thought guitars plugged into wall sockets, did not. And that division, very hard to disguise, could only incubate the more his back was turned.

At Windsor Brian was welcomed with open arms and absorbed totally into the family. Violet Lawrence says, 'He really was a lovely, gentle boy, always kind and courteous. He and Linda were very much in love.' Being part of a healthy, noisy family was good for Brian. Mrs Lawrence did his washing along with the family's and Mr Lawrence would chuck him the car keys across the breakfast table whenever he needed them. He felt involved and important, his feelings mattered. And, as she says, with Linda he wasn't afraid to show nerves:

> *When he stayed at our home, I used to wash his shoulder-length hair for him. Then I'd sit behind him combing it for twenty minutes and more, sometimes at three in the morning. It seemed to soothe him when he was tense.*

.   .   .

Their first tour kicked off on 29 September. Before it Brian had gone shopping for the clothes the band would wear on stage – somewhere on the ballroom circuit they had heaved the hound's-tooth jackets, mulishly determined to maintain their individual, dress-anyhow appearance. As the group photo proved, taken for the tour poster of them in cords and polo-neck sweaters standing on a Thames jetty. They opened at London's New Victoria Cinema. Linda remembers standing with him in the wings:

> *He was terribly nervous – all the Stones were – and he needed constant reassurance that he looked all right. I told him how good he looked. He glanced at me and smiled, and he was okay then, ready to face the screaming teenagers waiting out front.*

The tour was quite remarkable. Although the Everly Brothers headed the bill, by now they were fading legends, and Bo Diddley was still the cult R&B king. Brian was ecstatic to be playing upsides his idol and to show respect, dropped all Diddley material from their act. Bo was flattered. He liked Brian very much, was amazed that Jones had actually cracked the secret of his style and in the end asked the Stones to back him at his forthcoming *Saturday Club* date.

Then, eight days into the tour, they hit Cheltenham Odeon, the first time Brian was to play to his home crowd. Pat had got tickets, but had no intention of making a fuss. Slipping quietly into the front row, it was a bittersweet experience to watch the curtains part and see Brian step out on stage. She had no idea that just as she had seen him, so despite the powerful stage lights Brian had also seen her. He still felt bad at what had happened in the summer and as soon as he came off stage he sent Stu out with a message to Pat. 'Stu suddenly appeared in front of me,' Pat remembers 'and said that Brian wanted to see me.' Too confused to heed the envious looks from girls around, Pat went backstage with Stu at the end of the first performance, where Brian was waiting for her and, taking her hand, led her somewhere private to talk. They talked and talked right up until it was time for him to go back on stage, when Brian arranged with Pat to meet him the next day.

But the night's surprises weren't quite over for Brian. Lying in wait for him at the end of the second performance was another backstage visitor – a private investigator, hired by Bernie Taylor, doggedly on the trail of his depreciating £12.00 rent money. Firmly nabbed, Brian had no option but to cough up not only his two-year-old debt, but also an extra sum to cover Bernie's expenses.

In the High Street next morning Brian linked hands with Pat again and they drifted off to old familiar haunts. Brian told her about what was happening, his ideas for new sounds, his music, listening, too, to how things were going for her. Mainly he wanted to talk about their relationship once and for all, which they both knew was finally over. Pat gave him no hysterics or sobs. Realistically, she had faced this long ago. There was a maturity between them now far sounder than it had ever been. Brian talked too of Mark and of sorting out things financially. Then all too quickly it was time to go, to leave Cheltenham with the tour bound for their next stop. That October afternoon Brian said his last personal goodbye to Pat and moved on.

Not forgetting Linda back home in Windsor he wrote her a steady stream of letters, the following one night from Manchester.

MANCHESTER, WEDNESDAY

My darling Linda
I'm so very very sorry I haven't written until now but really we've been
so busy and you know I hate writing letters anyway. The tour is proving

a great laugh, but playing in theatres is definitely a drag. We've had a lot of fun, and met many people. I'm sorry I didn't ring you on Saturday night. I tried again and again but the connections with London were broken and I couldn't get through. Honestly, darling, that's the truth.

The new record will be out soon. It's great. We wrote the B-side. It's called 'Stoned'! I'll play you a copy of it when we come back. Can I stay with you next Monday? We're coming back on Sunday night. Can we stay in Windsor perhaps? Reading? We shall have to be off again on Tuesday morning.

Honestly, darling, I can't wait to see you again. Although you may have given up hope. I love you so very much. I always think about you and wonder what you are doing, and who you are with. I don't trust you an inch! I'm being good and haven't broken my promise, and I won't either.

We played in Hull last night at a concert with Johnny Kidd and the Pirates and Heintz. The girls were mad, the screaming nearly split my eardrums. We stole the show. We have to be up early tomorrow (I'm writing this in bed on Wednesday night) to go to Scotland. Do you remember the Mindbenders – Wayne Fontana's mob? Well, do you remember the coats they had at Watford that night they came to see us? The grey check ones with black collars, pockets etc. I bought one today. It's real gear! I like it better than my leather one, and that's good! Did you buy one for your birthday?

I wish I could be with you on your birthday, darling. But I'll be thinking about you all the time. Now, will you be in Windsor on Friday night and I'll ring you about two o'clock in the morning; I presume from Newcastle.

Well, my darling, I'll tell you all the rest when I ring you up on Friday. Please be good and faithful, and don't forget all about me. I love you more than ever darling and I always will.

BYE, SWEETHEART
BRIAN XXXXXXXXXXXXXXX
XXXXXXXXXXXXXXX

As the tour wore on the gilt began to flake. Night after night they trotted through tawdry dressing-rooms, down freezing dank alleys littered with rats and smelly rubbish. The one bright spot was their radio début when they backed Bo on the 26th on *Saturday Club*; not only did Brian realize a lifelong dream, it also turned out a profitable exercise: they were asked back themselves to do a lead spot on the show.

But tempers too had begun to fray, nerves accumulating, until one night petty squabbling flashed into full-scale assault as Brian and Keith came to blows. Interviewed for *Playboy* magazine Keith gave his version of events:

> *One night in my dressing-room, the stage manager sticks his head in the door and yells, 'You're on!' So we're pickin' up guitars and headin' for the stage and as we're walkin' downstairs Brian passes me and I say, 'You cunt! You et me chicken!' And I bopped him in the eye. We went on stage and as we're playin' Brian's eye starts to swell and change colour. In the next few days it turned every colour of the rainbow.*

A nasty business, but it was frustration which accounted for most of the heat. Frustration at the lack of a follow-up to their first single. It was only after Oldham blurted out his plight to Lennon and McCartney that the problem was resolved when magnanimously he was handed a new song on a platter, penned by pop's hottest songwriting sensation.

'I Wanna Be Your Man' became the Stones's second single, released on 1 November, just two days before the tour ended. Recorded at Kingsway Studios, in order to ensure their own Chicago blues effect Brian took command. The Beatles's harmonies were pleasing, but Brian preferred a rougher treatment. Ruthless and belligerent, his slide guitar assaults the number, investing it with a meatier altogether gutsier appeal. The B-side was a solid twelve-bar blues instrumental 'Stoned'. By the time the tour wound up 'I Wanna Be Your Man' had made such an impact, it caused the tour's presenter acute embarrassment for, instead of the crowd coralled in the Hammersmith Odeon shouting for the Everly Brothers, the war-cry went up, 'We want the Stones . . . We want the Stones!' They had begun the tour little better than ballast and ended it usurping the stars.

Keenly watching the charts, Brian revelled in their number thirteen slot, while even 'Come On' was still lurking tenaciously in the lower depths. The difference in its reception was easy to see and now journalists were flocking round them for a quote. Indubitably, the focus at the press receptions was Brian. When asked the inevitable question, 'How did you come to play R&B', Brian replied,

> *It's really a matter for a sociologist or psychiatrist or something. If you ask some people why they go for R&B you get pretentious answers. They say that in R&B you find an honesty of expression, a sincerity of feeling and so on. For me it's merely the sound. I mean I like all sorts of sounds like church bells for instance. I always stop to listen to church bells. It doesn't express damn all to me really. But I like the sound.*

Articulate and approachable, he became the natural magnet for reporters from then on.

By now club dates were blind pandemonium; Ken Colyer's Studio 51, in particular. It was a long room with a very small stage at one end and a low ceiling you could almost touch. On a Sunday it would be so packed that sweat poured down your arms and almost down the walls, and the humidity kept making the amps go wrong. But the music was fantastic.

One Sunday lunchtime mid-December, the crush was so fierce that several girls, not able to fight their way to the nearest airhole, fainted. One of them was Shirley Arnold. She came round in the Stones's dressing-room just as the door flung open and they all barged in. Girls fainting on them was a novelty and, concerned, Brian went straight up to her to ask if she was all right. In a blink of an eye, she was. Later, talking to Andrew Oldham, Shirley brought up the question of the Stones fan club. Of course, there wasn't one at that time and so Oldham offered her the job on the spot, promptly stuffing a fistful of postal orders, amounting to some £300, into her hand to make a start. Eric Easton's Argyll Street office was used as the official mailing address for the first fan club and for the next nine years Shirley Arnold lodged herself as a valued secretary and close friend to all the Stones, her loyalty implicit.

Before the year was out Brian's loyalty came under fire when the others at last discovered that he was getting more money than them. It was inevitable that it would come out, and as soon as it did things turned very nasty for him. Despite his contention that he felt entitled to it, the others considered him a cheat and for ever more hailed the fact as evidence of his total lack of leadership – a leadership which quite clearly was no longer politic for the other band members to acknowledge.

It has been argued that in the band's opinion there should not be anything as uncool and outdated as a leader. However, that laudably musketeer attitude of all-for-one-and-one-for-all would turn out to be conspicuously lacking later when it came to songwriting. Whether it is comfortable to credit or not, subtly there surfaced a set of rules for Brian and a different set for the rest. It is little wonder then that, in times ahead, Brian would never quite know where he stood with the rest. But, if nothing else, the animal uproar over money showed him one thing: as the odd man out he would be very vulnerable. Behind his carved handsome looks, there entered a certain hard-eyed glint.

FIVE

NOT FADE AWAY

In the same year that Cassius Clay would defeat Sonny Liston to become boxing's World Heavyweight champion, the Rolling Stones fought a warm-up bout before 1964 was hours old. Not, however, among themselves.

On New Year's Day 1964 the first *Top of the Pops* spun into life. The brainchild of Bill Cotton, BBC's Head of Variety, it followed on from the runaway success of *Ready Steady Go!* and was hosted by DJ Jimmy Savile. Recorded in a Manchester converted church hall, it went out that night at 6.34 p.m. 'It'll either be off after six weeks,' said Cotton, 'or it'll go on for ever!' It boasted a star-studded cast that night with Dusty Springfield, the Dave Clark Five, the Hollies, the Swinging Blue Jeans, Cliff Richard, Freddie and the Dreamers and, of course, the Rolling Stones.

North-south rivalry was strong, and half an hour before transmission the uneasy peace between the Stones and the Swinging Blue Jeans, who had been needling each other incessantly since they'd arrived, finally snapped. Who drew first blood is debatable, but one almighty scrap erupted, sending tables tumbling and studio staff scurrying for the cavalry. They had to be wrenched apart physically, just in the nick of time before appearing live on national television.

'I Wanna Be Your Man' was hovering at number fifteen in the charts and just about to be released was their first EP – Extended Player with four tracks – with 'Bye Bye Johnny' and 'Money' on one side, 'You Better Move On' and 'Poison Ivy' on the other. Recorded at Regent Sound Studios, it was to coincide with a tour due to start in barely a week's time. Before Brian could leave London, however, though not yet twenty-two, he received the daunting news that he was to become a father for the third time: Linda had discovered she was pregnant and announced that the baby was due in the summer.

Brian's reaction again was mixed. On the one hand he was happy with Linda, comfortable with her parents, and enjoyed the stability of a family home which the Lawrences provided. With bald honesty, however, Brian knew very well that the last thing he wanted was to be tied down. He was brimful of ambition and his relationship with Pat and Mark already stood as a sad sacrifice to the fire in his belly. Now, it was all just happening: the road to stardom stretched before him and with his foot firmly strapped to the accelerator the last place Brian was about to put his hand was on the brake.

Linda knew this:

Just before I got pregnant we were talking about the idea of getting a place together. Then when I got pregnant we actually looked for houses. But as all that was happening the Stones were all happening too. I mean it was like he was being pulled between two things. One thing that I felt he really wanted. And the other thing that he felt he really needed to do, to achieve his musical satisfaction, which is understandable now. I was very young, and he was very young too to be entering the music and a relationship all at the same time. And the way I saw it was – Andrew made it quite clear – that a Rolling Stone shouldn't be a family man. That's not a good image. So I felt Brian got drawn between the two images that people were expecting of him.

There wasn't much time to absorb the news and its implications. Their departure marking the commencement of what was to become a punishing round of tours spanning the next four years, the Stones set off on their first tour of the year. By now they were big enough to share top billing with the American all-girl group the Ronettes, part of the hugely successful Phil Spector Phillies record-label stable. Worried that his girls would become too friendly with the shaggy-haired monstrous Stones, Spector sent a blistering telegram to Oldham warning grimly that his boys were to, 'Leave my girls alone!' He would have been wiser to have left well alone, for the order itself guaranteed that the beautiful black trio and the outrageous white quins would form a pact.

Attraction between them was inevitable. The Stones were as wild and uncut, as the Ronettes were honed and graceful, and both held a hot fascination for the other. Bill already married, Charlie faithful to his fiancée left Brian, Mick and Keith circling the girls like the sharks they were reputed to be. The difference was, while Mick and Keith dithered about plucking up courage and debating the impossible choice of which girl was the most ravishing, by the time they had made their decisions Jones, dangerously appealing to all three, had made off with them. Spirited girls, they took delight in being photographed snuggling up to Brian, just so as to rub Spector's nose in it. But their public teaming up had another bonus. The music press somewhat jaded with Beatlemania had something dicy and spicy to latch on to. The fans loved it, and now both genders in the audience had something to squeal at: the tour was a box office smash, setting the trend for the years ahead.

On their bruised but exhilarated return, it was straight into Regent Sound to record their third single, a Buddy Holly number 'Not Fade Away'. Again the Stones lent it a very different sound from Holly's original. This time Brian applied his skill on harp and, played at twice its speed, each verse came under savage attack from Brian's yelping harmonica bursts. The Stones were very independent minded in the studio, a rarity in those days, and didn't accept graciously what they saw as interference. For this recording they hit on the highly irregular idea of recording through the night when no one was about to bother them. 'Not Fade Away' was therefore the product of a boozy bash whose guests included the pacified Phil Spector, Alan Clark and Graham Nash of the Hollies and a welcome brandy-bottle-wielding gatecrasher Gene Pitney. Its release date was the last week in February.

Only weeks before the Beatles had made the intrepid voyage across the Atlantic for their first American tour, making their début on the country's top TV slot the *Ed Sullivan Show*, thus paving the way for the British invasion to follow. The Beatles, however, were running into danger of being nice. Parents had begun buying their LPs, which revolted the kids. Who wanted mum beaming indulgently at their pin-ups! But, when 'Not Fade Away' came out with its opening sexual demands of its lyrics, it hadn't the remotest chance of being either approved of, or smiled upon, by any right-minded adult. The kids were delighted. The *Daily Express* wrote:

> They look like boys whom any self-respecting mum would lock in the bathroom, but the Rolling Stones, five young tough London-based music makers with doorstep mouths, pallid cheeks and unkempt hair, are not worried what mums think. For now that the Beatles have registered with all age groups, the Rolling Stones have taken over as the voice of the teens.

A deep smile dented Brian reading and rereading that last part.

Now television appearances fell fast into place, giving the country at large the chance to see them, to cough, splutter and feel suitably scandalized. Looking at those early clips it is hard to conceive why they attracted so much spleen. On the *Arthur Haynes Show*, Mick looks long armed and harmless, smiling through the words of 'You Better Move On', while Charlie stoically gets on with the job. Keith with his fingers superglued to one chord, tongue self-consciously in cheek, looks like he's landed a Jimmy Savile 'Fix-It', and emotionless Bill shares back-up harmonies with a dandy-looking Brian strumming smoothly on acoustic. Yet even before the performance was over, the barrage from the establishment began.

Producers of *Thank Your Lucky Stars* and *Ready Steady Go!* began to receive hate mail demanding why they couldn't stick to allowing only nice boys like Cliff Richard on air. Hair was the biggest beef with the viewing public. Although the Beatles shocked everyone with their four identical top mops, the key word was 'identical'; they were all scrupulously barbered, whereas the Stones had varying lengths, not to mention qualities, of hair.

Brian's, in particular, came in for harsh slating. By now he had grown his blond mane into an instantly recognizable dome-like heavy page-boy, which framed his flawless face and, barring an irreverent breeze, guaranteed that his ears and eyebrows were never again seen in public. This so offended the President of the National Federation of Hairdressers that he felt impelled to offer to give the next number one pop group a free haircut and, by thinly veiled inference, a delousing. He hit out, 'The Rolling Stones are the worst. One of them looks as though he has got a feather duster on his head.'

Brian was deeply insulted, not only by the tenor of the attack, but also by the narrow-gutted assumption that hair longer than conventional must be dirty. By now Brian washed his hair twice a day, something which unaccountably irked the other Stones even more. Their Mr Shampoo nickname had taken on, to Brian's ears, a malicious twist and whether it was deliberate or not their taunts began to nick him.

But Brian and the Stones were a godsend to the press. With no holds barred and the full co-operation of all except the record-buying youngsters, they could fire on them at will with both barrels. The more parents and establishment attacked them, the higher their popularity soared and the more their mould was chiselled. Being surly, radiating menace and unhelpful hostility became their hallmark, presenting the middle-aged journalists with a problem as they floundered for the words to describe the phenomena. Into this breach, more than competently, swaggered Andrew.

This was Oldham's forte. With a word here and there he fed the avid press exactly what they searched for vainly, until he came out with a one liner which became the national catch-phrase of the decade. It appeared in *Melody Maker* on 13 March in huge banner headlines: WOULD YOU LET YOUR DAUGHTER MARRY A ROLLING STONE? From that issue on, virtually every write up began with the words, 'They are called the ugliest group in Britain . . .' or 'Loved by kids, Hated by parents . . .' Mothers were said to turn pale, fathers reined in their little girls as the bogey men turned their sights on their town. Lock up your daughters, the warning rang out. The Stones are rolling your way!

Caught up in all the hype, few would come out and champion them. Jimmy Savile was the notable exception. Speaking up for his friends, he made known with all the clout his word carried through his pop column in the *People* newspaper: 'They're a great team for having a laugh and dress very clean and smart when they relax.'

Seeing how complete and instantaneous their image was, Brian distrusted it. It also seemed to him as if the press were running them, and he didn't like being that malleable. He had a sovereign remedy.

Whenever the Stones got cheesed off with the hectoring newshounds, at a silent signal from Brian simultaneously they would pull a Nanker – that was pulling down their eyes and ramming their fingers up their noses. Harmless enough really, but done in unison, at invisible command, it had an unnerving effect on the battery of cocky journalists surrounding them. Satisfied, Brian by his aloofness afterwards would spell it out: they were in control.

Behind the scenes, however, a more divisive battle for control was waging. Jealousies within the band had begun to eat away at it. Notoriously, blame for this had been lassoed and jerked tight around Brian's neck, citing his jealousy of Andrew for taking over the Stones, of Mick for stealing his limelight, most of all for Mick and Keith seizing the monopoly on songwriting. But it was not a one-way street.

Having slogged hardest of all to build the Stones from nothing, though Brian realized Oldham's potential use to them in certain quarters, he resented what he saw as a flash loudmouth, who knew nothing about music, moving in and grabbing overall control. That resentment and understandable professional disdain for their young brash manager was taken as groundless jealousy. On stage, it was another matter. Here, it boiled down to naked rivalry. Brian was the dynamic one, but stood right of centre. Mick as lead singer was set centre and out front. Brian did feel beefed that the spotlight hogged Mick, but as a Stones's friend candidly revealed, Mick was just as guilty. Bass guitarist with the Jimi Hendrix Experience, Noel Redding, says:

> *Mick tried to take over right at the start because Brian frankly was getting more attention than him. It's well known that Mick really resented the attention Brian got. I mean really hated it. And you know, that bloke really stood out. Brian was the true centre of attention and so easily that I don't suppose they would've liked it!*

In addition to this, once off-stage another element was separately working against Brian. Because he lived with Linda at Windsor, the other Stones ragged him relentlessly for being the comfy country squire, while they slummed it in the city. Their barbs, particularly after a bout of tit-for-tat upstaging, would fill Brian's anxious head full of doubts as he drove home, analysing every last remark, each subtle nuance. If he'd had a thicker skin, he would have spared himself the mass of insecurities that this eventually invited. But, he hadn't, and often later alone with Linda at the house whose name the Lawrences had changed to Rolling Stone in his honour, he would anxiously ask her whether she thought the boys liked him, or hated him. It bothered him deeper than anyone at the time fully realized.

But it was the songwriting issue which cut the deepest. Andrew had been encouraging Mick and Keith to try their hands at writing their own material. Both were totally amazed, since it had never occurred to them to consider this. Keith's initial reaction was, 'Naw. That's somebody else's job,' but gradually they both warmed to the notion. There was no earthly reason why Brian shouldn't have been invited likewise. But he wasn't. Indeed, though he already had inclinations to pen his own material for the Stones, it was something which was never given a substantial outlet.

According to Keith Richards, the one thing Brian would never do was physically show one of his compositions to anybody within the Stones, so possibly the others didn't know of Brian's desperate wish to air his songs. But it is hard to appreciate an atmosphere in which he was not able to convey that perhaps shyness attributed to why he was reluctant to barge into the studio and state his case, that he had a song and it went like this . . . After all, both Mick and Keith have openly confessed to needing to pluck up guts before they could present anything to the rest of the boys. Brian was no different. If anything, he was worse off because he was isolated; at least the other two could back each other up. What Brian longed for above all else was involvement.

Linda, absorbing many a backlash of this, knew just how important it was to him.

For sure it was a thing where they didn't let him get involved, as far as I could tell. Because he was writing too and he also wanted to share with the boys. He did often come home quite upset, almost crying because they would be doing their thing and he wouldn't feel that they would even be interested in listening to what his other ideas were, and things like that.

And Linda's mother Violet also stressed, 'Oh, yes! Brian would often sit up well into the early hours of the morning writing songs at the kitchen table. It was very important to him. And they were such good songs too!'

85

In many ways, living with his girlfriend's family, although good for Brian in so far as it provided a calm centre in which he could unwind, had a definite downside because it took him, and kept him, out on the perimeter of the daily developing cabal. Hypersensitive he may have been, but his sixth sense of being squeezed out was worringly persistent. Times, however, were hectic, the Stones in the ascendancy. As he would have to accustom himself to do so often in the future, Brian shut down that insecure part of himself and concentrated on perpetuating their blindingly successful formula of grinding, tingling, chilling R&B, encouraging aggression, chauvinism and rampant sexuality. Where the Beatles howled, the Stones growled. No sops were handed out to soften the message. They extolled sex for the unvarnished pleasure of it. Not for mushy romance.

Despite his inner frustration, or more likely as an extension of it, Brian, a physically urgent man who enjoyed performing anyway, began throbbing home the warning, 'We're out to bed you, not wed you,' all the harder. So much so, he had girls even just watching him on television at home squirming in their knickers from wet warm urges and aches most were barely old enough to understand. On stage he gave out defiance and cynical abrasiveness, shown in his driving guitar rifts, his angry grating harmonica slashes, the way he still had of materializing at the lip of the stage and smashing a tambourine viciously into the wave of faces as if to say a collective 'Fuck You' to the whole world. In as many ways as he knew how, he buried a stream of discontent which, no matter how often it drained, would seep to the surface to flow inside him again.

Then came the long-awaited first Stones album. Recorded in limited time at Regent Sound, the album had been a headache from the start. The necessity of compiling a twelve-track LP to capitalize on the singles' success highlighted the shortfall in their material. So far the first song produced by the kitchen-bound duo was 'It Should Be You', eventually recorded by the obscure white soul artist George Bean. The ballad 'That Girl Belongs to Yesterday' faired better courtesy of Gene Pitney. But only one number 'Tell Me' was considered good enough for inclusion on the début album. For the other eleven tracks they fell back on reflecting their rough and ready club days. Still they were short, and had to throw in an instrumental which Brian brought alive by tremendous breaks. For many the showcase of those twelve tracks is the authentically torrid sting that Brian's slide guitar work gives to the insinuating lyrics of Slim Harpo's 'I'm a King Bee'.

But the album's *tour de force* was its cover. That first LP broke every rule in the book. Despite big battles with Decca's design department it was released with no title, and no band name emblazoned on the front sleeve. Just a moody picture of five young men grouped together staring deeply into the camera. The lighting was a masterstroke. Across shadows so dense their Carnaby Street clothes were barely visible, a discriminating light picks out their faces. First left, Brian sticks out a mile. The only one not wearing a jacket, he looks rakish in a pin-stripe vest, white shirt with gold cufflinks, his oh-so blond hair impeccably groomed. The defensive curiosity in all their eyes makes the look, even today, timeless.

No title meant you had to recognize the cool audacious faces to know the LP. You were forced actually to ask for 'the Rolling Stones new album' by the group's name across store counters and once it was in your hands then came the biggest stunt of all. The liner notes on the back were pure Oldham with his charge: 'The Rolling Stones are more than just a group. They are a way of life.' By its release date the album had sold 10,000 copies in advance orders. Better than the Beatles début album *Please Please Me*, which had notched up a mere 6000. And more, their album displaced *With the Beatles*, their second album, on its way down the album charts.

.   .   .

By now Brian wanted space. As he would often do, he took off suddenly for Cheltenham for a quick visit to his parents and, in particular, his friends the Applebys. On previous trips he had taken Linda with him, making no mention, however, of their expected child. But this time Linda, very obviously pregnant, stayed at home and he went alone. Brian's first stop was always Park Place to see John Appleby. John's widow Raie recalls:

> *Whenever Brian was home he would call at the flat for a chat with John. They were always close. After a while they'd usually up and go to the pub. Brian did enjoy the few odd hours he could spare with old friends.*

87

At the pub, local youngsters would flock around Brian and John, shyly hoping to speak to him, to cadge his autograph. Good naturedly Brian wouldn't only comply, but better still he would thrill the kids by inviting them to pile in about him. John, weighing up his young friend, inwardly worried about the strain lines he could see developing prematurely around Brian's eyes and mouth. Often John would be mistaken by fans for Brian's dad and though he would quickly put them right, invariably Brian would spin about beaming, 'He is my father, my second father!' To Brian, John was a touchstone – a bridge to less complicated times. He didn't have long to linger in Cheltenham however; the Stones's schedule didn't permit it and very quickly he was back in harness with just long enough to kiss goodbye to Linda and their unborn child before embarking on what was their toughest challenge yet: their first American tour.

It was a prospect which both thrilled and appalled the Stones. Painfully aware that they were not washing in on the reassuring tide of a hit single, they were full of reservations. They tried very hard though to draw comfort from the fact that the Beatles had done this all before them. Bill once recalled, 'Other groups had had a number one, done a good tour, good TV. We'd got nothing like that to look forward to. No wonder we were depressed on the way over.' Owning up later to their patchy reception, Brian was philosophical.

'Well we need to make an impression on audiences first, before we can expect to sell them our records,' he said.

Few newspapers bothered to report their coming and those who did all dwelt heavily on their supposedly unbelievable dirtiness, which hardly helped. There was one exception: *Vogue* magazine, under the inspired editorship of Diane Vreeland, described them as, 'quite different from the Beatles and more terrifying'.

Treated to a tepid reception at Kennedy Airport, although hundreds of girls screamed from the rooftops – thousands had greeted the Beatles – they were quickly knifed with the demand, 'Hey? Are you guys wearing wigs?' Only the West Coast fraternity extended a warm welcome and Phil Spector also saw to it that they were awarded the VIP treatment in New York which, after all, was the world's recording capital. But Midwest America was a graveyard for them. Small-town local sheriffs, hotel flunkeys, even store girls flat hated them on sight.

After an unnecessary, oppressive escort of twelve motorcycle cops with wailing sirens, they were delivered to an auditorium in Omaha, Nebraska, equipped to seat 15,000, containing only an embarrassing 600. What's more, unused to alcohol laws, they ran foul of the police and at one point were subjected to the unnerving experience of being forced at gunpoint to pour scotch and coke down the toilet.

Their tour was in dismal contrast to the Beatles's earlier triumph. Then, all four had been very publicly imprisoned in the Plaza Hotel. With the best will in the world that wasn't about to happen to the Stones, no matter how hard Oldham tried, although the *Daily Express* was persuaded to run a story that the Stones were barricaded inside their Manhattan hotel for fear of scissor-wielding fans. This might have worked, if Brian hadn't been spotted happily strolling – sadly from the publicity point of view – unmolested down Broadway in a loose silk shirt and sleeveless bolero thoroughly enjoying freedom of noon in midtown Manhattan. But if they had felt depressed that their American television début had been on the limp *Les Crane* chat show, it was far preferable to what was about to befall them two nights later in Los Angeles.

They had been looking forward to appearing on Dean Martin's *Hollywood Palace* television show, only to be shamefully treated. What the Stones represented was far removed from the showbiz schmaltz epitomized by Dean Martin and perhaps he felt threatened, but Martin exposed the raw, nervous Rolling Stones on their very first American tour to quite inexcusable ridicule with his belaboured, boozy jokes all, blatantly, at their expense. He didn't mind how personal he got either.

Brian was white-lipped, livid at the abuse. Keith wasn't in a much better state and behind Brian all the way in his bloody-minded determination to walk right off. He clearly came within a hair's breadth of defiance too, if a clip from that programme is anything to go by. Brian sucking harp, jammed against a microphone, has naked fury etched in his chiselled cheek bones, his eyes expressively fiery as he plays lead in 'I Just Want to Make Love to You'. The agony of it all was that, because the show had been pre-recorded in segments, it wasn't until they sat down before a television set days later, that they fully realized the awful send-up they had undeservedly been given. Years later, Keith looked back at that:

If Dino had thought a little more, he mightn't have been quite so flippant. But then I don't blame him thinkin' about it now. But in 1964 it was a deadly insult. But all it did . . . all those things did was make you want to prove yourself all the more, so we could come back and bite their heads off.

For Brian the highspot of the whole trip came when they were booked for a two-day session into the famous Chess recording studios in Chicago. That it let them hobnob with great bluesmen Willie Dixon, Buddy Guy and Muddy Waters, who helped to carry in their gear, was grounds for delight, but his delirious excitement stemmed from having the opportunity to benefit from the advanced technology and imagination that Chess and its house engineer Ron Malo – the man responsible for the best works of Chuck Berry – could offer.

Under Malo's strict supervision the whole band's performance tightened. Brian threw himself enthusiastically into it, determined to milk those two days for everything on offer. Of the fifteen tracks recorded, four remain unreleased; of those, one originally entitled 'Stewed and Keefed', later known as 'Brian's Blues', is an intensively evocative instrumental showcasing, long held to be Brian, on stunning lead guitar, at his slow-blues best. Singer/songwriter Donovan reflects: 'There is a saying, "The Blues ain't nothin' but a good man feelin' bad".' Listening to a bootleg of that 2.18-minute track, you absorb a constrained captivity in Brian's playing, an unintentional loneliness.

For the Stones the recording session produced the Bobby Womack composition 'It's All Over Now', which would soon give them their first UK number one. After the session, an impromptu press conference was held in the middle of the road outside the building on South Michigan Avenue, creating a tremendous traffic jam, mass confusion and almost resulting in the Chief of Chicago Police carrying out his Bolshie threat to 'lock up the whole goddam bunch of them!'

'Tell Me' was released as a single in America as their tour ended on an encouraging high, with two concerts at the Carnegie Hall, when fans started to run amok before even a note was struck. Instead of closing the show as planned, the police forced them to appear half-way, then sneaked them out during the first interval. It seemed that just as

Americans were starting to warm to the Stones, the Stones had to leave.

In fact they broke their tour to return home to honour a long-standing engagement at Magdalen College, Oxford: the annual Commemoration Ball. Magdalen were frankly stunned that the now famous Stones turned up at all. Though generally fastidious about such things, the Beatles had failed to appear at a £500 gig at Christ's College May Ball, and the Stones were strongly tipped to give Magdalen a clean bodyswerve. The fact that they literally couldn't afford to stay in the States an hour longer, combined with the attraction of Howlin' Wolf on the Oxford bill, probably had much to do with their honourable conscience, but anyway they turned up.

Initially that was the strength of it. Performing dispiritedly at first, they seemed to take perverse pleasure in the jeers they deservedly got. Then for no apparent reason they snapped out of it and turned on the style. By doing so they instantly created what was later termed a counter-culture, as suddenly the louts of no account became the new aristocracy.

.   .   .

When they had flown into Heathrow Mick had been met by Chrissie Shrimpton. Brian had to wait to get to Windsor to see Linda. The whole experience in the States, even the rough patches, had thrilled him, keeping him on his toes. Yet he had missed Linda badly. The pile of postcards he had sent, the expensive gifts he had bought for her and her family hadn't made up for his need to see her. His welcome return, however, brought the sobering reminder that his heavily pregnant girlfriend was soon to give birth. It brought back too the unavoidable issue of what he was going to do about it and, despite the slow walks he and Linda resumed around Windsor with his beloved Billy G. faithfully in tow, tension tinged the happy homecoming. Noticeably Brian had changed. Too scared of what she might hear, Linda didn't probe. He was back. For now that would do.

That they were back meant Oldham picked up the reins again, racking his brains for ways to whip up some stunts, anything so long as it promoted them at their most loutish. A favourite ploy was to send three of them to any of London's top hotels, knowing full well they would get thrown out. Prior to that, of course, he would have tipped off half a dozen journalists to be on hand to photograph their ignominious ejection. After bouncing off the tenth pavement in as many days, Brian was heartily sick of the fiasco. It was all very well for the fans to love seeing their heroes being martyrs to establishment, but now Brian began confiding in friends that it seriously worried him.

Probably the most talked about outrage of that summer happened when the Stones were invited to be panelists on the British television show *Juke Box Jury*, where new releases were played to a celebrity panel of four, who had to vote it a HIT or a MISS. The Stones's invitation was unique in that it was the only time that five panelists were permitted. Oldham saw it as a tailor-made chance to go to town. Act disgracefully and be as abominably rude as possible about the discs were their instructions.

But Brian was fast losing patience and he vented his frustration thoroughly behind the scenes that day. BBC presenter David Jacobs hosted the show and he vividly recalls Brian's attitude, his deep irritation at the rank stupidity they were supposed to portray:

I remember very clearly that they started their antics just the moment they got on set. I can't recall whether this was at rehearsal, or whether we went straight into transmission. But there is no doubt in my mind that Brian called them severely to order and much to my surprise said something to the effect that they were being thoroughly unprofessional and were to let me run the show in its usual manner. This had an instant effect on them all and after that they behaved themselves in a most unexpected, conventional manner.

It wasn't enough. Shell-shocked viewers countrywide, after watching the Stones ruthlessly vote every disc a resounding MISS, went flying for their writing pads. One lady bitterly complained that they had all smoked throughout the programme, and that only Brian had had the courtesy to stand up when shaking a lady's hand.

'On hindsight,' Brian later reflected, 'I think it was a mistake inviting all five on at once. Perhaps two one week, and the others another might've been better.' Although he also defended the Stones by his perception that 'People are rude to us and it's a laugh. That's okay. But if we're rude to somebody it's . . . aw, that's terrible!' From that day on Brian found himself treading a tightrope. On the one side he would lose his temper and privately challenge the group's moronic image, so much so that he earned the cold shoulder from the others. But he was also staunchly loyal to the Stones as a group and, of them all, was the most vocal in hitting back publicly at the flak hurled at them, which then rebounded on him too. Not surprisingly, confusion seeped in.

Jimmy Savile was close to Brian for many years. He confirmed that 'Brian was very deep and always asking questions of life. Misunderstandings hurt him a lot and as it went on he would wonder . . . where is it all going?'

The Stones hit the coveted number one slot in the UK singles chart on 4 July with 'It's All Over Now'. Jones's assault on the number from his ominous opening chords alone commended instant attention and advance orders of 150,000 copies catapulted it into every Top Ten, zooming up the charts to displace the Animals's 'House of the Rising Sun'.

Just weeks after this Linda presented Brian with his third son, another beautiful blond little boy whom they christened Julian Brian. He was as proud of Julian as he had been of Mark. Says Violet,

Oh yes! Brian came dashing to the nursing home to see his little son and, of course, Linda. In fact, he asked Linda to marry him right there in the nursing home. Alec and I were there and he came to us first. You see Brian was always very correct. I mean when he wanted to date Linda, he came to the house and asked our permission. There, in the room he asked Alec and I for our permission to propose to Linda.

Violet's advice was for them not to rush into marriage simply because of the baby. As it happened, Brian was already busy struggling with stronger emotions. It hadn't been a rash impulse. At that particular moment in time he had meant what he said. But really he was, if anything, further away from settling down with Linda than he had been with Pat. Though Violet had given him some slack, ultimately he knew what would be expected of him. It didn't take long for him to realize then that trouble lay ahead.

The Stones's horrendous schedule mapped out for the second half of the year conveniently allowed him to avoid facing the issue. But it was not going unnoticed and, far from bringing them closer, the birth of Julian and the attendant pressure it carried, stretched their

93

relationship in the coming months to the point at which, after a heated and long overdue confrontation, he would move out of the Lawrence house. With their very first hit disc, television dates in three countries, stop-over gigs in France and Holland, and three tours taking him round the globe, all to fit into six months, quite simply he had too much on his plate.

Plainly these were also incredibly invigorating times for Brian. Existing somewhere between exhaustion and exhilaration, probably his only lucid memories were that nightly feeling he loved of waiting in the wings before going on. Their concerts now were synonymous with a rash of riots. Describing how he felt about live performances he once said, 'The atmosphere is more than electric. It's something tangible, like a vast elastic band ready to snap at any moment.'

From the Hague to the Isle of Man, a quick trot round the Channel Isles and through a British tour which incorporated some Irish dates, that nerve-tingling edge kept Brian going and exciting, thrilling audience after ear-splitting audience. After the mad clamour of fans swaying like palm trees in a tropical storm, the screams and trampled cries of girls crushed and gasping hysterically in the gloom just beyond the footlights, there came the terror of trying to get out of a gig alive.

Battle plans for the getaway were meticulously drawn up hours before a gig. In no danger by now of underestimating the threat to their physical safety, it was vital to effect a smooth or at least swift exit. As Bill Wyman sums it up:

> These kids would just tear you to bits, rip your hair out, tear your clothes . . . go mad . . . just jump on you, screaming. As we ran out of TV stations and then to the car, there'd be kids, and the door would be just wrenched right off and we'd go up the road with the car door missing and mayhem left behind.

It was a very tense life with the added complication of having to live in each other's pockets twenty-four hours a day. The disagreements and difference which existed between Brian and Mick and Keith in particular were having a knock-on effect. In such an airtight cocoon the darker sides of some personalities had begun to emerge.

Always susceptible, Brian was finding it a struggle to deflect the abuse to which he felt particularly subjected. At times he might have believed that the others held him in utter contempt, and that hurt. But it would have been difficult for him not to have believed that. By this time, by their own admissions Mick and Keith had perfected very hurtful impersonations of Brian, which they would take great delight in doing to gales of cruel laughter, based on what they saw as his physical deformities – short legs and a short neck. Their harsh and wicked mimicry gathered unruly momentum during their spell in Ireland and brought Brian down badly.

At the same time Brian, already at loggerheads with Oldham, could see little hope for any improvement in that relationship since his irritated anger at nonsense like the *Juke Box Jury* lark was in direct defiance of the image Andrew was determined to bludgeon to death. Finding his back to the wall too many times then, Brian began to drink.

When Pat was with him he hardly ever drank. 'He was always too busy playing music,' she says. As he moved to London and ventured forth, he had started to down a dram to boost his confidence. That drinking had been increasing insidiously without him noticing, until he was by 1964 a fairly heavy drinker. His smoking, too, another nerve-settling habit, soared to an incredible sixty a day which aggravated his chest already weakened with asthma. He also suffered, as they all did, from the lack of a balanced diet. No regular meals meant bolting a burger between pit stops. Home became where their tour ended, and since what little time he actually spent in bed was rarely spent alone and sleeping, with the perennial shifting sands beneath his feet the insecurity he carried deepened all the more. He would drink to overcome that scary feeling, but in trying to overcompensate he would drink too much and his behaviour then would become erratic. The confidence he was pursuing forever eluded him and his combination of hurt, frustration and confusion far from being blotted out only became magnified, which left him prickly and awkwardly belligerent.

What galled Brian most was that after having been made the butt of some heartless bout of mimicry, which it must have been obvious was hurtful to him, when it came time for a performance he was still expected to get up and do his stuff. No one could deny, and it is often said, that the strength and drive of the Stones came from Brian's musicianship. All asked to be forgotten by the band as soon as he picked up his slide guitar or played harmonica, his cheeks filling and hollowing, the quick light dancing breath that kept the whole sound together.

But, for Brian all was probably not forgotten after a performance, nor forgiven. He would end up drained and alone, feeling very defensive. That lurking suspicion that the others would love to see him squeezed out had spread to a firm foundation. There was a decision-making trio from which he was convinced he was being carefully excluded, until, that was, they needed his musicianship. Although he tried to seal it, a canker set in. Not everyone, by a long way, sympathizes. According to Glyn Johns, 'Brian by now was an outcast in the band and it was his own fault.' Other people also frankly saw Brian as deliberately putting himself out on a limb, when he should have tried to integrate. The Stones, presumably seeing no harm in their behaviour, have always distanced themselves from any blame for Brian's hurt and as for his feelings of being excluded they reckoned that his excommunication was his own fault because of that self-same belligerent behaviour.

The gruelling touring, meanwhile, went on, with nothing to choose by now between the bedlam generated while they were on stage and that spilling over into their getaways. Brian always had been frightened of crowds. Paradoxically, though, he got a kick out of the chaotic enthusiasm; yet deep inside his was a basically shy and nervy nature, not at all suited to public life; and mass hysteria terrified him. It terrified all of them, especially if anything went wrong.

While playing St George's Hall, Bradford a whim to nip across to their hotel between shows had disastrous results for Brian. Stu recalls:

Between the shows they didn't want to sit around their dressing-room until the second half. They said, 'Shall we chance running across the road to the hotel?' They all made it except Brian. Before Brian got to the hotel entrance the fans surged on him. He turned round and ran the other way. So all these people are chasing Brian through the streets of Bradford, tearing clothes off him. The police finally brought him back without a jacket, without a shirt and he'd lost a shoe and great handfuls of hair.

It happened again in Sheffield. Fans out to strip him got him cornered in the city square. According to Bill:

There was Brian running around Sheffield Square with, like, fifty girls to begin with behind him, tearing his clothes off bit by bit while we were in the hotel looking out of the window laughing. Then there was a thousand of them after him!

.   .   .

By the autumn of 1964 Britain had virtually divided itself into two camps with just one relevant question in life. Were you a Beatles fan or a Stones fan? It was unthinkable to be both. The rivalry was needle sharp and, once voiced, your choice tended to label you. To confess to being a Beatles fan conjured up a nice sort, amiable and safe. To be a Stones freak gave you an edge, a non-conformist stamp tattooed invisibly on your forehead.

While London was rockin' to the Who, the Small Faces and the Kinks, the Stones continued to inflict a trail of destruction around the country. Splintered chairs, torn drapes, cost theatres a fortune in repairs. The boys out to put an end to Brian's fatal attraction now numbered four at a time. At one highly memorable gig his Steinway grand piano was wrenched from right under his hands and torn off stage in their desperation to thump him. Countless concerts were summarily cancelled for fear of what had happened back up the road. And the virus was spreading to Europe where Stonemania far out-stripped Beatlemania.

October brought a brief respite in Brian's hankering to compose, but only a minor one when a song recorded by the band carried a Jones songwriter's credit. It was 'Dust My Pyramids', recorded for a BBC general overseas programme. The cut, lasting less than a minute, was more of an improvised Elmore-James-style jam used to open the programme and was of little significance. That same month after they announced they would not be touring South Africa, and Charlie defied Oldham by upping and marrying his sweetheart Shirley Shepherd on the quiet, the Stones hit Germany and Belgium.

On the 18th, in the teeth of an attempt to ban them by Belgium's minister for the interior, the Stones played to a howling sea of heads at the Brussel's World Fairground. In actual fact there was an even larger contingent outside the venue who had failed to be selected for the audience. These, the true fans, were held back by grim, doghandling and armed state police. Two nights later anarchy was unleashed in the streets of Paris after they had played Olympia; fans this time so bold they took on the gendarmes with quite insane nerve. Then, in late October, the Stones returned to America for their second twelve-date tour, this one, though, included two prestigious appearances: one at the Academy of Music and, more important to them, their coveted début on the *Ed Sullivan Show*.

It was a decision Sullivan regretted the second the Stones stepped out on stage. Though there was nothing wrong with the way they looked – Brian even wore a suit and tie – viewers were still outraged by their informality and besieged Sullivan for an explanation of why he had let them perform at all. In his defence he maintained he hadn't seen them till the last second before they had gone on air, and therefore had no idea they looked so outrageous. But he vowed faithfully he would never have them back.

During this tour Mick was going through his second camp period, hamming it up to the nearest camera, particularly when one interviewer strove to elicit an explanation of why the Stones were more popular this time around. For Brian, as ever, his involvement was in the music and just as in June the highspot was a visit to Chess and this time, too, the RCA Studios in Hollywood. Fitting in time to film for the TAMI awards and Jack Good's popular television show *Shindig* along the way, Brian managed to pick up a virus which laid him low, leaving him listless and tired.

Then their last release of the year came in November with 'Little Red Rooster', a bold gamble as a follow-up to 'It's All Over Now'. It was back to pure unadulterated blues. The sexual innuendo in the lyrics were skilful, but what made the number so successful was the compulsive throb of Brian's lone slide guitar. As the song's life-blood, it invests the music with a pump action that palpably takes over, swooping and slashing, snaking quiveringly higher. Though greeted mutely by the fans, 'Rooster' gave the Stones their second consecutive number one and remained one of Brian's personal all time favourites. To promote it the Stones returned to their regular haunt at *Ready Steady Go!* and before letting them launch into their controversial number, the show's presenter Keith Fordyce interviewed both Brian and Mick. The conspicuous difference between Brian's classy performance and Mick's boyish bumbling characterizes the then essential distinction between the two men.

Of all the Stones, Keith liked Brian the best. 'He was a lovely guy,' he stresses. 'Really! The outstanding one of them all by a very long way.' As Keith explained, the refreshing thing in 1964 was that although they were breathlessly exciting times, there was a very relaxed atmosphere around studios like *RSG!*, all the bands totally astonished at, and grateful for, their success. With the single exception, according to Keith, of the Stones. He elaborates how:

> *No, to a certain extent they would be temperamental. Except for Brian, that is. It was invariably Brian then that the team worked with. You see he took a keen interest in everything about the show. I mean the mechanics of where they should position, what setting best served them etc., yet he was also modest. He never dictated. He'd always suggest . . . ask. Say, 'Should we do this?' or 'Perhaps that? What do you think?' And he took advice. Oh, if no one else did, he knew that we were all out there to do them good.*

On that particular edition Brian announced that the Stones were looking forward to their six-week break which would take them through to the end of the year. 'I think we all need a holiday,' he told Keith. He was, of course, alluding only to their public crazy timetable and not to the brewing barney beneath the surface.

With Charlie's secret hitching just the month before, Oldham was still spitting bullets, dementedly obsessed with guarding his three unattached big wheels. He was furious at Brian for being a new dad again and made it plain that come what may Julian's birth had better be kept secret. Brian Jones was not even supposed to be having a serious relationship, let alone be the father of a third child. Like Mick and Keith, Brian was supposed to be an eligible bachelor on the loose – every young girl's pubescent fantasy.

Being leant on heavily in this way by Oldham was the final emotional straw for Brian yet, although a major contributory factory, it was not the sole reason why his affair with Linda was breaking up. Brian had talked of marriage and to a certain degree fantasized about the notion. 'He dreamed of a big house and an estate where he could keep lots of pets,' says Linda. Yet, although there was that part of him which craved the emotional anchor of a loving wife back home, he was only twenty-two and a long way from putting a ring on any girl's finger. Music was what drove him and, if push came to shove, relationships were dispensable. That kind of callousness was not unique to Brian, and neither did it mean he didn't mourn the loss deeply. But his situation with the Lawrence family naturally was altering as it began to become clear that he wasn't about to fulfil their expectations, and matters came to a head when an argument finally split the tenuous bond around the end of November.

Brian moved out and back into a flat in London, this time as far removed from Edith Grove as could be imagined. To celebrate his official return to life on the tiles, he splashed out on a fast sleek Humber motor car. He raided the Carnaby Street boutiques spending upwards of £40 on a single French jacket from Cecil Gee, every week living up to being the Stone *Rave* magazine voted Best Dressed Pop Star. He also began haunting the many teeming clubs like the Ad Lib and Whipps, meeting new people.

His social sphere was subtly about to change. In would come the likes of Robert Fraser, a London art dealer who used his influence in the art world to champion the works of Andy Warhol and Jim Dine. He had met the Stones in Paris after their Olympia concert when he had hung out with Brian. Along with Fraser came his old Etonian chum Christopher Gibbs, a young antique dealer with a store in Chelsea. The nephew of the Governor of Rhodesia and a friend of royal photographer Cecil Beaton, Gibbs along with the rest of his Chelsea set were all too willing to extend open arms to Brian.

Until this time, Brian's friends had been almost exclusively fellow musicians, not the arty crowd. In time Brian would become cloistered, separated from his solid old acquaintances. But no one yet envisaged that, or even saw the flaw in it. The pop world was a fickle thing, anyway. They all thought so. The projected lifespan usually, with luck, around a couple of years. As the end of their first meteoric year drew to a close Brian himself predicted laconically, 'It won't always be a gas like this.'

SIX

READY, STEADY, GO!

T he sixties by 1965 had really started to swing – into a free-living, free-loading, free-loving orbit. Morals and inhibitions altered and dissolved as the seams of society at last gave way. It was the beginning of one of the most glamorous periods in pop music. An arts explosion was happening in every field: fashion, theatre, photography, spearheaded by music whose stars were rapidly creating a new echelon of their own, attracting the eager curiosity of society's sophisticates. The popular perception that the poor little rich kids were wickedly seduced into sex and drugs by rock's ruffians is a fallacy. Already well heeled, well travelled and in many cases thoroughly jaded, they had already been experimenting for some time with purple hearts and the like, and it was often they who sold dope to the naïve pop stars as a way of bribing their way into this new and shockingly delinquent nobility.

Within the Rolling Stones it can easily be argued that by now Mick was more than handsomely bestowed with the lion's share of the spotlight. Yet despite fierce competition from him and others, no one would exude the energized aura that Brian so effortlessly personified, on a scale greater than the confines of the band.

Brian's face and image became, and have remained, one of the timeless quintessential emblems of the swinging sixties. At a time when, as Keith Richard concedes, image held greater sway than the music itself, it is abundantly clear from looking at photographs that Brian was in a superior class of his own. With his perfect blond impudence, his self-assured, extremely photogenic arrogance and reckless spirit of free love, he more than encompassed an enigmatically 'beautiful' heart-throb. More importantly, he represented the voice of youth against establishment, convention and tradition to become a cult figure of classic times. And teenage boys the world over instinctively homing in on him as being the pure essence of the rebellious age, zealously imitated him.

On stage, before a camera, he looked incredible – a predator on the prowl, as much for his lasciviously potent smiles, as his uninterested camel-like stares. In the most fashionable and expensive nightclubs like Scotch of St James in the heart of London's West End, the second he walked down the flight of stairs to the small highly exclusive bar, with its dance floor and tiny stage bracketed by framed stretches of tartan cloth on the walls, he exuded a physical presence indefinable, yet so vibrantly alive, that an immediate awareness of him being in the room would temporarily paralyse proceedings as heads turned to watch him. Furthermore, and probably of most importance to Brian, it was a well-established fact among his peers that Brian Jones was the authority on music and that his advice was well worth seeking. In a year which would see the rise of folk heroes Bob Dylan, Joan Baez and Scotland's Donovan, it wasn't unknown for future stars of the seventies, tentatively groping their way forward in the hotbed of competition, to approach him for his opinion, knowing his advice was sound.

For the Stones 1965 kicked off with the release of their second album *Rolling Stones No. 2*, backed by a quick tour of Ireland. At a concert the previous year Belfast fans had become so demented that several of them had had literally to be carted out in strait-jackets by ambulance men. Fortunately, this time events didn't reach quite that drastic level, though it was still a case of reading riot for gig.

Theirs was no longer a performance, rather a wall of sound created in an attempt to penetrate the bedlam of hysteria which crashed on stage like gigantic tidal waves. As their overworked amplifiers struggled to cope, delirious girls now took enormous risks to try and reach their idols, at times flinging themselves off balconies, while boys waving flags beat their fists on anything before them. Anything from a concert programme to a potentially blinding six-inch metal bolt would be hurled on to the littered stage. Brian sitting cross-legged – a position in which he always felt distinctly uneasy – with his sitar across his lap saw a patent-leather shoe unerringly on target for his head. Ducking elegantly he smiled and kept playing, but all the while he was waiting for the second he'd have to spring up and sprint off with his delicate instrument, as sweaty, desperate girls clawing their way towards them were being tossed brutally by their madonna-length hair back into the surging press.

At the end of January the Stones took off again – this time for Australia where their reputation had long preceded them. More and more Brian was kicking against their increasingly degenerate image. He was perfectly aware of the integral part it played in their success and certainly wasn't above enjoying the fruits of his fame. But, it still did not stop the sensitive side of him from recognizing that it was definitely now going too far. To Brian they were in severe danger of becoming caricatures of themselves, and that to him was worrying, especially when personally his Stone image was so very much at odds with his true character. Trying to justify it within himself was extremely hard, as Jimmy Savile explains, 'It was very difficult for Brian. He was quiet and sensitive by nature but had the Stones terrible tag to live with.' Brian didn't believe either that it had to go so far. He had already had bawling matches with Andrew in a fruitless effort to tone it down, but by the time their plane touched the runway in Sydney he was ready to speak out.

The Australian press, already prepared to be hostile, turned to Brian for a comment on Andrew's latest proclamation before leaving British soil that the Stones should 'alienate the parents, and get the kids on their side'. With a forest of microphones thrust under his nose, Brian didn't mince his words.

I think it would be a very negative policy, wouldn't you say, for any entertainer to set out to attract one section of the public, any public, in any country by deliberately antagonizing another section. It's a very negative way of going about things, and it's quite a stupid thing to suggest.

Doubtless Andrew loved him for that. But the defiance was just another notch up from the incident when, after Oldham had snubbed hundreds of waiting fans by announcing that the Stones did not give autographs, Brian, outraged at the slapdown, though nervous of the agitated mob, promptly stood jammed in a theatre doorway for an hour signing until his hand ached. To Brian, the fans were very important. He never lost sight of the fact that but for them buying their records they would be lost. He carried his duty to his public, at times, too far for his own good.

Savile says:

Once he was very upset that he couldn't answer a whole sack of fan mail which had over 6000 letters in it. In the end I took it from him, promising to keep it just until he could sort out some secretarial thing. There was just no way he had time to deal with it. And that was only one sack.

Meanwhile, in Sydney, one-third of the 10,000-strong welcoming committee had gone on the rampage, smashing the airport to bits, ripping up chain fences and Customs hall rails. Of the twenty girls injured, two were seriously hurt. Australian newspapers lashed out by digging up the worst dirt they could find, and if that wasn't sordid enough the more inventive hacks were only too happy to embellish. Brian, wading through the scurrilous flak, hit back in a mood of subtle defiance. He rang up a radio station that night, told them who he was and asked them to play 'Have I the Right?' by the Australian band the Honeycombs at 78 r.p.m.

Then came the first landmark of the year when 'The Last Time' was released, the first Stones Jagger/Richard single. It was the first number Mick and Keith had felt confident in presenting to the others. It is claimed that this important development stoked such flames of resentment in Brian that they eventually ate him up. In fact, he was inflamed, though to a less dramatic pitch. He had festered already about this for nearly a year and, not without cause, felt very sore that from that moment on virtually all the band's records were composed by Mick and Keith, his compositions ignored. But he once confided to his friend, journalist Don Short, 'It's not that I dislike their music. It's great. But there must be a fair crack of the whip. As a group we've got to consider all channels of music. Mine included.' Not an unreasonable request.

What hurt deepest was the arrogant assumption that he couldn't write songs. Said Stu once, 'I mean Brian was incapable of writing music, so I'm really not sure what else he wanted them to do.' Yet this ignored the glaring fact that Brian, apparently so incapable, somehow managed later to score an entire movie brilliantly – an achievement outwith Mick and Keith's capacity then.

Alexis Korner saw it quite differently. 'It's not true to say that Brian couldn't write music,' he said, defending his friend, 'but his reticence in putting his music forward for consideration by the group seems to have been due to a mixture of shyness and lack of confidence.'

Allegations are strenuously denied that there was any question of forcefully stifling Brian. Although Mick has admitted, 'We probably sort of didn't think, and we didn't try to bring it out of him which was, I suppose, a bit insensitive of us.' Mick also freely concedes that the more you get involved in songwriting, the more creatively satisfying it is. No one who knew Brian to any degree could possibly have failed to understand that the single most insatiable craving in his life was the struggle for creative satisfaction. It is a sad waste then that the door wasn't even eased slightly ajar for him. Although true to say that it was in Brian's own hands to force it open, he feared rejection too much to do that.

If it had to come down to practicalities, the feeling that his contributions, adjudged to have been too sentimental, would be inappropriate, might have served as an excuse. After all, rock music is basically very traditional and ballads are part of traditional folk music which in 1965 was already enjoying its boom. Just the following year 'Lady Jane', a love song whose entire Tudor tenor succeeds through Brian's virtuosity on harpsichord and dulcimer – a tiny delicate stringed instrument, half mandolin, half harp – would find its way on to an album. Rumoured to have derived from love letters between King Henry VIII and Jane Seymour, which Mick and Keith had come across in a museum, nothing more sentimentally sweet than 'Lady Jane' can be imagined. It would seem that room could be found for sentimentality, as long as – it must have felt to Brian – it didn't carry a Jones songwriter's credit.

Back in Britain after their Australian visit, a major English tour began, punctuated by an incident on the way back from a gig, which was to be whipped up into an inflated national outrage. It happened when their chauffeur-driven crammed Daimler pulled into the forecourt of the Francis Service Station in Romford Road, Stratford, in London's East End. According to manager Charles Keeley a 'shaggy-haired monster' – apparently Bill Wyman – got out and asked in 'disgusting language' whether he could use the toilet. Keeley stiffly replied it was out of order and refused to let them use the staff one.

At this, according to Keeley, eight or nine youths and girls including Brian and Mick got out of the car, pushed him aside saying, 'We piss anywhere, man,' and, chanting and dancing about Brian, Bill and Mick allegedly walked across and urinated in a line against the wall, thoroughly upsetting the attendant. Since this occurred in the dead of night, in a fairly isolated spot, it is remarkable that the newspapers got wind of it. Without someone's deliberate contrivance, it must be suspect who tipped them off.

Keeley's account differs radically from Bill's. To Bill Wyman it was a silly incident, typical of the exaggerated abuse they encountered. *We stopped there just to use the bathroom. I asked him, and he immediately got very uptight and said, 'There's no toilet! You can't use it.' And so in the end we went out of the garage, down a side road and just went up against a wall. Next thing, we were arrested. We had to go to court, accused of urinating all over the forecourt of the garage, swearing abuse and everything.*

So, the seamy Stones – three of them – were arrested. Granted not for the most heinous of crimes, but the papers still made the very most of it and their case was set for 22 July.

· · ·

Just as all this was going on, Brian's private life was catching up with him on two counts. Unbeknown to him letters had been passing back and forth between Linda's parents and his own. The Lawrences were angry about Brian's treatment of Linda, and in their frustration felt they couldn't keep Julian's birth a secret any more. Violet Lawrence had written first to Lewis and Louise, telling them that they had a nine-month-old grandson and warning them of their proposed course of action. Lewis's reply was a distant mixture of regret, confusion and fear of the folly of risking exposure in the press. 'It could only prove to be a triple-edged sword, harming us all equally,' maintained Brian's father thinking, it seems, primarily of his son's tendency towards depression.

Obviously the Jones's response was not at all welcome to the Lawrences but, in fairness to Brian's parents, although Julian's birth was a first for Linda's mum and dad, for them this was Brian's third child. Having gone through the trauma twice before, now that Brian was a vulnerable international star, they had come to realize there was a great deal more at stake and their anxieties about talking to the press were understandable. Still, it smacked of cold rejection to Linda and her parents and they went their own way as Brian would soon discover: with the relationship between himself and Linda now adrift, plans to sue him for child allowance would threaten later that year.

The hectic round of heavy touring, meanwhile, trundled on, which meant Brian, like the rest of the band, spent very little time at home, this time 13 Chester Street, Belgravia, a very swish palatial place. Brian had the basement flat which he shared with a friend, Mike Jackson. Staying in the apartment above were two members of the group the Pretty Things, lead singer Phil May and ex-Rollin' Stone and friend Dick Taylor, whose hair was even longer and more outrageous than the Stones. Dick says:

Brian lived in the flat below us. We were working so much – the Stones and the Pretty Things – that we didn't see a lot of each other as such. But it was great to see Brian again. He and Phil would go out drinking together a lot. Brian was tight, you know. Even when they were very drunk he would be reluctant to fork out for a taxi home.

Dick laughs:

Oh, but I must tell you this. Our rhythm guitarist was Brian Pendleton. He wasn't popular, poor guy. But anyway, Pendleton and me went shopping in Carnaby Street for a pile of new gear. Pendleton bought this black and white striped jersey. Next day Brian spotted it in the flat. 'Oh, that's real nice!' says Brian. 'We're doin' RSG! live tonight. Do you think anybody would mind if I borrowed it?' I laughed and said, 'Yeah, go on and take it.' Poor Pendleton never saw it again. But you know the best bit? We were all sitting in the flat that night, before the telly, and on comes Brian, you know, like

107

wearing this jersey. 'Oh, look!' cries Pendleton. 'Brian's got a jersey just like mine!' Well! We all fell about laughing. He didn't twig. He never twigged! He kept saying, 'I wonder whatever happened to my jersey like Brian's?' And I wouldn't mind but every boy in the land the next day went out and copied Brian's jersey. He was photographed in it too, so many times.

About that jersey, Phil May says, 'There's no way Brian would like a jersey and go out and buy one like it. He'd just nick it. That was just Jones.' Phil and Brian were good mates and knocked about together both, as Phil politely phrased it, 'enjoying their success'. But beyond the girls and high jinks, Phil came to understand Brian pretty well. Though he liked Jones a lot, Phil feels Brian's own personality was his own worst enemy many a time. He remembers that:

It was very hard not to upset Brian. He thought so much about things, you see, and he took things to heart so easily. His biggest problem I think was that he never quite managed to tap into someone else's sense of humour. If someone would say something and mean it in a joke, Brian would take it to heart – very much. For instance, I was with him several times when Mick would say something and personally I didn't think he meant it to hurt. But instead of turning it aside, Brian would analyse it down to the last detail and get hurt.

For a time a frequent visitor to Chester Street was Linda. She would turn up to see Brian and at first he would be pleased to see her. More often than not, though, they would end up rowing and both Phil and Dick tell of hearing many a serious shouting match, usually ending with slamming doors.

Through April and May, though, personal problems were to take a back seat on the non-stop treadmill of live television shows in Germany, a two-day date in Paris, then back to the States for another tour, recording *Shindig* with Jack Good along the way, as well as the *Ed Sullivan Show*. The last time they had appeared in 1964, Sullivan had vowed never to have them back. However, with 'The Last Time' at number eight in *Billboard*, he couldn't justify the ban. And so, on 2 May, after eating humble pie, Ed introduced the Stones.

Imprisoned for eight hours before transmission they had compromised this time by visibly smartening up. It still didn't appease middle-aged Americans. After the show Sullivan sent the Stones a telegram saying that he had received hundreds of calls from parents complaining bitterly about them. But, he added, 'I've received thousands from teenagers praising you!' Magnanimously Ed wished them the best of luck with the rest of their tour.

It was a tour which would bring out the shadier side of life on the road. Backstage Brian would be confronted by a ferocious-looking cop brandishing a Stones LP, demanding on pain of splitting his head open that he should autograph it. Nothing if not prudent, ignoring the charge of being a long-haired sissy, Jones would dutifully pen his moniker. In certain cities the cops would wait to see the extent of the hysteria, and therefore the Stones' plight, then offer them protection – at a price. Bribes were big business around those enlisted to protect rock groups.

The Stones's relationship with the police was never good in any country. In Ontario, the cops stopped a show after only fifteen minutes, turning up the house lights and pulling the plug on their amps. Feeling sorry for the disappointed fans, the Stones promptly turned on the police. CRUDE AND RUDE ROLLING STONES HURL INSULTS AT THE POLICE shrieked next day's headlines. This time the papers didn't get away with it. Canadian teenagers jammed all the radio stations and switchboards exonerating their idols, and laid the blame squarely on the doorstep of their own national police force.

Then it was back to Britain. In mid June came a short Scottish tour. Clearly remembering the date they played in Aberdeen, Brian's friend and flatmate Dave Thomson recalls:

> *It was just the day before the city was sealed off for an outbreak of Foot and Mouth Disease. The fans went mental. I was acting as Brian's decoy that night. Brian had given me his jacket after the gig so that I'd be mistaken for him.*

With a mob hard on his heels Dave just made it headfirst into the back of a van before it careered off, rocked by a frightening and agile posse, while Brian slipped away discreetly in the other direction.

The following month Brian, Bill and Mick appeared in court for the first time to face charges over the garage incident. LONG-HAIRED MONSTERS and YOU CANNOT BEHAVE THAT WAY headlines rolled off the presses, but the judge only fined them £3.00 each. What was not made particularly clear was the significant fact that the prosecution had not been brought by the police. It was a private action by Mr Keeley and a garage customer Eric Lavender. Their addresses were kept out of print for fear of Stones's fans' reprisals. However, the slurs heaped on them managed to magnify the already difficult problem of the abuse they received everywhere they went now.

From that moment on they were refused leave to stop at nearly every roadside hotel and café, and were forced to pull into lorry driver pull-ups and motorway service stations – thereby thrust slap bang in among the very people who resented them most. All five Stones suffered insupportably from horrendous insults, but no one argues that Brian took it worst of all. He could never adapt to being accused of having lice in his hair or wearing filthy clothes. He tried writing to the newspapers and invariably brought it up in interviews, as a way of pointing out the sheer injustice of it. But it was like spitting in the wind. It just came back in his face. Frustration and annoyance built up and friends could see the outward signs of the strain beginning to tell on him. Michael Aldred from *Ready Steady Go!* reveals:

> *He was prone to violence when he was very drunk, but not generally against other people. I went with him to a club one night and we walked home and he kicked the dustbins and he kicked the wall, and if he could possibly have thrown himself into the wall – he would've.*

Other times he could weather it well. Ray Coleman, former editor of *Disc* and *Melody Maker*, had a long-running private joke with Brian of, 'Coffee, madam?' At a swish London restaurant that summer a sneering waiter, unable to hide his active contempt for Brian, had eventually let it spill over by asking Brian pointedly, 'Would you like coffee, madam?', making a scathing dig at Brian's by then generous hair. Ray knew Brian and knew he could have easily, and justifiably, lost his temper and decked the waiter. Ray recalls, however, that:

> *It was an electric moment. Brian was a sensitive man who often showed anger and I expected him to at least punch the waiter's face. But Brian, showing a big heart and far too much self restraint, burst into laughter. 'That's very funny, man!' he said to the waiter. 'What's your next film?'*

Ray was also privy to the personal frustration Brian felt more immediately connected with the music, and the claims that he was riddled with jealousy at the attention Mick received. He puts the view that, 'Brian didn't actually resent Mick's leadership, but he was musically unfulfilled. He didn't really love the Stones music though he realized Mick and Keith wrote songs much more commercial than his, which tended to be more bluesy.' Aldred also related to this.

One just has to understand the lifestyle of somebody like that. He was a musician, with a musician's mentality. A musician is a race apart – and striking chords, playing well on the guitar. When one hears that back, it's like . . . it's a spiritual thing. It would be, I should imagine, like, I dunno, plasma. It's like seeing or feeling the very essence of one's self. God, it's so hard to explain if one isn't in there doing it.

.   .   .

Late summer would see many changes. The previous autumn Harold Wilson had led the Labour Party to 10 Downing Street after thirteen years in opposition wilderness. Now within the Stones a new government was also in transition. Eric Easton was given the ignominious bum's rush in favour of an American businessman, Allen Klein. Easton's star had faded rapidly with the arrival of the glittering and flamboyant Klein, who courted the Stones with his aggressive management style, which it was felt would further the band's financial success.

Meanwhile, more private matters were being transacted. Oldham had been furiously trying to make Linda's intended paternity suit go away, and finally managed to get Linda into their solicitor's offices. As she says:

It was all pretty scary. I mean, those high-powered attorneys in their plush offices pushing bits of paper at me to sign saying that I would never at any time say or claim that Julian was Brian's son, and so on. It was all very overwhelming.

Brian was there, and though he didn't say anything I knew he didn't like what was going on one bit. You must understand that there was an awful lot of pressure being piled on Brian. It was all wrapped up with the Stones image and whatnot. He was as much forced into it as I was and it upset him. That's why I signed in the end. It was to make it easy for him.

Brian did feel badly, so badly that not long afterwards he swept Linda off to Morocco as some kind of thank you. She admits:

111

I thought it was to reconcile, but it wasn't. Brian wanted us to talk through what was best for us both. He felt he had to go on with his career and that I should spread my wings and live more. It might sound selfishly one-sided, but it really wasn't like that. No. I had no choice in our break-up, but the way I see it is that it was Brian who took me into the world, if you like . . . shook me out of small town mentality.

There was strain, nevertheless, and heartache for them both which could only be exacerbated when some kind soul tipped off the media that Brian had taken his girlfriend abroad with the notion of proposing. Everywhere they went they were dogged by hoards of gossip-hungry hacks. On top of everything else, this was the final straw; what had been a difficult situation in the first place was now magnified, and the trip dismantled in disaster, as they returned home separately.

Then came another – this time professional – turning-point for Brian with the Stones's first dual UK/USA number one, 'Satisfaction', a recognized milestone in Brian's life and, according to common report, the beginning of the end for him when it was claimed that Brian was now virtually dead in terms of his importance to the band: a second-class Stone. He supposedly came to realize that he was no more than a dispensable appendage that could be lopped off at any time, since the two songwriters had emerged to prove themselves beyond doubt the prolific talent in the band. Brian, in short, was officially redundant. Many close to the situation, however, frankly dispute that.

It is said that the famous riff upon which 'Satisfaction' is built came to Keith one night in a hotel room. Recently Richards recalls:

I actually woke up in bed, I think in the London Hilton, although I've read somewhere that it was somewhere else. Anyway, it was a hotel room and I had had a little tape machine next to the bed and I just woke up and had this riff and, I thought, I had to put that down. I did one chorus and then apparently fell asleep because when I woke up in the morning the tape had run out. I didn't remember. All I remembered was leaving it ready to go. When I played it back there was this maybe thirty seconds of 'Satisfaction' in a very drowsy sort of rendition, then the guitar goes clang and then it's like forty-five minutes of snoring. I'm glad I played it back.

112

Proof is often offered of Brian's panicked pettiness in tales of him childishly vamping, 'Popeye, the Sailor Man' during any stage rendition of the number. But Brian's disgusted dissatisfaction with 'Satisfaction' might have had its roots in something more serious. It is sometimes said privately among several of his closest musical contemporaries that there was a possibility that Brian thought up the riff for 'Satisfaction'. One of those contemporaries, bassist Noel Redding, goes further and claims: 'It is said it was Brian who thought up the riff, played it to them. Then the lads said, "Yeah, right – thanks," and took it.' Unsubstantiated by the Stones, and by no means a confirmed and official line, if this were the case, then Brian's much accused sense of hollow bitterness would have some justification. It is, however, a matter of speculation and an open verdict must be recorded.

The tension which had elasticated the band for long enough, just cranked up some more. Someone who experienced first hand the choleric conditions around Brian was photographer Gered Mankowitz, who worked closely with the Stones between 1965 and 1967. Personally Gered didn't get along with Brian and in many ways didn't like him. Gered remembers:

The first time I met Brian was in a restaurant and he was very charming, polite and nice. As I got to know him, though, I felt the charm was only surface deep. Beneath it he was curiously awkward, manipulative and a rather difficult person to rely on.

Brian's relationship at this time with the other Stones was variable. It would be very nervy and edge. It was often static, and by that I mean electric. Then there were other times when they all got along very well. As a guy, Brian was a strange mix. He would be very difficult, then he'd be very jolly and good company. I always felt he was the odd one out. Certainly you always knew, if someone was going to rock the boat, it would be Brian.

Gered spoke of episodes such as when they would all pull into a roadside restaurant for a meal. Brian would say he wasn't hungry and stay in the car as the others trooped out. Then when they returned he would decide he was hungry after all and would get out of the car and march in. In answer to why Brian did these petulant, contrary things, Gered replies, 'I don't know. Perhaps he was feeling insecure or something. He had a fragile character.'

113

It was a very difficult time for Brian. Long-standing problems only seemed to be compounding. Even the matter of him having paid himself that extra fiver back in 1963 still rankled resentfully with the others. Feeling that his songwriting had been suppressed was bad enough, never mind the speculation over 'Satisfaction', on top of this the implication that he could be dropped and no one would miss him must have been crushing for his confidence. Of course, he was too close to the situation to see that was arrant nonsense – a farcical fallacy – but others were not.

Musically, no one could touch Brian. Gered continues, 'I was with them at recording sessions and when they were on stage, and he would be brilliant!' But incredibly, as well as his musical genius Brian, as a creative entity, added a dimension, had a quality which was uniquely his own.

Phil May was adamant.

Brian was very very important to the Stones, incredibly essential. You can see that by the fact that the Stones have never been the same without him. I'm not saying they aren't good. But they've never been the same without Brian. Anyone else up there, and I've nothing against either Micky Taylor or Ron Wood, is just another guitarist. It was something spiritual with Brian. He was a left wing – a spiritual element. I dunno, but it was vital. You could've cut off Brian's guitar arm and he'd still have had it. Even the problems surrounding him within the band were central to the electricity of the Stones.

And, believe me, it wasn't an ego thing, although it has been made out through the years to appear like that. You know, this shit about who got more fan mail than who? It was really far more serious than that. The divisive force was strong, this pulling in opposite directions. Hearsay has it that Brian wanted to sing his songs and do his numbers too, but Mick and Keith were a 'mafia' thing unto themselves.

When Phil spoke of the Stones knowingly hurting Brian he was making particular reference to what was rumoured to have happened one night when the Stones were playing in Portsmouth. He tells how:

In those days there was only one road to Portsmouth. Well, Mike Jackson was driving Brian there in Brian's old Rover and they broke down. They couldn't fix it, but Brian said, 'Look don't worry the boys

114

will be along in the limo in a moment.' Brian always was picky about
setting off on time to get to gigs, and so he was always the first one on
the road. Well, anyway, the limo did come along, and here's Brian
waving them down like hell and Mike too. And what happens? The
limo draws level, the fingers go up from inside and they drive on
laughing their heads off and left him stranded on the verge. What I'm
saying is, they would rather play with one short than pick him up.
That really hurt Brian. Maybe some guys would take it differently,
but not Brian. It really cut him up. And I mean it's murder playing
with one short. It changes the whole balance.

There would come a time when, for one reason or another Brian didn't
make a gig, the other four would near crucify him for making them
play a man short.

If that Portsmouth incident happened, then it may not have been
isolated. Tales have been told of other times when once, for instance,
Brian had a bad sore throat and asked to stop at a chemist after a gig.
Stu who was driving is supposed to have found one and stopped while
Brian ran in to buy some lozenges. Apparently they then noticed that
the fans had spotted them. According to Stu, Keith saw the mob
converging and looked at Brian inside at the counter. 'Leave him and
drive off,' he is alleged to have told Stu, who promptly obeyed him.
When Brian emerged, so the story goes, it was to find the car gone and
a pack of screaming girls ready to tear him to shreds.

At this time even their management was at war. The advent of
Klein, with his dramatic flair and impeccable timing just as Decca's
two-year contract had expired, meant the professional demise of Eric
Easton who had kept the Stones financially afloat when they hadn't had
two pennies to rub together. He was very shabbily treated by Oldham
who, with all the insolence of youth, bluntly told him his services were
obsolete. Quite rightly Eric instantly instigated legal proceedings for
breach of partnership agreement against Oldham, although he had
difficulty serving the papers on Andrew as he would literally leg it away
from any civil writs.

After pulling a stunt straight out of a B-grade gangster movie,
when all five Stones were instructed to get themselves a pair of shades,
look mean and moody and, above all, keep their mouths shut while
Klein negotiated with Decca's Sir Edward Lewis himself, Klein and

Oldham from that moment reigned supreme and Easton was history. The deal with Decca was lucrative and full credit for it belongs to Klein, but as the new management team was made official on 28 August, Brian never felt happy about how Eric had been ousted, no matter how much he loved making money.

.   .   .

Out of Our Heads became number one album in the States in September 1965, about the same time as Brian was voted by a *Record Mirror* poll to be the Most Handsome Man in Pop. It was a title which, though flattering, personally embarrassed Brian. Dave Thomson says, 'I was with him when he read that. He threw down the newspaper and said, "Keith Relf [lead singer with the Yardbirds] is better lookin' than me. It should've been him".'

Modesty apart, however, despite the reality of stress and strain, which had to be hidden at all times from the fans, he strutted his stuff very well and knew when to turn it on. Outwardly, to the world at large, Brian was aglow, the trendiest person alive with a personal charisma as powerful as a physical punch. It radiated no more so than when *Ready Steady Go!* gave them the singular honour of devoting a whole show exclusively to them.

In the year about to dawn and, certainly all through the one after that, the camera would have a field day zooming in on the increasing ravages that would begin to wreak havoc on Brian's looks. But in 1965 the lens couldn't get enough of him. One of the most memorable clips ever recorded of Brian must be when, with Cathy McGowan, presenter of *Ready Steady Go!*, he mimed a send-up of the now classic Sonny and Cher hit 'I Got You Babe', with backing from the other Stones and Andrew Oldham. In tight white trousers, brown polo and a white fury waistcoat Brian appears at his most rakishly dangerous as he plays Sonny to Cathy's Cher. Closing one wide well-shaped hand over Cathy's shoulder, while their heads clunk romantically together, female heartbeats broke the Richter scale up and down the country; there wouldn't have been a father watching who would have trusted him within yelling distance of his daughter. Wickedly sensual, Brian's inbred elegance subtly robbed his bedroom eyes of any offence.

Above: Pursuing a childhood passion, Brian enjoys the Tramway Museum, Derbyshire, in 1961, in a photo taken by his friend and mentor, John Appleby.

Above: Cheltenham, 1951. Brian, aged nine, in his hated school uniform and glasses, both of which he often refused to wear.

Left: Brian's childhood home, Ravenswood, 355 Hatherley Road, Cheltenham. It was here that he deafened the neighbours with his first saxophone.

Above: Brian's first flat in Selkirk Street, Cheltenham, around 1961. He occupied the top floor, left, with his friend, Graham Ride, a fellow musician and alto saxophonist.

Left: Julian Mark Andrews, Brian's son with Pat Andrews, who was born in Cheltenham in 1961.

Opposite: New love. Linda Lawrence in 1962, taken by Brian in Windsor, Berkshire, where he lived for sometime with her and her family.

Below: First love. A very young Brian dances with Pat Andrews in 1961 at a private party.

Above: Linda Lawrence
and Brian in Morocco,
1965, where they went to
relax and attempt to
mend their relationship.

Right: Julian Brian
Jones, Brian's son with
Linda Lawrence, born
in 1964, who now lives
near his mother on the
American West Coast.
(*Joel Sussman*)

Above top: Looking
decadent on the 1968
original album cover for
Beggar's Banquet, taken
at Sarum Chase stately
home, hired for £40 a
day.

Above: The Rolling
Stones – fresh-faced and
eager in 1963.

Left: Clubbing it in London, 1966, at the *Flamingo. From left to right:* singer and composer, Lindsey Duncan, Brian, Georgie Fame's trumpeter, Eddie Thorton, close friend, Ronni Money and wife of Zoot Money.

Right: And clubbing it earlier in Cheltenham, Brian went to the famous basement jazz club, 38 Priory Street. A low stone wall conceals the oak-panelled basement, which runs the length of the house, and which saw such stars as Lonny Donnegan, Terry Lightfoot, Acker Bilk, the Temperence Seven and Tommy Steele.

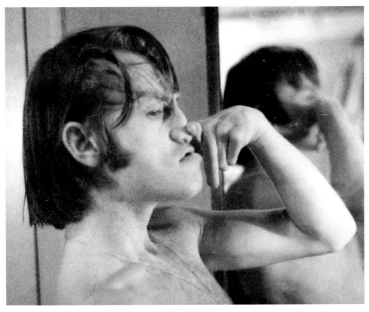

Left: Brian displaying his penchant for pulling faces – in the dressing room, 1966.

Overleaf: Rival Stones, Mick Jagger and Brian in 1966 concert at London's Royal Albert Hall. (*Hulton*)

7

Above: 1965: patiently posing for an admiring fan outside his Chelsea mews flat.

Right: Is this Brian? No, it's Phil Kent joining the Jones lookalike craze sweeping Britain in 1965.

Above: 5 December 1968. Chaos reigns at the Beggar's Banquet as Les Perrin, Stone's PR man, attempts custard-pie revenge on a cowering Bill Wyman. Brian sits centre table, and on the right Mick Jagger watches, laughing gleefully.

Left Les Perrin at work again.

Above: In Green Park,
London, in 1967.
(*Hulton*)

Below: Signing an
autograph on the arm of
one of the many fans

hanging around his
mews flat in London.
To the left, his friend,
David Thomson, looks
on.

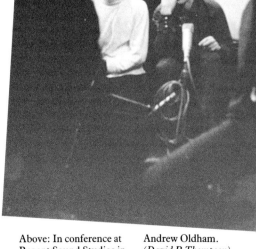

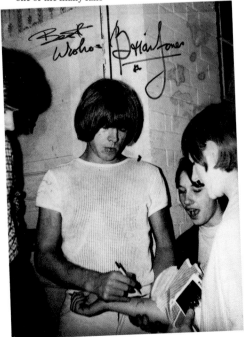

Above: In conference at
Regent Sound Studios in
1964. *From left to right:*.
Allen Klein, Brian,
Mick Jagger and

Andrew Oldham.
(*David B Thompson*)

Above: On guitar
(Gered Mankowitz).

Right: And keyboards
(Gered Mankowitz).

Right: In drag in a New York back street off Third Avenue for a publicity shot for *Have You Seen Your Mother, Baby, Standing in the Shadow?* in 1966. Jean Harlow lookalike Brian is first left.

Left: Rock 'n' Roll Circus, Wembley, north London in 1968. *Back row:* Bill Wyman, Pete Townsend, Brian, Mitch Mitchell; *Front row:* Keith Moon, Charlie Watts, Yoko Ono, Julian and John Lennon, Eric Clapton. *(Hulton)*

Above: Tangier: Bachir Attar and the Master Musicians of Jajouka during filming for the BBC in 1989. In the sixties, it was Brian who was largely responsible for drawing attention to their music. (*Cherie Nutting*)

Left: Fans invade the stage during a Stones concert at the Royal Albert Hall, London, in 1966. Brian's broken left hand is bandaged after a fight with Anita Pallenberg.

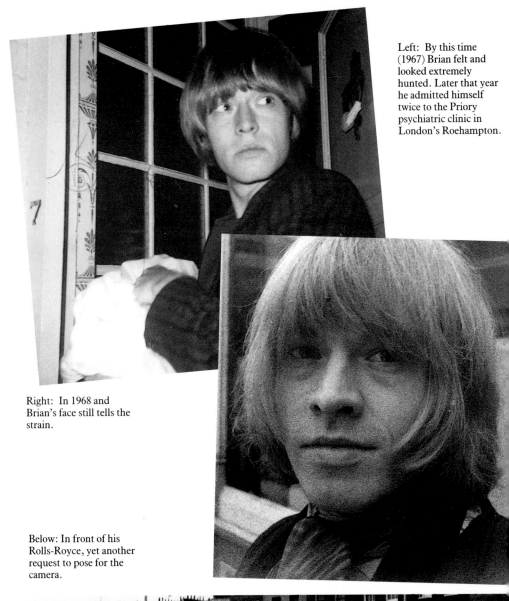

Left: By this time (1967) Brian felt and looked extremely hunted. Later that year he admitted himself twice to the Priory psychiatric clinic in London's Roehampton.

Right: In 1968 and Brian's face still tells the strain.

Below: In front of his Rolls-Royce, yet another request to pose for the camera.

Right: Mary Hallett, who looked after Cotchford Farmhouse and to whom Brian was emotionally very close.

Above: Brian's rural retreat, Cotchford Farmhouse, once the home of A. A. Milne, which Brian bought in November 1968. First floor, third window from the left was Brian's bedroom, and the ground-floor door on the far right leads out into the garden from his studio.

Left: Hay Waggon Inn, Hartfield, Sussex, where Brian was very popular with the locals.

Overleaf: Brian, in his prime in 1965, stares down from under his heavy blond fringe.

Cathy McGowan once dubbed Brian more of a pop idol than any of the others. 'He seems to glow in front of the camera. He loves it. But he is also very strong willed and tends to speak his mind. That's why he gets a lot of criticism. He's a bit like John Lennon in that respect.' But whatever troubled waters he had tread, without knowing it, Brian was about to hit the rapids. The Stones took off for a tour of Austria and Germany the day after that special edition of *RSG!* and it was in Munich that a certain young lady bribed her way backstage to meet the Stones.

Anita Pallenberg came from generations of painters of German/ Swiss origin who had emigrated to Florence. Anita and her sister were fluent in four languages and completely at home in the company of painters and writers. After studying picture restoration and graphic design, Anita travelled to Rome, ostensibly to study art. She began standing in for models and soon her photographs began to appear in top fashion magazines. An unusual girl with cropped hair, lean and lissome as a thoroughbred, she had an unsettling air about her. By the time her path converged with Brian's in 1965 she was twenty-one and had worked in all the major European capitals. She had gone to West Germany on a fashion assignment and was in Munch the very night the Stones were appearing.

'That's how I met Brian,' she once revealed. 'He was the only one of the Stones who really bothered to talk to me. He could even speak a little German.' Having watched Brian on stage, Anita had been captivated by the way he moved, the fabulous aura he projected. 'Brian was so far ahead of Mick and Keith, you wouldn't believe it. They were just schoolboys beside him.' Only hours later, off stage, however, Anita confronted the reality in its grim light. She says:

There had been some kind of disagreement within the Stones. Brian against the others and he was crying. He said, 'Come and spend the night with me. I don't want to be alone.' So I went with him. Almost the whole night he spent crying. Whatever had happened with the other Stones, it had absolutely devastated him.

That crisis notwithstanding, Anita saw to it that she forged a relationship with Brian. Brian was hardly unwilling; he was totally knocked out by Anita. She was the first woman to fascinate him and the one woman who would dominate him as all her predecessors had failed

117

to do. In many ways Anita became a harder, more insidious drug than any he would soon sample, and the effect in the long run was perhaps even more shattering.

Never a man to run an uncomplicated love life, Brian was already seeing French filmstar Zouzou from an earlier trip to Paris. For a while both actress and model were cutely conned into believing they were the sole woman in his life. Usually Dave Thomson had the task of ferrying one discreetly out of the back door, as the other blew in unexpectedly at the front. A nerve-racking business for his young Scots friend.

Anita's attraction took many forms, but certainly her daredevil streak dangerously matched Brian's, and together they made a dynamic, though not always pleasant, couple. After having withstood so much pressure, having Anita as a cohort was very satisfying for Brian. A manipulative streak in him detected by Gered had now found a soul mate. Says Gered:

One was always uncertain of Brian, of what he was going to do. He would engineer a situation and stand back and watch the results. When Anita came along? Well, she was exactly the same. They took great pleasure together in manufacturing those sorts of situations. The two were undoubtedly very much in a world of their own. Disconnected, you might say.

That disconnection had two sides to it. On the one hand – and this was a factor which appealed greatly to Brian – Anita was an asset. She was like no other girl. Certainly none of the other Stones had a girlfriend who came close, and as a result she had been greeted with wary hostility, especially, it is said, by Mick. Anita claims to have been able to crush Jagger with a single word. And as for Keith? She terrified him. Mick's girlfriend at this juncture was still Chrissie Shrimpton and it appears that disenchantment – already brewing ever since a seventeen-year-old beauty with hair like a bolt of silk called Marianne Faithfull had appeared on his horizon a year ago – set in whenever he saw Brian swanning about with the classy Pallenberg on his arm. Perhaps Mick's wariness, which Brian was quick to appreciate, played a part in how deeply he was prepared to plunge in. With all his insecurity, quite simply his ego needed a good fillip.

Yet on the other hand, Anita was far more than a simple crutch for his shaky confidence. He did fall deeply and irrevocably in love with her. He was impatient of the time they had to spend apart and his eternally jealous nature worked overtime. Having found someone with whom he really felt he could want to spend his life, he was petrified from the start of losing her.

Anita's motives, though, have always been a grey area. The picture painted is very much that Anita, while loving Brian, went through the mill with him, suffering many beatings at his hands because of his wild insecurity, and that in the end she was simply unable to take any more. But other sources, some closest to Brian, read it quite differently. They suggest that Anita, whom no one took for a fool, first thought the power of the Stones was Brian. But once behind the scenes it became obvious that Brian was in a minority of one and going through great difficulties, then her allegiance wasn't so hard to shift.

But Brian had no way of knowing what the future held. At that point he was on the crest of a wave. He looked set to be one half of the hottest, most sexily ruinous item on the social circuit. And the more it appeared outwardly that he was more concerned with that than concentrating on the Stones, then the harder life got for him in the studio. Matters climaxed one night during their September British tour. As he was playing organ in the number 'That's How Strong My Love Is', Brian couldn't help but feel the bitter irony of it. Here they were singing of love, when he was playing with people who he felt humiliated him and reduced him now almost nightly to tears. As the fans' hysteria whipped up, so too did his own. In the darkened hall he threw his head back into the spotlight suddenly and let harsh and cynical laughter crackle out.

By the time the Stones toured America and Canada in late October, the strain he was under began to cause him to miss gigs. The prospect of getting up on stage with the band was starting to affect him so badly that it made him ill. By this time personality clashes were effecting performance. It wasn't that Brian physically couldn't play, rather the problem lay with his will to do so. All the tension had naturally begun to bend his mind.

Brian's failing to make the gigs put pressure on the other four to carry the show without him, and they deeply resented that. Thus, what had begun as an invisible fracture was widened to a gully running with a river of ill will which would overwhelm Brian when he did return to the fold. In an ideal world they would have sat down and tried to talk their way through the things that were going wrong, but personalities, jealousies and egos got in the way. They were also all very young and living heady lives and the continual round of appearances played its major role too. It was hard enough to grasp which country they woke up in, let alone be rational and generous enough to mend sails. As a result it became a vicious circle.

For Brian the one good thing to come out of New York was that his friendship with Bob Dylan blossomed there. It was a valuable friendship to both men. Gered was introduced to Dylan for the first time in Brian's hotel room, although he missed the famous Lost Jam Session. It was the night of the New York harvest moon black-out that Dylan spearheaded a party of revellers up five flights of stairs to Brian's suite at the Lincoln Square Motor Inn. That night they played acoustic guitars and sang together by candlelight. No power meant that the historic happening was never recorded for posterity.

Another happy legacy of those times is that Brian's dress sense was by now beginning to take off in an international direction. In the years to follow Brian would elevate dressing to an art form, and become the prototype for today's pop star. It was he who first brought glamour to the Stones, leading the way with frock coats, fedora hats and Berber jewellery. The pop fraternity followed him slavishly. He was a highly artistic man in every sense, not only musically. He was good with his hands and had crafted marquetry as a small boy; he painted on canvas and designed too. The sleeve for his album of Moroccan music *Brian Jones Presents the Pipes of Pan at Jajouka* was a product of his personal design. He once professed an ambition to be a clothes designer and certainly he experimented with silks, satins and acres of velvet, proving by bold example that a man could wear these sensual fabrics with style and grace and retain every ounce of his masculinity.

Unfortunately, his experiments didn't restrict themselves to sartorial pursuits. After a small drama in Sacramento when a live mike knocked Keith out for a full seven worrying seconds, the tour wound up in Los Angeles on 5 December. To celebrate the end Brian and Keith went off to an Acid Test party given by the writer Ken Kesey and his crowd. Needless to say, Brian passed the test as did Keith, which was to try out a manmade drug so new it had not yet been declared illegal – lysergic acid diethylamide, a hallucinogenic drug, abbreviated to LSD and more commonly known as acid. That night he dropped acid and set his ever curious feet on a new and, this time, destructive path.

When Brian arrived back at Heathrow he had a touching reunion with Anita, who melted submissively into his side, looking leggy and lovely for the popping flash bulbs in a floral-print miniskirt and thigh-high suede boots. Brian, it appeared, was a man who had it all. Rumours flew that he was about to marry Miss Pallenberg. However, they were dashed when Brian with economical abruptness replied, 'That's not my scene, man.' It didn't prevent him, however, from also being quoted as saying that, 'Anita is the first girl I've ever been serious about.' She was certainly the first since his rise to fame to be invited to come share his luxurious London home. And as Anita moved in, the old year moved out with a guest appearance by the Rolling Stones on a special edition of *RSG!* on 31 December.

SEVEN

THE ACID
TEST AND
RUSSIAN
ROULETTE

.

THE GIRL WHO LOVED A ROLLING STONE is how the *News of the World* headline ran on 16 January 1966. The accompanying full-page spread unsparingly detailed Brian's harsh and humiliating neglect of Pat Andrews and Mark. His love life had never been more complicated and time consuming. Having headed off at the pass Linda's intention to sue him for child allowance for Julian, he had failed, nevertheless, to keep it out of the papers. It had been this trigger that drove Pat to take her story to the *News of the World*.

For a long time Pat had been disappointed that Brian had not kept his word to see her and Mark right financially. When she opened a newspaper and read not only that he had another child, but that it was a boy whom he and Linda had also called Julian, in her own words, 'That, more than any hardship Mark and I had yet endured made me blow a gasket!' Living in Camberwell, working as a £11 a week shop assistant, Pat decided she had no option but to seek a paternity order against Brian. Till then she had kept Mark's father's identity a secret, but all that changed as she set court proceedings in motion.

Recognizing that this was no idle threat that would vanish with a pacifying trip abroad, the Stones machinery went into action and Pat came up against, not Brian, but those handling his affairs. 'What mattered most to me,' explains Pat, 'was that Mark was acknowledged as Brian's son, for Mark's sake.' In the shortest time imaginable Pat was whisked into a prestigious Bond Street solicitor's office, where 'They offered me thirty shillings [£1.50] a week until Mark was a certain age,' she continues, 'but I had to sign a bit of paper which would guarantee that I would never say or claim that Mark was Brian's son. I told them to stuff it.'

Pat had no intention of selling Mark's parentage down the river, and wished above all else that she had been allowed to meet and speak with Brian in person: 'By this time there was about as much chance of that happening, as getting on a plane for Mars. Brian was nowhere to be seen. Very little got through to him in person come this stage.' Brian, of course, wasn't entirely powerless. Yes, they were so big and therefore so vulnerable that the slightest attack on them, justified or not, was handled swiftly and efficiently by those paid colossal retainers to save them any annoyance. But, that doesn't go any way to exonerating Brian for not taking a personal hand in matters.

The upshot was that Pat was granted a paternity order at South West London Magistrates' Court. Sir John Cameron awarded the maximum sum allowed in those days of £1.10s (£2.50) a week for maintenance, along with £78 costs. He justifiably lashed out at Brian: 'The Bench finds it deplorable that the child who is now four years old should not have been recognized and helped by his father. We find it impossible to understand the father's attitude. If we could make a larger order, we would do so.'

Brian had recognized Mark as his son, and in far more tangible ways than the few lines of a letter which Pat had had to use as proof for legal purposes. But, unwilling, or unable, to take on board any more pressure, regrettably he left it entirely up to others to sort out. One story, however, which consistently circulated, to Brian's detriment, for many years to come was completely groundless and is worth scotching: this concerns Brian's apparently callous denial of Pat's request of a Petite typewriter for Mark's fifth birthday. For years, Pat carried hurt, not to say bewilderment, at the Brian she had once known and loved having changed so radically as to be so cold hearted. Years later, quite by accident, Pat discovered through a reliable source that her private letter to Brian had deliberately been withheld from him and, in fact, Brian had never even known of her minor demand on his by then considerable pocket.

All these machinations had been overlapping at the end of 1965 and it was in January when he had thought it had all been dealt with that Brian was confronted with the *News of the World* headline. The day before that he had flown out to Copenhagen with Anita. Not just time consuming, his affair with Anita was emotionally leeching for Brian to the point of rendering him anaemic. Certainly the romance was there, just as strong, and the lust showed no signs of wearing thin. But, Anita drained Brian so dry that, combined with the creatively exhausting sessions in the recording studio and his steadily increasing insidious drug habit, it is hardly surprising that by the time the Stones appeared on *Ed Sullivan* in February 1966, Brian looked baggy eyed and washed out. Impeccably dressed, yet the packaging doesn't conceal the fact that he was frankly knackered.

Despite the clear need to drop anchor, the constant round of partying had really only just begun. He had moved with Anita to a larger and stunningly beautiful studio flat in Courtfield Road, near Gloucester Road tube station. With its heavily carved wooden minstrel gallery, thirty-foot-high vaulted ceiling and a gallery bedroom concealed above the studio, accessed by rope ladder, their home became the magnet for all the beautiful people. The biggest names in rock made a bee-line for Brian's pad as blond host and hostess became the pivot of social London.

The Rolling Stones new single was '19th Nervous Breakdown', a punchy aggressive number which appealed to Brian very much, even though, on both sides of the Atlantic, its highest chart position was number two – the first single of the past five not to reach number one. The title itself wasn't too far off the mark with regard to Brian's state of mind. He had been pushing himself too far, too fast and too long. All five Stones were feeling the strain of a new year on the road as between mid February and early April they battered and clanged their way through one tumultuous riot after another in Australia and New Zealand, including an extra tour of Europe.

The violence too was becoming more vicious. Mick ended up with stitches to his right eye after being clobbered by a chair hurled on stage in Marseilles. Ferocious riots broke out, with running battles with police in the streets of all the major capitals, resulting in mass arrests and thousands of pounds' worth of damage in a wake of destruction, and making their already intense getaways even more hair-raising.

The times Brian spent on the road separated him from Anita and because of this, his mad jealousy soared to new, often manufactured, heights, which he found very hard to control – but his energies were by no means solely or even mainly directed towards anything so destructive. Far from it. For months the Stones had been working on their fourth album *Aftermath*, which would be released in April. This may have been the first Stones album to boast entirely Jagger/Richard originals, but its strength lies not just in that, but also the invention and intuition which Brian brought to the compositions. With unbridled inquisitiveness, Brian thought nothing of breaking every rock rule in the book as he brought instruments into the studio which rock had never dreamt of exploiting – in many cases instruments hardly anyone had ever seen, let alone knew how to play.

Phil May says of Brian, 'He really was a true musicologist, much earlier than anybody else.' Brian's incredible musicianship was a sheer gift; a natural gift which one doesn't choose or try necessarily in the beginning to cultivate, but with which one is born. To Brian there should be no limitations.

Gered Mankowitz explains, 'He was amazing. He could literally play anything you put into his hands, regardless of whether he'd ever seen it before. He must be remembered for that.' And Brian's brilliance extended even further. He had immense talent as an arranger. Intuitively he knew just what sound to apply to any composition handed to him by the songwriting pair. Neither was he dictated to by convention. He blithely introduced flutes, harpsichord and dulcimer, thus instilling an intelligent, new and subtle dimension into rock.

Stones and engineers alike looked on in awed fascination as no one ever quite knew what Brian would bring next into the studio under his arm. When he was turned on with his creative juices flowing, he elevated the whole standard of performance for all concerned. In time he would turn his skill to mastering an endless stream of increasingly exotic instruments, setting the pace for fellow musicians across the pop board, for them either to copy or combat furiously.

Aftermath has Brian's stamp marked all over it. On it he plays lead and rhythm guitar, marimbas (African xylophone), bells, sitar, piano, organ, a baroque-sounding harpsichord and that evocatively period-invoking dulcimer. Undoubtedly Jagger's excellent range from sweet yearning to scornful chauvinism on the track 'Under My Thumb' – which produced howls of protest from every feminist in the land – is clever, but it is Brian who took the album by the scruff of the neck and shook it out of the ordinary into startling, vibrant life. What was perhaps most peculiarly unique to Brian was the visual quality he could capture in his music, the ease with which he coaxed a kaleidoscope of colours to the mind's eye. On *Aftermath* he can also be heard as creditable co-vocalist on the track 'It's Not Easy'.

Hailed as a triumph for Brian, the album must have restored a sense of confidence and stability in him because, for a while, he looked a little less frayed at the edges. His romance with Pallenberg more than ever the focus of attention, rumours were gathering fresh fuel that a wedding was imminent. Bob Dylan, known to be close to Brian, was tipped as best man. This time, though, Brian, already unpopular for having dubbed marriage an anachronism, put the rumour firmly to rest, just when hard on the heels of *Aftermath*, their latest single 'Paint It, Black' sent his standing among his peers soaring all over again.

Originally the track had been intended as a comic take-off – Bill Wyman even played organ in mimicry of Eric Easton's one-time job as a cinema organist. But, no matter how hard they tried, the number wasn't working and they knew it. When Brian took a hand and played over his version, suddenly it became a whole new thing. His work on the Hindu sitar will always rate as the most innovative and downright disrespectful ever, with his intuitive understanding of the intricate instrument lending him a far different interpretation of it from George Harrison on the Beatles's number 'Norwegian Wood'. Where Harrison's treatment is careful and tender, Brian blatantly attacks it with vigour. His spiritual affinity with the hot exotic jangling dissonance was something which sprang from deep inside him. Speaking of the day he watched the sitar with its long neck, bulbous body and movable frets being placed into his friend's hands Dave Thomson remembers, 'I guarantee Brian took no more than one hour to have it figured out. Out of this world!'

The whole of the musical fraternity, already sitting up, were now on their feet applauding. Modestly Brian would merely say in interviews, 'It has completely different principles from the guitar, and opens up new fields for a group in harmonics and everything.' Still, because of Brian, the Stones regained their top notch in the singles chart once more both in Britain and in the United States. Because of him too the rock world, which had lurked furtively in the shadows of Indian and electronic music, now dared more boldly to venture out into the light.

Despite the fact, however, that there weren't many musicians, arguably none, around of Brian's calibre, still the squeeze which Brian felt compressing him continued to magnify for him behind the scenes to the point at which, it has been alleged by a friend of the Stones, he believed that far from genuinely affording him his due over 'Paint It, Black', resentment stirred in the band at all the talk about his musical prowess and sitar playing. The other Stones, however, have never confirmed his suspicions. And, in fact, Richards's has once credited Brian with the number's strength. Referring to the way they had floundered in the studio before Brian's intervention, he has this to say: 'We'd been doing it with funky rhythms and it hadn't worked and he [Brian] started playing it like this and everybody got behind it. Brian playing the sitar makes it a whole other thing.'

In part to compensate for his insecurities, Brian's answer was to accentuate his other attractions, especially his stance as the ultimate fashion symbol. Already the personification of irresponsible and dangerous glamour, extravagantly he pushed this to its androgynous limits, introducing laces and robes, flowing scarves and floppy brimmed hats to London fashion, such as hitherto had been the strict preserve of Ladies Day at Ascot. Frock coats and silk shirts, striped trews and furry waistcoats, not to mention dazzling candy-striped blazers from which he would protect himself with tinted oblong-shaped glasses, brought the camera zooming dementedly in on his exotic figure. To the delight of the boutique owners, it also sent the masses on furious shopping raids as 1966 began the momentum for the psychedelic era and the explosion of flower power in the year to come.

. . .

Though Brian adored the frivolity of clothes, and lived and breathed music, he had a needle sharp brain and was very much a political animal. As with everything else, he held strong political beliefs and his characteristic bluntness could turn arguments among friends into a furnace of disagreements. Censorship frustrated him, the injustices meted out to homosexuals and other minority groups offended him as keenly as the contemporary suffering in Biafra, all of which invested him with a deep guilt at their own decadent lifestyles. But by the time the year was half done he had troubles closer to home to concern him as Linda Lawrence, who could still never stop hoping for a reconciliation, briefly returned to his life.

By now his social circle of the new élite was as false and unreal as the stupor-inducing cloud of grass upon which they all communally floated. Theirs was a selfish, overindulgent clique, where human emotions like sadness, weakness and fear were uncool. They all had these feelings, of course; they just never admitted to them; and certainly never showed them outwardly.

One day in summer as the joss sticks burned in the midst of yet another boozy bash, Linda appeared on Brian's Courtfield Road doorstep. Accounts claim that Brian's reaction was not only to keep Linda waiting outside in the street with Julian, but also to laugh uproariously down at her standing on the pavement, flagging over his drunken guests to the window to join in the jeering at his dejected and cast-off girlfriend. But someone who was there that day fiercely refutes this. Dave Thomson claims:

That's shit! Brian had some friends in. There was a knock on the door and I went to answer it. Linda, Julian and another woman, I think was her mother, were standing there. I didn't know what to do, so I let them in. Just then Brian came out to see who it was. When he saw Linda he asked me to keep the rest, particularly Keith, who was in a bloody annoying laughing mood, out of the way while he took Linda and Julian away to his bedroom and closed the door.

Later, Linda left and Brian stayed upstairs crying for a whole two hours. He was missing Linda, thinking of her and kept saying how good it'd felt to have held his son.

Brian's private misery had to remain just that, for no other reason than that to have shown himself distressed by Linda's visit to his merry-making guests would have potentially exposed him to unbearable ridicule. That wasn't hip, not the image. It just happened to be reality.

An extension of that carefully cultivated image had only recently been highlighted when the first of the five Stones's films, announced on New Year's Day 1966 by Klein, was reported to be about to go into production. *Only Lovers Left Alive*, in conspicuous contrast to the lightweight farces through which the Beatles had innocuously skipped their way, was to be adapted from the novel of the same name by Dave Wallis and told the story of an England taken over by teenagers after a nuclear attack. Stressing their fundamental differences, Mick Jagger told *Melody Maker*, 'I can't see, for instance, Ringo with a gun in his hand, being nasty in a movie and going to kill somebody. It just wouldn't happen. But I don't think you'd think it was very peculiar if you saw Brian do it.'

In truth this was a somewhat backhanded compliment to Brian. But it was that very cloak of ruthlessnesses, so far removed from the sensitive, thinking man he was, that Brian detested. In the end the world never did digest the spectacle of a villainous Brian brandishing any hardware – the movie was never made. Instead, he took off with Anita and Christopher Gibbs, the Chelsea antique-shop owner later credited with providing the first outlet of the eastern explosion, to Morocco, taking the episode of Linda's visit with him. Torn up inside, he was hoping this break would provide him with a welcome lift.

Morocco in the 1930s and 1940s was to American literati what Paris had been the decade before. The famous writer William Burroughs lived in Tangier, the nucleus of a clutch of talented, artistic expatriates including the composer and novelist Paul Bowles, and painter-cum-writer Brion Gysin. By the sixties it was really the nearest eastern country to visit, as Turkey wasn't opened up so much then. Americans and Europeans flocked to sample Morocco's more licentious delights such as kif and male prostitution.

Sinister, corrupt and incurably exciting Morocco had a profound effect on Brian. He adored everything about it. The mayhem of the Grand Socco Bazaar, the rabbit warren of crowded covered streets where he could buy lavish caftans, djellabas (a loose cloak with a hood), cushions, and luxurious tapestries to drape over the banister of his minstrel gallery. Not to mention the dope – hashish to inhale lovingly through a hookah, or unknown, unnamed concoctions mingled in mysterious pots. Even the lighting was gorgeous as the very strong sun reflected off the ultra white sands. He loved too the simple sensuality of eating with his fingers.

In Tangier he would stay at the fabulously opulent Hotel Minzah, at night eating kebabs and couscous, idly appreciating the charms of the silver-hung bellydancers while he drew on the bubbling dung-like tobacco which, mixed with fragrant traditional substances, was only newly becoming known as 'shit'.

Morocco was a country made for Brian. Natively attuned as it was to physical beauty, its way of life, both spiritual and secular, most importantly was thoroughly indivisible from music. None of the tempting attractions offered, even within the ancient red-mud city walls of Marrakesh, absorbed Brian more than the street musicians who would sit on the ground playing delicate 1000-year-old Berber melodies on pipes, or thrashing out African rhythms on drums providing a permanent backdrop to daily life.

Brion Gysin had given his life to the music of Jajouka. After over a year in Morocco spent listening on the road, he had returned to stay, searching for the particular sound which had haunted his every waking thought. In the end, one of the villagers had brought him to Jajouka. For Brion Gysin not to come across Brian Jones would have been flying in the face of destiny. Their meeting was inevitable.

It was from Gysin that Brian first learned of the Master Musicians of Jajouka in the foothills of the Rif mountains, whose music pre-dated Islam. Gysin, so besotted with this sound that he never let the sun set without listening to it, easily conveyed his passion to the wildly receptive Brian, who begged him, practically on bended knee, to take him there immediately. Brian was beside himself with anticipation, but it would be another two years before he would actually travel there. But, then, it was also from Gysin that Brian learned of the G'naoua, whose music would play a slightly earlier role in his life.

This was the trip which was first to become marred by Brian's alleged mistreatment of Anita. Friends tell of them constantly feuding. Christopher Gibbs once recalled:

They fought about everything – cars, prices, restaurant meals. Brian could never win an argument with Anita, although he always made the mistake of trying. There would be a terrific scene with both of them screaming at each other. The difference was that Brian didn't know what he was doing. Anita did know what she was doing.

Their tirades spilled over into physical violence, which allegedly resulted in Brian assaulting his girlfriend so badly that he ended up with a broken hand. Whether he actually did break it on Anita's head, as is suggested by some, or, as is equally suggested by others, on the metal window frame meant to absorb his rage, he wound up at the end of this trip – which had supposedly been aimed at easing his mind – with relations taut with Anita, brittle with the rest of their friends, and with a bust useless hand which, by putting him out of action, degenerated his popularity with the other Stones to zilch.

The official handout was that Brian had broken his hand during a climbing accident and the warning INJURED BRIAN JONES OUT OF ACTION FOR TWO MONTHS went out to fans eagerly awaiting their Stones gig. It appears as if the Stones considered a substitute guitarist at one point, although publicly Oldham was careful not to be drawn on whether a substitute would even travel with the group; the last thing Brian could take was replacement. Already anxious, he was so conscious of his tenuous cord to the band's mainland that undoubtedly he would have read far too much into any move to have an understudy, as he would see it, breathing down his neck. He boarded a plane and flew to England to see a specialist.

When the Stones embarked on their fifth American/Canadian tour, he was up there on stage as usual, bandaged hand and all, as can be seen during the performance on *Ed Sullivan* of 'Paint It, Black'. Stunning in white from head to toe, cross-legged with his sitar, the bandage half-way up his left hand is almost impossible to detect. The tour opening in Manning Bowl, Lynn, Massachusetts did so with a riot in sodden rain. A paltry 85 cops held back 15,000 fans until the opening note of the last song 'Satisfaction', when the fans erupted. Tear gas was brought in, but rendered useless by a strong wind. As they tried to drive off, a hysterical mob surrounded the cars squashing up against them raining blows on the toughened glass. Of the girls clamouring desperately on to the back bumper of Brian's car, one of them was so distraught that she didn't discover till later that, as she was howling Brian's name at him, fighting to get even within a windscreen's touch of her idol, she had actually lost two fingers.

The tour was very well orchestrated. *Town and Country* magazine featured them on the front cover, with the headline SEX AND THE DEB. A press reception was held on Klein's luxury yacht, the SS *Sea Panther*, at which Brian managed to upset straitlaced reporters by wearing a badge proclaiming SEX IS HERE TO STAY. Then, before it came to an end in Hawaii, Brian fell foul of the authorities.

He was accused of making off with the American flag, having first irreverently dragged it across the floor of the War Memorial Hall in Syracuse. Brian claims he had considered it for a souvenir and, with his propensity to nick what took his fancy, it is not at all inconceivable that it could have found its way back to Courtfield Road. But, it is also just as likely that, having seen Brian dubiously finger it, a stagehand snatching it from him saw a headline in it for himself. Whatever, with American politics being as volatile as they were at that time, it was an unwise thing for Brian to have contemplated.

By now, Brian was smoking grass a lot as a way of relaxing himself. They were all at it and for a while life did lighten, but the cattiness was never far away and by the time their British tour opened with the Yardbirds and Ike and Tina Turner in August, it was back in full force. Keith once admitted just how bad it became in an interview with *Playboy* magazine. He said:

Mick and I were being merciless on him. The harder the work got, the more awkward Brian got and the more fucked up he would get himself when he didn't get his way, until we would be working three weeks in the Midwest with one guitar player. Namely, me. That was when I learned what the Rolling Stones were all about. You can't cover what you want from the Stones with one guitar.

On top of that, life with Anita had become even more of a rollercoaster. There was no stability in this relationship for Brian. His close friend of many years, Ronni Money, wife of musician Zoot Money, had been looking on for a long time and felt she couldn't keep out any longer. She says:

It got so bad I decided to go right over to Courtfield Road and sort him out. You've no idea what a mess that place was. Beautiful, yeah, but a tip. His fridge was full of liquid methedrine. There was no food, well nothing you could eat. It was all mouldy.

Blonde, beautiful and a forthright Scot, Ronni, although strictly a platonic friend, posed a real threat to Anita's hold over Brian. When the two women had met some months earlier it had had spectacular and, for Anita, startling results. Says Ronni:

It was in Scotch of St James, which was on two levels. I hadn't seen Brian for ages with his touring etc., and anyway I arrived and was on the second floor. Down below Brian suddenly looked up and spotted me. He leapt to his feet, ran like a maniac through the crowd right up to me, hugging and kissing me, making a rare fuss of me. I was laughing and hugging him back. I could hardly breathe for him. Then suddenly I felt a hand dig into my shoulder hard, wrenching me away from him. This was Anita. She ordered Brian at the top of her voice, 'I don't want you talking to this slag!' Well! I've never seen anything like it. Brian's hand snaked up so fast you hardly saw it. Really! She got it right on the nose – what a wallop! God, I'd never seen him hit a woman ever! But he was furious – fit to be tied! Anita got the biggest shock of her life, no kidding! She'd misjudged that one badly and you could see in her eyes that she knew it. Brian growled at her in front of everybody, 'Don't you ever talk to Ronni like that ever again! Do you hear me?' Anita didn't know where to look!

Brian calmed down and I assured him I wasn't hurt. But he was.

. . .

By the autumn the Beatles had poleaxed their fans by ceasing to give live performances, only assembling to make albums. The Stones meanwhile rolled on. Making early videos of themselves was becoming all the rage with bands around this time, the Stones included. This renewed their acquaintance with their old Marquee friend Harold Pendleton, who explains how:

By the mid sixties nearly all the groups hired the Marquee to perform some numbers. You know? To make a private film of it. This particular day it was the Stones's turn. Only someone had gone and covered up the Marquee sign behind the stage. The only prerequisite of using the Marquee was that the sign would remain visible at all times.

During this filming, which was never released, I came in to see how it was coming along and spotted what they'd done. I immediately stopped the filming. Keith was extraordinarily annoyed and extremely drunk, smashed out of his brains in fact. Well, he lurched forward to thump me with his guitar and I ducked out of the way. Keith completely missed me and crashed flat on his face on the floor.

After the sign was uncovered they carried on. Later Keith a bit more sober by now didn't even know it had been me he had swung for.

Meanwhile Brian was flirting dangerously with an all out depression. When the Stones hit Bristol he was totally unable to put up a show for his parents who came to see him play and to meet him afterwards backstage. Lewis remembers the drastic difference in his son that night at Colston Hall.

Brian seemed very different, all his spark seemed to be gone. He was very unhappy. We didn't stay. Brian was not friendly. Some indefinable change had come over him. It was typical of Brian, though, that he called later after the tour was over and apologized. He said, 'I wasn't very nice.' I said that's all right. He said he had been upset about Anita, who I understand said after his death that she did him wrong.

Brian's ability to cope may have been fragmenting gradually, but fellow rock stars feel strongly that an element of perspective has to be kept. As Ray Davies says:

When Brian was off-stage it did seem to me as if he had difficulty coping with the real world. But it's something I myself had similar problems with later on. Brian also though seemed to have the additional problem of being slightly schizophrenic. But then who wouldn't be in that band. Having said that, Brian was still easily the star of the Rolling Stones.

September marked the month when, in the eyes of many people, the outrageous Stones themselves finally flipped. Their latest single, with the extraordinarily long title 'Have You Seen Your Mother, Baby, Standing in the Shadows?', was a raucous energetic number, but it was completely overtaken by the stunt pulled to promote it.

Until then you bought a single wrapped in a simple white-paper sleeve. But, the Stones decided it would be a great idea to have a coloured cover picture on the front; it would sell more records. This was the single with which they chose to introduce the new format, and for the début they decided to dress in drag, enlisting the help of their film-maker friend, Peter Whitehead, to film the photo session in a New York backstreet off Third Avenue. Its release caused an uproar of outrage which reverberated as much within their own ranks, as among their fans.

To have contemplated taking such a risk, in the words of Peter Whitehead, 'took a lot of courage'. It wasn't seen in that light at all. SICK. PECULIAR. TASTELESSLY VULGAR. All these words and worse were levelled at the Stones. Yet anyone catching Peter's film of them preparing for the session can have no doubt that far from sinking to the depths of depravity, it was no more than one gigantic giggle; a harmless lark for which they all adopted female pseudonyms. Bill became Penelope, a chairbound sullen WAC with skinny legs tied in spinster knots. Charlie was Millicent, a god-fearing housewife. Mick was rechristened Sarah for the day, a coloured singer. And Keith became Molly, the minister's lush wife. While Brian became Flossie, a sexy peroxide blonde WAAF officer proficient in pouting smoke rings while showing off her well-upholstered bust.

As the camera lurches in on them in the dressing-room all five are near collapsing with hysteria, barely able to concentrate on their own metamorphosis for giggling at how the other was coming on. For the first time in his adult life Brian actually looks unsure of what to do with a slinky black stocking, an incongruous accessory to his homely chunky Aran cardigan. Emerging as the limb-slithering, sensual blonde bombshell, Brian smirks subtly at the camera, ungallantly amused at Keith's failure to control his slipping boobs. The ultimate freak out was no more than a gas, which ultimately ended in Flossie making an inelegant dash, propelling Pen still in the wheelchair at a rate of knots to the nearest pub for a drink.

Twenty-three years later Mick Jagger still laughs gently about this. 'Well, it's just a thing about English men,' he excuses his race off-handedly, 'we don't need much encouragement to dress up. I mean, if you've got friends over for the weekend and you get bored and want to dress up as women and go down the pub, that's all right. You don't need more than that one time asking.'

If the world at large had thought the Stones had gone stark raving mad – if they themselves had suspected a hint of insanity creeping in –

then help was already at hand. Newly in their midst they had welcomed a man who would become an invaluable friend, a calming influence and who, above all else, was a first-rate public-relations officer: Les Perrin.

It was the Stones themselves who had contacted Les Perrin and asked him to take over their PR. Les had been in the business for many years and was very highly respected. It was a major coup for the Stones that he agreed to take them on. Les never had a written agreement; their arrangement was if, at any time, the Stones were not happy with his services they could drop him. Just as if he wanted to leave them, he could walk away. From the day Les took hold of their affairs, there was never any danger of the band being so stupid as to let him slip away.

While the masses were enjoying their apoplexy over the Stones making spectacles of themselves, Les issued a caption to accompany the picture which, by way of explanation, contained Andrew's latest profound proclamation:

> *The number is about the attitude that exists between parents and their children. The shadow illustrates the uncertainty of the future, this uncertainty triggered by the thought whether [sic] we slip into a national and global depression or universal war.*

Whether the nation was coming with him or not, Brian had finally lost his foothold and was definitely slipping down towards depression, even though he fought it as best he could. It was a fight in which the wife of their PR man, Janie Perrin, would quickly prove crucial in helping him to win. The reasons for Brian's decline were a combination of things whose roots had begun at the outset when, curiously, he had appeared anything but depressed.

The rivalry within the Stones always had transcended musical issues. The fact that Anita outclassed Chrissie had rubbed Mick up so badly that in the end he had finally thrown over the model's sister for the winsomely lovely ex-convent girl Marianne Faithfull. Marianne more than compensated, in Jagger's mind, for any deficiency. She was also socially good for him. Tony King of Rolling Stone Productions once volunteered, 'I think Marianne was responsible for giving Mick the more cultured image he required at that time.' Which left Keith, though hardly barren of female company, without any one particular girlfriend with whom he was publicly associated, and certainly no one on offer remotely in the same league as either Anita or Marianne. Moreover, Mick's increasing absorption with Marianne meant three was a crowd. Left out in the cold, Keith turned to Brian.

Brian's need of a friend within the band unfortunately blinded him to any possible calculation in Keith for cultivating a renewal of their Edith Grove closeness. Wrongly, Brian took it to mean that Keith was now in his camp and that pleased him no end. It is indicative of his desperate need for an ally within the Stones that his basically ultra-suspicious nature when it came to women didn't immediately trigger alarm bells in his head.

Keith pounced on Brian's generous invitation to come stay with them at his spacious flat; Brian by his own hand thereby bringing into being the unholy, unhealthy triad. For a while the three of them had a riotous time during which common sense completely flew out of the window. Already ruled by Anita in most things, Brian was highly susceptible to pranks, especially if he happened to be high at the time. But foolishly he allowed himself to be caught up in one particular prank which would redound badly on him.

Brian and Anita were much sought after for modelling work. As the high-profile, highly successful couple they were, they would tog up and snuggle up together in any amount of sensual poses for the glossy magazines. The West German magazine *Stern* had wanted the photo-genic Brian to feature on the cover of its November issue, but when they were presented with the photo, it showed Brian looking hideously magnificent in the hated SS Nazi uniform crushing a doll beneath one jack-booted heel while Anita cowered submissively at his feet.

Obviously, they rejected it out of hand. But disastrously the photo leaked out and one almighty furore broke over Brian's head. The press got him into their jaws and were determined to draw blood. The photo was emblazoned across the land. It is doubtful that Brian himself fully realized what he had done when he had sobered up, but trying his best to explain he spluttered, 'These are realistic pictures. The mean-ing of it all is there is no sense to it.' A frighteningly thin-sounding muddle of an excuse. The bottom line was, it had been the most horrendous gaffe. Of a certainty, Brian did not sympathize with Nazism in any shape or form, and he deeply regretted the lunacy of having got caught up in it. It distressed him greatly for a long time afterwards to think of the offence he had caused. It is unlikely, though, that he would have got much sympathy from Anita. Referring to it years later her response was, 'It was naughty! But what the hell! He looked good in an SS uniform!'

With the criticism coming down like rubble about his ears, it is about now that suspicion of Keith's motives began to thread into Brian's brain. He didn't need it. Life was fairly fragile for him and he was consuming a staggering amount of LSD which heightened all his insecurities; highest on the heap was the worry that nefarious moves were afoot behind his back. Because of his fears, his temper which had always been fiery worsened. He hated himself; the black rages he flew into and the memory of his blasting fury the next day only added to his guilt. This made him insecure and vulnerable all over again.

To compensate for this, he dropped acid all the more. Its effect is that of Russian roulette in that it is entirely unpredictable how it takes you. A good trip would have Brian seeing the world through a beautiful shimmering cascade of crystal. He would be loose, relaxed and quite often would end up capering about, grinning harmlessly. On the other hand, a bad trip would send him scurrying terrified to crumple and cower in a corner, whimpering with fear. He would see monsters climbing out of the walls, closing in on him. Yet despite the horror of a bad trip he would, when life got too much for him, crave the chance of the hallucinatory numbness that a good trip would give him.

Brian also believed that dope enabled him to make better music. This was all very well if the trip was a good one. Many a bad trip even prevented Brian from turning up at recording studios. Once, he got as far as the studio door only to become convinced that the place was crawling with giant black beetles waiting for him. Terrified, he turned and stumbled away. Of course, not turning up put him right back on the delicate tightrope which threatened every day to snap from under him as resentment at more missed sessions increased the handicap he continually carried.

It is very hard not to sympathize with Brian for feeling that he couldn't win whichever way he turned. Especially when, to make matters worse, he did make it into the studio, it was to discover that in his absence a new wind was blowing, and one very definitely not to his taste.

Even if Brian had felt confident to criticize the Stones's new musical direction at this early stage, it is doubtful that there would have been willingness to take account of his opinion, though, when it came to the music, no one would deny that this was an area which remained exclusive of his personal paranoia. Never when it came to musical direction did Brian let his judgement be clouded by any personal grievance he harboured. It is the one area where he was always able clearly to define that line. Chris Barber picked up on this:

Indisputably, Brian was a genuine blues man. He was more into blues than the rather commercial stuff that the band were playing. But then he knew that that's where they were popular and what the punters wanted. So no matter how frustrating it was for him, he gave them what they wanted.

That hadn't changed. Now the problem was that he was in disagreement with the band over whether they were about to embark on the right road. On top of that, returning home from the studio with Keith, his dissatisfaction would turn then to disquiet.

The nagging suspicion that his two flatmates had something going, however, earned a brief respite when Anita landed the lead in a new feature film being made by German film director Volker Schlöndorff, entitled *Mord und Totschlag (A Degree of Murder)*. Twenty-seven-year-old Volker had won the Cannes Critics Award the previous year. He also had to his credit the San Francisco Golden Gate Award for *The Young Toerless*. Rob Houwer Films, Munich had undertaken to make this film and it was as Volker was casting that German photographer Werner Bokelberg proferred Anita for the role, describing her to Schlöndorff as 'this incredible girl he had photographed on the Zugspitze [Germany's highest mountain]'. Volker says:

She had a flat in Paris at the time and I flew there to shoot a screen test. Before it was even developed, I knew that we'd do this together, even although she'd never done movie work and ducked down when she had to cross in front of the camera on the first shooting day.

Volker's other certainty was that he would commission Brian Jones to score the music for the film. He had quickly agreed to allow Brian and Anita the run of his apartment on Tengstrasse 48, and so had already become friends with Jones. He was also well aware of Brian's reputation as a musician; conscious too, as he puts it, that although

Mick and Keith wrote the Stones's music, it was Brian's true ambition to be a composer. But he had another, overriding reason for making Brian his offer. He says,

I liked Brian and trusted him. You could feel that he had a lot of creativity. He was a poet, an enfant terrible *it's true, but he was very much in touch with his time and he was also very much in love with Anita, the only actress in the movie – and its soul. She was bound to inspire him, if he was to write the music for her.*

He continues:

When the editing was done, Brian came back to Munich and sat in the editing room with me as we discussed, just as with any other professional movie composer, where to put music and what kind of music. It was a small movie of a nouvelle vague *spirit, no message. 'Fuck the message' we used to write all over the walls. It was just the true story of a girl who accidentally kills her boyfriend with his own gun, but instead of going to the police she hires two men for a few hundred marks to drive the corpse to the country where they bury him in the construction site of an autobahn. No moral implications, no guilt trips. It's more like an outing on a beautiful autumn day. Brian's score then was to provide a reflection of those rather callous feelings, while somehow managing to hint that of course she was mourning her boyfriend's death.*

Keen to submerge himself in something new and, moreover, in his threatened state of mind, something which would directly cement him to Anita, Brian threw himself into it right from the start. He had a succession of brilliant ideas. First he wrote a theme, suggesting folk music, like a dance rhythm, for the jaunt through the countryside before it segues into a particularly poignant piano piece.

The opportunities were endless to Brian. The latitude was there to indulge the vast variety of styles within his massive capabilities. Later he would draft in the services of guitarist Jimmy Page and pianist Nicky Hopkins, but they were superfluous for his own dominance was complete. Personally Brian played sitar, organ, dulcimer, harmonica, autoharp, flute, jazzy piano, violin, banjo and sax. Even the faint vocals are his. On its completion Volker was delighted, as he explains:

And it wasn't just that his music was special, it was that the score was so spontaneous, vital. Only Brian could've done it. He had a

tremendous feeling for the lyrical parts and knew perfectly the record-ing and mixing techniques required to achieve the best sound for drums, his guitar or flute et cetera.

In the making, however, beneath pleasure there had been pain. For it had only been a brief respite. The shield which Brian had man-aged temporarily to create deserted him the moment he decided to return to Olympic Studios for the actual recording. Says Schlöndorff:

When I joined him in London he was back fighting again with Anita. I know he loved her, and I think she loved him. She was certainly in love with his lifestyle. But Brian was very passionate and their affair had problems. Brian was also doing a lot of drugs at this time which messed everything up and work on the score then was slow. He still had lots of ideas, but when I got there for the recording he'd written none of them down.

We started to do it right there in his flat, together. That's when I could drag him out of bed. He was up and down a lot. I mean sometimes he'd be really switched on, his irresistible smile beaming out, and he'd be really enjoying making great music. Then other times he'd be depressed and uninterested.

That compressed moodiness came straight from the return of all the defensiveness he had been trying again to stave off acknowledging and against which he was gradually losing ground. Volker maintains, 'There was obviously tension within the Stones too. It was very clear that Brian wanted more profile or he would go his own way.'

Volker, however, didn't see the problem as lying squarely with Mick and Keith. Just as Gered had done before him, Schlöndorff felt that Brian put an extra obstacle unnecessarily between himself and the Stones, by dint of his sheer volatility.

What I mean is, Brian was extremely likeable. He really was! Yet he wouldn't often allow you to like him. Strangely at times he'd rather challenge you, provoke you. There was also something definitely devilish about Brian. He'd sense your weakness with incredible intuition and, if the mood took him, he'd exploit it. On the other hand, he could turn around and be incredibly nice to you. I liked Brian, but he was a complicated guy. It must've been hard.

With so much material amassed, now Brian faced the daunting prospect of pulling it together. He turned to Glyn Johns. Due to a clash of personalities the two men detested each other, but with his hands already full Brian recognized the need to seek an engineer's help. The best engineer in the business was Glyn Johns and not without some reservation he approached him. Says Glyn:

Brian came to me and asked for help. He'd lost so much self-confidence by this time and really was in need of a hand. In a way I felt sorry for him. It wasn't that I didn't think he was capable of handling the project himself. But clearly he wanted help in the engineering. So I agreed.

The lack of confidence Glyn refers to again significantly related only to Brian's personal life. It had nothing to do with his musical prowess. Having had something into which he could fling himself so completely had actually turned out to be the best thing that could have happened to him. Confidence in his intuition had crept back and he found purpose and enthusiasm once more – something he had been missing badly in his Stones work. Though on the surface he was still a mass of problems, it had given him an underlying causeway to walk along for a while.

In 18 December Brian lost a good friend in a car crash. Tara Browne, the Guinness heir, died when his fibreglass sports car, a blue Lotus Elan, collided with a stationary van in Redcliffe Gardens, Kensington. In the car with Tara was his girlfriend, model Suki Potier. Tara was killed outright. Suki survived. Brian flew at once to Ireland for the funeral. Suki was utterly inconsolable until Brian arrived. 'He gave me a shoulder to cry on,' she says. 'He picked up the pieces and made me feel like a woman again.'

Years later Suki maintained that given the chance she and Brian would have married. Right then she completely depended on him to get her through day-to-day living for some considerable time after Tara's death. In time they would pick up the reins of a relationship together, but for then Anita was more than enough woman to handle and, despite three trips to the Munich set, in between also recording 'Let's Spend The Night Together' at Olympic, worry over her refused to go away.

By the end of 1966 Brian was convinced there was something kindling between Keith and Anita. Later, in interview Keith apparently questions his motives by asking why he had moved in with Brian.

'Was it out of friendship? Or subconsciously did I intend moving in on Brian's bird, after making Brian think I was his mate again?' Only Keith knows what was in his heart and mind, but the invisible waves that were washing over Brian by the day took with them another layer of him when they receded, leaving brittle bones half exposed under a thin skin. In just outside of six months' time, they would shatter almost irrevocably.

EIGHT

BUST, BROKEN AND BETRAYED

For the Stones the year started with controversy. The lyrics of 'Let's Spend the Night Together', blatantly promoting promiscuity, were deemed irresponsibly *risqué* for American ears. A couple of years before they had had the inflammatory lyrics of 'Satisfaction' bleeped, supposedly to avoid offence. Although as Bill Wyman has pointed out, with typical phlegmatic logic, 'When you bleep things it only makes it worse because you automatically think of worse words than the words on there. Trying to make some girl? What're you going to think it says? It certainly ain't make! Is it?'

This time if the Stones were to be allowed to perform their new single on *Ed Sullivan* the deal was that Mick would have to alter the words to sing, Let's spend some time together. That this degree of censorship more than irked the Stones was common knowledge and, at least for a while, Mick and Keith were hell-bent on digging in their heels. Finer sentiments, though, had to be sacrificed when one considered that the show hit sixty million viewers. With American radio stations already boycotting the disc, it would have been sheer idiocy not to compromise. And so Mick went on and slurred his way through the opening lines, only temporarily baffling the besotted fans busy stuffing hankies into their mouths.

Back in Britain where no such censorship prevailed, unfairly that compromise had smacked of spinelessness and the British faithful were not pleased. They had just one week to stew, however. On 22 January, when the Stones took part in the televised weekly show *Sunday Night at the London Palladium*, with satisfyingly reassuring arrogance they committed the sacrilege of refusing to join the other performers on the customary revolving stage at the end from which they were expected to wave sweet goodbye to over ten million viewers. The bad boys were once again the baddest on the block.

Between the Buttons, however, from its first release in January 1967 attracted no more than a lukewarm reception. Critics panned the album as samey and boring. While Keith continued to perfect his basic rhythm guitar, Brian had added more stringed instruments as well as recorder and other wind instruments to his repertoire. Yet, following *Aftermath*, the new album was no more than pallid, stencilling a tired apathetic beginning to a year in which music would take very much a back seat to the personal plights about to unfold.

At the turn of 1967, the *News of the World* had been running a series of exposés aimed at prising open the secret debauched lifestyles of the rich and shameless. And who better filled the bill than the licentious Rolling Stones? One article maintained that Mick Jagger was seen in Blaise's nightclub gaily passing around bennies – the amphetamine tablet, Benzedrine. It appears that the culprit had actually been Brian but, whatever, the upshot was that Jagger was quick to slap libel proceedings on the newspaper for wrongful accusation.

Less than one week later, on 12 February, acting on a tip-off said to have been from the *News of the World*, the police raided Keith Richards's stately country house Redlands, in West Wittering. Brian had been working on the finishing touches to his film score and had decided to call it a day. He rang Keith to tell him that he and Anita would be joining the party within a couple of hours. His timing was impeccable. Just at that exact second a squad of detectives led by Chief Inspector Dinely had swarmed into Keith's house, flashing search-warrants into stunned faces. 'Don't bother, Brian,' Keith told him, 'we've all just been busted!'

The story broken by the *News of the World* hit the pavements with a resounding thud within hours: STONES ARRESTED ON DRUG

CHARGES. Also facing charges was their art gallery owner friend, Robert Fraser. The media went haywire. The public's wildest fears of the Stones's behaviour had finally been confirmed. Traces of cannabis had been found in a pipe, more in a tin on a table, and ransacking wardrobes officers had fallen upon four pep pills in the pocket of a green jacket of Jagger's. A search of Fraser had also produced a few tablets of heroin.

A great public display was mounted to show that neither Mick nor Keith was unduly concerned and indeed, years later, Jagger maintains that the entire episode looks like a bit of a joke. But at the time it was deadly serious and its reverberations within the band were very real. Already undermined, Brian's grip on himself received a severe knock by the bust and he welcomed the universal snap decision to bail out of Britain – which some took to calling a police state – while the prosecution prepared their case. Morocco was the natural choice of destination. Marrakesh, in particular. For Brian it was a trip doomed from the outset.

He travelled with Keith and Anita in Keith's Bentley Continental driven by Tom Keylock, a former paratrooper skilled in combat techniques more in keeping with a minder than a chauffeur. But Keith had an incurable penchant for hard men. On the 2000-mile trek across France and Spain, they stopped off in Paris to make room for a friend, film-maker Donald Cammell's girlfriend, Deborah.

The route they took was mountainous and before long Brian became distinctly uneasy as the thin air began to affect his asthma. Despite using his puffer, it worsened by the hour. Soon a fever developed, sending his temperature soaring sky high and they had to make for the nearest hospital. Suspecting pneumonia, he was admitted on the spot. Supposedly at this point, Brian urged Anita to carry on into Spain with Keith and the others without him, saying he would join them in Tangier later when he felt better. Anita says:

> It was Brian who suggested that we drive on without him to Tangier where we should wait for him at the Hotel Minzah. That meant that Keith and I could be alone. By the time we reached Valencia we could no longer resist each other and Keith spent the night in my room. In the morning I realized, as did Keith, that we were creating an unmanageable situation so we pulled back as best we could during the rest of the journey.

At Minzah the desk clerk handed Anita a pile of cables from Brian telling her to return to Toulouse for him so that they could then fly together straight to Marrakesh. Keith, trying to do the decent thing urged her to do just that, but 'From the moment I arrived in Toulouse,' complained Anita, 'Brian treated me horribly.'

While Anita and Keith had been spending the night together in Valencia, Brian had been lying sleepless in his South of France hospital bed, tormenting himself about what was going on. When he came face to face with Anita, he sensed immediately that his fears were grounded. Rancid suspicion had been vile enough, but there had always been the chance that he was wrong. Now he didn't even have that. By the time he flew in with Anita to join Mick, Marianne, Robert Fraser, photographer Michael Cooper, Keith and Deborah, he was haggard and drawn and psychologically a wreck.

The beatings, which Anita insists Brian dealt her, started that night when, after having spent hours staring hatefully across tables at Keith, they retired to their bedroom suite. Every second from then on was fraught with unbearable tension. Occupying the entire tenth floor they threw acid parties, hoping to alleviate the palpable strain, but in Brian's case it only created more pressure in his head.

Almost on arrival Brian had renewed his friendship with Brion Gysin and he remembers one spectacular row erupting between Brian and Anita. She had flounced off and locked herself in the bedroom, while Brian in a black, destructive mood went off out into the night and returned with a Berber whore. *Ménages-à-trois* were by no means uncommon for them, but this time Anita wasn't in the mood and would have none of it. It is said because of this that Brian beat her up again.

By morning the atmosphere rolling in around the pool come breakfast time was thick enough to cut with a knife. It wasn't going unnoticed by Brian and the others that Anita spent all her time gazing passionately at Keith splashing about in the pool, for his part not adverse to returning her secret taunting smiles.

Summing up Anita, Keith once said, 'Brian tried to beat Anita but instead ended up breaking his own ribs. That shows you how tough Anita is.' It was well known too that Anita enjoyed to the hilt the mantle of being very untypical of her softer sex, more wild and

147

masterful than most men. Yet strangely in a total about face, she was now cast in the role of cringing damsel in distress, Brian as the manic monster and Keith slots into this cast as the most unlikely Sir Galahad. And so the stage was set for the final act in this drama in which Brion Gysin was inveigled as an innocent pawn.

Unbeknown to Brian the others had collectively decided to leave, Gysin by then gulled into believing the tale that a posse of British reporters was about to touch down at the airport. It was urged upon the artist that, for Brian's own good and that of the band – with their trial pending – he should be kept out of harm's way in case he talked to the journalists. Gysin was persuaded it would be best to take Brian out for the day – which he did.

Unaware that it was a ploy, Brian warmly welcomed the invitation to plunge back with his friend into the Djemaa El Fna – the huge town square – to record music, soak up the hazy surreal atmosphere heavy with the pungent scent of spice and other aromas. In fact the brief was, 'Lose Jones for as long as possible!' It was easy enough. Once Brian got caught up recording he happily wandered about his beloved maze of bustling souks, taping for hours with a heart lighter than it had been for a very long time.

Meanwhile, back at the hotel, Operation 'Skin Out' was in full swing. They were all going. Eventually Keith and Anita got into the Bentley together, with Keylock once again behind the wheel, and drove off without a note, with no warning, without any apparent thought for the consequences to Brian's state of mind on finding himself alone and abandoned on his return.

Keylock drove them like a bat out of hell from Marrakesh to Tangier where they boarded a ferry for Malaga, eventually catching a plane from Madrid to London. Instead of returning to Marrakesh, Tom then drove his winding slow way back to Britain, leaving Brian, with the entire party having joined in the evacuation, completely high and dry.

His feelings, when he returned to the hotel brimming with excitement about his tapes and clutching a long stemmed carved pipe he hadn't been able to resist buying, on discovering what had happened had almost horrific results. So frantic did he become that for a while all he could do was run about the hotel madly, totally unable to believe that just no one had stayed behind. Time and again he asked the desk clerk to check there was no note for him, as all the while tears weren't far away. His worst dread had come true and he came within a hair's breadth that day of committing suicide. Ronni Money remembers:

> *Brian rang me up that night from Marrakesh all but incoherent. He was in an awful state. I said to him, 'Calm down, Brian! You must calm down and tell me what's wrong!' He said, 'They've left me, Ronni! They've taken everything – my cash, credit cards, even my cameras – and left me! I'm stranded!' He was frantic. I said, 'Look, first things first. Don't panic. Now think about it. Ring the office and tell them you need money cabled to you at once. Now listen, Brian, I kept saying, think straight! You know you can get yourself out of this fix.' Thankfully I got that part of it through to him, but that was nothing really. He was completely devastated. Christ, he could've done anything to himself that night.*

Amazingly in the circumstances he managed to pull himself together. But he desperately needed to talk to someone. Stopping off in Paris he made for his friend Donald Cammell's flat, arriving on the doorstep distraught and dishevelled, and with no baggage. 'They left me,' was all he could blurt out again to Cammell as he opened his door. 'They just fucked off and left me!'

That night too confused for clarity, his account of the desertion wandered drastically and at times all he could blab on about was the wooden pipe he had bought with Gysin in Marrakesh. But Donald had no difficulty in recognizing the horrendous impact this abandonment had had on his friend. Brian kept muttering that he couldn't think where they could have gone. In fact, the fugitive pair had taken bolthole refuge in a tiny St John's Wood flat.

Next day unable to put it off, Brian forced himself to continue on his way back to London, despite his rage and misery his one thought to beg Anita to come back to him. His pleas fell on deaf ears. 'He caught up with us in about a week, back in London,' recalled Keith, 'and there was this tearful scene. Anita says, "No, you're just too much of an asshole to live with. Keith and I have got something going."' It was the biggest, most gigantic slapdown Brian had ever suffered and many are quick to pinpoint it as being the most crucial turning-point in his life. It certainly, as Keith admits, was the final nail in the coffin between them as mates. Brian could never forgive Keith for what he had done.

Brian reeled from pillar to post for a long time after that, unable to stop himself. The only thing that mattered to him was winning Anita back, yet the more he asked and was rejected, the greater the betrayal he felt. His drinking soared alarmingly. He downed double Bacardis and coke like water, but they failed to swamp his excruciating insecurity. Where his apartment had only recently overflowed with friends, there were few around him now with the patience or the will to help him. He had hit rock bottom and even that turned out to be quicksand. His drug intake escalated dangerously as blowing his mind was at least a means of forgetting the agony that gnawed away inside him and, for the duration of a good trip, he could lose the immense sadness and blanket of loneliness which had settled on him. Ronni confides how:

That in many ways I'd say was the worst bit of all. You see ordinarily Brian never was a fool with drugs. He knew his limit and he wouldn't touch certain drugs. And I can tell you for a fact, it didn't take a helluva lot to put him right off, which he knew. So unless he was trying to hide from something, he never did go anywhere near as mad or as far with drugs as folk and newspapers have loved to make out. This time though, yes, he was just out of control.

He was a broken man – with no confidence or trust in anything any more, vacillating between paroxysms of tears and rage – and he finally succumbed to the inevitable and sought help. On 9 March 1967 he admitted himself to the Priory Clinic in Roehampton, suffering from depression. Here his stay at the private clinic was far too brief and any benefit gained evaporated practically over night as he had to check out just over two weeks later, in time to join the Stones on their European tour kicking off in Sweden. To share a stage with Keith, to perform for the masses as if he wasn't holding on to sanity only by his fingernails was a living hell. It is probably true to say that no one can even begin to grasp his depths of despair. Every time he looked across that stage at Keith, there stood the symbol of what Brian saw as his failure and inadequacy.

This kind of crushing personal pressure in any walk of life would seem impossible to cope with, and of a certainty the charge that Brian fast degenerated into becoming the band's chief handicap rather than its asset is well reported. Yet curiously an interesting conflict emerges. The opinions of two men, both of whom knew Brian at this time and perhaps, more significantly, both of whom had no liking for him, could hardly differ more. While Glyn Johns maintains, 'His ability went right down, so much so he couldn't even hold a chord down,' Gered Mankowitz reveals the opposite: 'He was so extraordinary that even when he was way way out of it [on drugs] he could play brilliantly! Yes, even when he was virtually unable to stand up!'

The tour had other external pressures too. Because of the fact that in every one of the nine European countries through which they charged, the story of the Redlands bust had long preceded them, whenever they passed through customs all the Stones were subjected to rigorous baggage and body searches, often to the humiliating extent of having to strip naked.

Then, four days before the end, the Stones played an historic concert behind the Iron Curtain. The Palace of Culture, Warsaw was the venue; the date, 13 April. The official Polish News Agency barely reported it. 'The audience consisting mainly of young people received the performance with an enthusiasm that was too noisy,' it complained. What it didn't report was that outside 10,000 youths, rioting at being barred from the concert, were being suppressed with barbaric ruthlessness. Having failed to disperse the mob with batons and high-pressure water hoses, the police unleashed Dobermans and tear-gas, making scores of arrests.

The whole shocking truth was being captured, unknown to the authorities, on film by an extremely nervous, but determined, student. Somehow he managed to pass the small spool to Tom Keylock to smuggle out of the country, who promptly took it to Don Short who had travelled with them. Initially Don agreed to try to smuggle the indicting film out, but quickly – quite naturally – had second thoughts. 'I gave the film back to Tom,' Don says. 'There was no way I wanted to be caught trying to take anything like that out of Poland.' It was most fortunate that Don had had qualms, for he ended up under arrest anyway. After, that was, Les Perrin was arrested first.

Janie Perrin explains:

151

At that time you weren't allowed to take any Polish currency out of the country. The number of times my husband was searched just because he was with the Stones was unbelievable. The Stones, mind you, thought this was hilarious because really no one looked more respectable than Les. But, anyway, they were searched and of course Les had some Polish money on him. So they arrested him. They said they'd free him on condition he first spent it all before he left in the Duty Free shop. While all this was happening, our friend Don Short for a laugh began singing the theme song to From Russia With Love. *He was promptly arrested too!*

Janie goes on:

Les had to spend the lot, buying up the most ridiculous things. There was this great bearskin coat that no one in their right mind would wear. The thing that got me, though, was that Mick slipped Polish money into Les's pocket on the plane after that. My God! If he'd been caught with that? I'm sure it was meant as a joke, but I didn't think it was very nice. Les would've been in serious trouble.

Finishing on 17 April that memorable tour, though they didn't realize it, marked the end of touring for the Stones for over two years. For Brian, it was the very last tour he would ever be on.

. . .

Back home Brian tried to put his troubles behind him, but really all he did was mentally cram them all in a closet and shoulder-shut the door; a door which continually strained at the lock. Since the Perrins had come into his life he had come to depend heavily on them both. He confided in Les a lot, who helped him whenever he could but, as Janie stresses, 'Les was in a difficult position because he acted for all five of them. For me it was different.'

Janie Perrin was Brian's best confidante. Despite having a family of her own, she always made time for Brian, to the extent that her children looked on Brian as a brother. Mostly the help Brian sought was an ear into which he could pour out his worries. Although, curiously, many times when he actually got on the phone the last thing he would speak about was what was actually upsetting him. Janie explains how:

Brian would ring me up and talk about anything and everything. Once he had raging toothache. 'It's driving me mad, Janie,' he said. I said, 'Well, get a dentist to see you.' 'But it's Saturday,' said Brian, 'I can't disturb him on a Saturday!' I said, 'Blimey, the fees you pay that Harley Street dentist, he'll come out all right and charge you accordingly. Get him out.'

Whether Brian actually had toothache was immaterial. The fact that he needed that sort of response was what was important. Shrewdly, however, Janie knew where the underlying problem lay. Touching briefly on it she says:

What Keith and Anita did to Brian was the dirtiest thing of all. I thought nothing of them for that. Brian was completely head over heels in love with Anita. He was badly betrayed. Not that Brian ever discussed his feelings with me, no matter how many times we talked. Because Brian was the kind of man who never discussed his women. His private life remained his own problem.

Noel Redding confirms this. 'Brian wasn't the kinda guy who laid his personal problems on you and he would never discuss his love life because he was a class bloke. If you knew him, you'd know that.' From the moment Brian and Noel met the two became good friends. Initially Noel was very much in awe of Jones. He confesses frankly:

I've never stopped being amazed that Brian had anything to do with me. I mean there was me, all of twenty – a nobody right? But there I was hangin' out with Brian Jones. There was an ingrained kindness in Brian, really. He was soft spoken, soft natured and yet terrific fun.

In Noel's own words Brian took him under his wing. They went everywhere together, in Brian's silver Roller to the Speakeasy or the Ad Lib, two ex-grammar school boys enjoying each other's company. It was a friendship which, though Noel makes no such claim, in fact helped Brian then a great deal.

His other lifeline was his film score. Recognition for it came when *A Degree of Murder* became Germany's entry for that year's Cannes Film Festival held at the end of April. But any pride he drew from that was robbed at the prospect of travelling to France for the festival. Anita's presence in Cannes as the film's star meant that what he had been trying to hide from, jumped up and bit him all over again.

But it was unavoidable. Anita was there as thick as thieves with Keith, Michael Cooper and an entire entourage. Pictures appeared of Brian with Anita in restaurants, but in truth they were as far apart as ever. Foolishly, thoughh, Brian hadn't learned his lesson and every chance he could, he headed off Anita on her own to plead with her again to come back to him. His wooing was a waste of breath. He humbled himself in vain and disastrously plummeted all the worse, bingeing on drugs and drink in a maniacal effort to slip into oblivion. Leaving the day before the festival wound up, Brian with his head already down flew back to London to find, within hours of his return, his doorstep filled with a dozen large Scotland Yard Drug Squad detectives, slapping a search-warrant in his face.

It was four in the afternoon. Brian still in a Japanese kimono and bleary eyed, unaware and uncaring of the damning debris of a heavy all night session, was moving about the wreckage. One guest was still rattling about the place: a Swiss nobleman friend of Brian's, Prince Stanilaus Klossowski de Rola, Baron de Watteville – otherwise known as Stash. Brian hadn't a leg to stand on. The detectives went methodically through the apartment, adding steadily to their tidy haul. Eleven objects were found in various places, all of which contained or bore traces of drugs: two canisters, two wallets, two pipes, two cigarette ends, a box of cigarette papers, a jar – even a chair caster which had been used as an ashtray. The total number of grains of cannabis found was $35\frac{1}{4}$, enough to make seven to ten reefers.

Looking on in tousled but by now stark alertness, Brian knew he was beat. However, when the policemen showed him a glass phial, which appeared to show traces of cocaine, Brian was immediately roused. 'Yes, it's hash,' he confessed to the other substances before him. 'We do smoke. But,' he pointed to the phial, 'not cocaine man. That's not my scene. I'm not a junkie.'

As if being busted weren't bad enough, when Brian with Stash was bundled by the officers to Chelsea Police Station he walked out into a mob of waiting reporters. Inexplicably the whole of London's press seemed to have known about the bust in advance and were waiting to swamp Brian as he ducked into the back of the police car.

By 5 p.m. Brian had been formally charged with, as the *Times* reported, 'possession of a quantity of cannabis and cannabis resin,

154

contrary to section 13 of the Dangerous Drugs Act 1965 and Regulation 3 of the Dangerous Drugs [No. 2] Regulations 1964 [SI 1964 No. 1811]', and also with 'permitting premises to be used for the purposes of smoking cannabis or cannabis resin, contrary to Section 5(a) of the said Act.'

It is an uncanny coincidence that the cops chose to bust Brian that particular day, 10 May, as this just happened to be the date on which Mick and Keith were appearing in Chichester Magistrates' Court at a preliminary hearing for their bust at Redlands. Electing to be tried by jury they had put up bail of £100 each, pleading not guilty and their trial was set for 27 June. To the country at large, it seemed obvious that the police were out to break the Stones; to anyone closely connected with the group, there is no doubt that they were being singled out to be made examples of.

Pat Andrews, reflecting on these troubles, holds strong views.

The cops were down on Brian. In many ways it was a political thing. The Stones were seen as a menace and threat to the establishment. Brian was known to be the brains of the outfit, the pivotal figure and, as such, to hit the corner-stone meant hitting Brian Jones. I know Mick and Keith were busted that year too but really they never let up on Brian. He was definitely the target from the police, press, friends, within the band – the lot. I felt so helpless at that time. I knew Brian needed taking in hand and I've often wished since that I had had the guts to go to him and try to help, but I was scared of being rebuffed.

I don't think Brian would've turned me away and he knew if anyone would say, 'Bugger you, Jones! Wake up to what you're doing to yourself,' it'd be me. But honestly by then it was a physical impossibility to get close to him for the thugs surrounding him.

Chris Barber adds another slant.

The press made a meal of it, but you know it's never right to blame people like Brian 100 per cent for losing their grip. Because there's more involved here. Your normal punter is frightened to drop acid, but very much encourages their pop star to do it. People like that want to live vicariously through their idol's life. Their fix is watching the stars do what they haven't the nerve to dabble with. The stars in turn are expected to live up to that image.

Chris was by no means suggesting it was the fans' fault that Brian popped pills, but he makes a valid point.

On 11 May Brian and Stash appeared briefly before Great Marlborough Street Court's stipendiary magistrate. Both chose trial by jury at Inner London Sessions and were released on £250 bail. Brian's first thought was for his folks in Cheltenham. He sent them a telegram which read:

> PLEASE DON'T WORRY. DON'T JUMP TO
> NASTY CONCLUSIONS. AND DON'T JUDGE
> ME TOO HARSHLY.   ALL MY LOVE.
>   BRIAN

At home alone his panic must have been profound, yet he wouldn't turn to Janie. 'No! Absolutely not,' Janie was emphatic. 'When it came to anything related to drugs he steered well clear of phoning me. I don't know whether it was because he thought I might disapprove. Of course, for myself, I would've. Or if it was perhaps that he would have felt as if he had let me down. I don't know.'

The solution should have been work. Back in the studio, however, for the Stones, although it had already been a bad year, it was about to get worse. In 1965 when Brian, Mick and Bill had been fined for watering a garage wall, their rivals had picked up squeaky clean MBEs. Now in the approaching summer of 1967, while Brian, Mick and Keith were looking at possible jail terms, the Beatles, with impeccable intuition, had focused all the spiralling directionless spoils of flower power into one dynamically different album, *Sgt Pepper's Lonely Hearts Club Band*.

From the first spin, its effect was catastrophic on every band on the pop scene. It definitely put the wind up Mick and Keith for, after listening to *Sgt Pepper*, their immediate answer was to produce an album of their own just like it, but even better. And frantically they threw themselves into a hastily manufactured whirlpool of psychedelic obsession. The failure of *Between the Buttons* lurked darkly in their memory. If they couldn't rise to what they saw as the challenge, it boded ill for their future.

Brian watching the hysterics didn't see it like that. He recognized the panic, and in essence felt just as threatened. But to him it would be abject folly to try and copy something so brilliantly original. Why be an imitator? had always been his philosophy. He tried suggesting that, Yes, *Pepper* was inspired. Yes, it was a Beatles triumph. But if they, the Stones, can't top it, then they ought not to try or they would not only fall on their faces, but worse would be seen to fall on their faces. That wasn't what Mick and Keith wanted to hear, and not only was he dismissed instantly as outvoted, he was also regarded askance for supposed disloyalty in not concurring with their reasoning. The musical direction within the band's repertoire had been straying way off base as it was. Now, sinkingly, Brian saw that he was going to find it even tougher to accept.

Fortunately a reprieve from it all presented itself the following month when the very first international open air pop festival was held in Monterey, California. A board – a Who's Who of rock – had already been set up to organize the event, on which Paul McCartney for one was invited to sit. Chas Chandler, ex-member of the Animals, now managed a stunning young black blues guitarist called Jimi Hendrix. According to Chandler, McCartney's condition on joining the board of Monterey was that the Jimi Hendrix Experience, which comprised of Hendrix, Brian's mate Noel Redding and drummer Mitch Mitchell, were invited to appear. Already a long-standing friend of Brian's, Chas had phoned John Philips – singer and songwriter with the Mamas and the Papas – in California and got Jones who was staying with him on the other end of the line. Spontaneously he asked his friend if he would introduce Jimi on stage. Brian agreed and was invited to be the board's guest for the entire weekend of 10–11 June.

Brian spent a very happy weekend there. Unlike his contemporaries, he refused to hide behind a barrier of bodyguards and wandered freely around the hippy bivouacs, fascinated by the colourful stalls and side-shows, enjoying the universal feeling of camaraderie. It is claimed, mainly by people who weren't there, that Brian was an ethereal shadow of himself, already showing signs of fading away. With what had recently befallen him it might not have been at all surprising, but the only etherealism firmly attached to Brian was the flute work with which he had brought the number 'Ruby Tuesday' evocatively alive. It was then riding high at number one in America. He was, as Noel, who had travelled at his side all the way out there for this spectacular gathering vouched, completely undrugged. 'He was grand,' Noel remembers, 'in fine shape. I know others say differently. But I was with him. I knocked about with Brian the whole time, even more than Hendrix did.'

Brian attracted enormous attention. Everywhere he went people draped in their own finery were dazzled by his presence. A pop deity, the epitome of rock royalty, in layers of velvet, lace and sweeping silk ikat robes, shards of lustrous sunshine glinting off his heavy blond hair, he was God to all the sixties hippies, yet sipping the ordinary man's beer, enjoying mingling with them. He always had loved meeting people and with his preference not to be treated as untouchable, those who began in awe of him rapidly relaxed and followed him about as he casually drifted from one crowd to another, staying a while, talking and listening, then moving on.

In quiet retrospective moments his bust obviously weighed very heavy on his mind, but contrary to widespread allegations that he tripped the whole three days on STP – a drug which induces a seventy-two hour trip – he did not get stoned. 'You want the bare truth?' asked Noel. 'He was too terrified to. With his trial coming up he knew he couldn't afford the risk.'

Brian was there to introduce the shy and introverted Jimi Hendrix to the populace. He had no intention of performing himself, though he could have. His sole intention was to launch the Experience, with all the authority his word carried, on to the world's stage. 'I want to introduce to you a friend of mine, a fellow countryman of yours,' said Brian and goes on to describe Jimi as the 'most exciting guitarist I've ever heard,' coming from him, an enormous compliment.

Having done his best for Hendrix, Brian, with his quick eye for talent, was keenly taking stock of the new wave of American blues stars, like the outrageous Janis Joplin. With typical outspokenness Brian startled journalists after seeing Otis Redding go down a storm the night before by baldly broadcasting, 'The Stones think we're the greatest band in the world. But you couldn't give me a million pounds to follow [on stage] Otis Redding.'

.   .   .

Mick and Keith's two-day highly publicized trial started on 27 June as they appeared before Judge Leslie Block. Despite testimony from

Jagger's doctor that the four pep pills found in his jacket pocket and legally purchased in Italy were similar to those regularly prescribed to Mick, Jagger was summarily found guilty. With Keith he was bundled into jail for the night to await his sentence after Richards's trial the next day. The unnecessary and heavy-handed sight of Mick emerging from the police car that morning handcuffed delighted the lip-licking media.

Keith's case was more involved, although the actual hard evidence against him was slim. He could only be charged with allowing dangerous drugs to be used in his home, but the prosecution still made the most of what they had and he went the same way as Jagger. After the jury returned their verdict, Judge Block sentenced Keith to one year in prison, Robert Fraser to six months, and Mick received three months. 'When he gave me the year,' Keith remembered later, 'he called me scum and filth.' Appeals were instantly lodged, but both still spent three nights in jail before their lawyers' motions were accepted.

In the meantime sympathy for the Stones and their outrageously prejudicial treatment was gathering gusto. The Who rush-released a hastily recorded single of 'The Last Time' and 'Under My Thumb' as a protest against the sentences, with the pledge that should Jagger, Richards and later Jones go to jail, they would see to it that the Stones music would be kept alive. Only Davey Jones of the American group the Monkees had a dig about not needing drugs to have a good time, despite which the three other members of the band, which Brian had caustically christened the prefab four, wore black armbands on stage one night. The voice of disquiet had even extended into the House of Commons with some MPs disturbed at what they saw as a blatant misuse of authority at work within the judiciary.

While the furore whipped up, culminating in the famous *Times* leader WHO BREAKS A BUTTERFLY ON A WHEEL?, Brian took advantage of the glare for a while not focusing on him to slip in to see his Harley Street psychiatrist. The sessions with the eminent Dr Leonard Henry were not enough, however. Together with his trial staring him in the face and the barrage of intimidatory harassment everywhere he went, Brian was buckling by the hour. Strain and exhaustion pushed him too close to the edge again and he knew he had no hope of coping. He agreed that a complete breakdown was imminent and for the second time that year he retired quietly, on 6 July, to the residential care of the Priory under Dr Anthony Flood. At least he tried to slip away quietly but, as ever, whatever he did, no matter how personal, made the papers and the headline BRIAN JONES IN NURSING HOME betrayed him next day.

His three-week stay began controversially when Brian arrived as flamboyantly dressed as ever, stepping out of his darkened Rolls-Royce with Suki Potier. All summer in an effort to expunge his feelings of masculine inadequacy, he had gone through an inordinate amount of women, like a torch to dry bracken. Suki had gradually come to terms with losing Tara through Brian's help and had been watching this. Turning the tables around, she had worked it so that she was the one from whom he could now get support. When Brian had woken up to the futility of his rampaging, recognizing that all he was doing was hastening his own burn-out, Suki was there. In bringing her with him to the clinic, Brian's total lack of confidence and fear at the fragility of his sanity is more in evidence than the accusation of it being a childish desire to flaunt his virility. As it was, Dr Flood snuffed any suggestion of allowing Suki to stay. Brian argued, but lost. Giving way, he watched her leave, nervous of being left alone. Then he was put to sleep for several hours so that treatment could begin.

At the start of his treatment Brian was in a very bad way. Initially diagnosed as 'Anxious, considerably depressed, perhaps even suicidal', Dr Flood felt that Brian didn't so much need treatment for drug taking, as for help to regain emotional stability, to negate his tendency to fits of depression when up against the strains of life.

It is clear from various reports made on Brian that the many interviews he went through carried an additional obstacle, put there by the doctors. For Brian represented a new breed. He was not your normal patient and to understand him, and his generation, required a comprehension of their thinking and beliefs. His anti-establishment tag, even within the nursing home walls, could not help but hinder a normal prognosis. The task of unravelling Brian and his problems was made therefore considerably more complicated.

Persevering, the redoubtable Dr Flood fought through the glittering garb to the frightened, insecure, unhappy young man inside. From first resenting the probing personal questions, which he would deflect with bouts of flaming arrogance, Brian's resistance gradually dissolved. He knew well that he needed help, and under his psychiatrist's care he at last not only exposed his more obvious open wounds, but rendered an insight into how agonizing it had already been for him for so long to uphold his aggressive, ultra-macho Stone image, with all its conceits and extravagances, and reconcile it with the real him. Punished by the pressures of pop, he seemed to hanker for the normality of being non-descript, of perhaps going to university and pursuing an academic career.

Flood was quick to stress that he wasn't too late. It wasn't personal bias. He found Brian to have outstanding intelligence, to which he would later strongly testify. During the many sessions together their debates were of a highly intellectual content on history, world politics, philosophy and ethics. Doctor and patient became friends.

Only once did Brian fall by the wayside. Feeling so much better even half-way through, he began pressing Dr Flood to let him out for a visit to Olympic studios. He told the doctor that their new album was in the making and impressed on him that he would be needed. Flood swithered, but reluctantly agreed on condition that Brian was back in bed by midnight. Brian staggered in the following morning around 7 a.m., so full of booze and pills that he could barely walk. Disappointed, Dr Flood had no alternative but to knock him out and start again from scratch. Ten days later Brian was discharged on 24 July having made, for all that, considerable progress.

Seven days later Mick and Keith's appeals were upheld. Keith's conviction was quashed and Mick received a conditional discharge. While their fate had hung in the balance, Mick and Andrew Oldham had responded to Peter Whitehead's suggestion to film a promotional clip in case the worst befell them. That filming took place the night Brian absconded from Roehampton, as is excruciatingly clear in Peter's film. *We Love You*, with backing vocals courtesy of Lennon and McCartney showing their solidarity for the besieged Stones, was released in August. Glazed and remote, bombed out on drugs, for the spectacle Brian thus made of himself, if nothing else, the BBC banned Peter's film. In the director's own words, 'It was the best thing they could've possibly done, because everyone then wanted to see it.'

This was the month which saw the emergence of the religious guru Maharishi Mahesh Yogi, whose arrival quickly attached to it the aura of the second coming and attracted disciples from people as influential as the Beatles. Mick and Marianne, not about to miss out, were quick to follow the faithful boarding a headline-hitting train on course for Bangor in Wales, just two days before the world was stunned by the tragic news that the Beatles's manager Brian Epstein had been found dead in his flat.

With Mick in Wales, Brian and Keith were foisted together to do most of the work on the new album *Their Satanic Majesties Request*. Brian's attitude hadn't budged: he still fundamentally disagreed that because of the panic over *Pepper* it was in their best interests to produce their own psychedelic album. That isolated unpopularity was the last thing he needed at this time. He had improved, but was still very fragile. His contributions to *Satanic Majesties* were reluctant. To function at his best, the drive had to be there and he found it just too difficult to get behind this album. If he turned up at all, feeling his lack of commitment, the others would accuse him of being no use to them anyway. It was a dense, unhappy atmosphere, not conducive to producing good music. Tensions ran high and spoiled any chance of finding a workable affinity again.

It was abundantly clear that Brian was too diametrically at odds with the others over this. To alleviate stress he could not afford, Brian took off with Suki for a quick run round Spain. To Brian the chaotic composition and knee-jerk response of *Satanic Majesties* was symptomatic of their life at that time. As he once said philosophically, 'Our entire lives have been affected lately by social and political influences. You have to expect those things to come out in our work.'

Much is made of Brian's failure to turn up at the studio, of his withdrawing his labour, which after all was his prerogative considering how deeply he felt, even to the extent of him being absurdly accused of messing up his life so much just in order deliberately to render himself professionally useless to them. Little account seems to have been taken of how close he was skating to an irrevocable crack-up. Undoubtedly it must have been infuriating for the others that Brian was not prepared to sit down, shut up and play at his considerable best. Yet, in the end, it was still Brian who contributed the most impressive and effective sounds to the album.

In the midst of all this, other problems arose. After four years with the band, Andrew Oldham decided to walk out on them. Leaving the Stones to produce their own records, he instantly filed a lawsuit against the company set up by Klein, Nanker Phelge USA, and even more writs began flying about among their ill-fated managers.

For Brian the strain of the *Satanic* sessions had caused him more damage than he knew. And it wasn't helped by pressures at home. Suki had a difficult time juggling with his nerves and came and went at his erratic demand. He felt hemmed in and hunted, never more so than the evening when, alone in his flat, he was catapulted from his chair by a furious battering on his door. His initial terror that it was the cops again evaporated at the sound of the voices of the two men outside shouting for him to open up. Brian bolted for the phone. As Janie Perrin explains:

Brian phoned me up in an awful state. The father and brother of a certain ex-girlfriend I'd rather not name were banging hell out of his door. I could hear them at my end. They were demanding money and being very violent and abusive about it too. Brian was really upset. He said, 'I can't understand why they're doing this, Janie. I've sorted things out already legally and morally. Why are they upsetting me like this?' I said, 'Look, Brian, go to the door, open it and biff them one, then close the door.' 'Oh, you're terrible,' cried Brian, 'I couldn't hit them.'

Unwilling to take Janie's blunt advice, Brian instead put down the receiver and sat huddled, listening to repeated insults and threats hurled at him through the wood until they eventually gave up and went away.

The solitude left Brian prey to his worst recurrent nightmare: he was terrified of being sent to jail. His trial was drawing closer by the day, relations were in tatters with the band and, with the exception of a select few, hostile faces surrounded him. Starkly he knew prison would kill him. Twice in that state of disabling despair, in a relatively short space of time, Brian threatened suicide. Janie reveals that:

Brian phoned me on both of those occasions, saying he was going to commit suicide. He was extremely unhappy. One of the times he was in

163

the Dorchester Hotel and he said he was going to throw himself out of the window. I said something like, 'Well, dear, go down a few floors before you do it. You don't want to make too much mess on the pavement.' 'Oh you're so terrible,' Brian told me. But inside I was absolutely sick at heart that he wouldn't respond to my tactics. It was the same the second time when he was determined to slash his wrists and I told him to go into the bathroom first so as not to splatter blood on the bedroom carpet. I was 99 per cent sure that he didn't really mean it and I always tried to be firm but light with him. But I worried so much! I felt so sorry for Brian at this time but I wouldn't tell him. That wouldn't have helped him, to keep saying, 'Oh, I feel so sorry for you. That's not what he needed.'

Janie admitted that it was very hard safely to gauge his moods and the nagging fear that she had misjudged him haunted her every second until Brian would call some time later after he had calmed down. 'The other Stones knew how very unhappy he was, just as they knew he was leaning on me.'

Brian's trial began 30 October at Inner London Sessions. When the charges were read out in court Brian pleaded guilty to possessing and smoking cannabis, but otherwise not guilty. The Crown prosecutor Robin Simpson told the court that when Brian was asked as his flat was being ransacked if he had any drugs, he had replied, 'I suffer from asthma, the only drugs I have are for that.' The prosecution case rested damningly on the eleven objects confiscated on that raid.

Brian's defence lawyer James Comyn QC put the case that Brian had suffered a major breakdown and had since been under strict medical care, to which he was responding. He made much of Brian's musical talent and intellect. Dr Leonard Henry was called to speak about Brian's state of health and said that Brian had improved greatly from the agitated, depressed, incoherent man he had been, but warned that he was far from out of the woods yet. Dr Flood also added his professional weight to this testimony.

Then Brian took the stand. In a navy suit with flared jacket and bell-bottom trousers, a polka-dot cravat and cuban heels he faced, as calmly as he could, Judge Reginald Ethelbert Seaton. When asked if he intended relinquishing drugs completely Brian maintained, 'That is precisely my intention.' He told Seaton that drugs had brought him only trouble and disrupted his career and he stressed the wish that no one should seek to follow his example. Obviously Brian was out to save his hide, but he meant every word and in his quiet well-spoken voice he was incredibly eloquent considering his inner feelings.

Comyn also made clear that Brian did not peddle, nor promote drugs. Indeed perhaps wrongly – but genuinely – he had held the belief that if he chose to take them himself in the privacy of his own home, then he couldn't see how he could be committing a crime against anyone but himself. Comyn also didn't fail to draw attention to the glaring fact that charges against Stash had been dropped and that Brian was being made to carry the can for everyone.

None of it was to any avail. He was promptly found guilty. Asking Brian to rise the judge said, 'I am very moved by what I have heard, but under the circumstances nothing less than a prison sentence would be correct.' Despite the fact that Brian's rap sheet disclosed nothing more heinous than peeing against a garage wall, he was sentenced to nine months' imprisonment for, as the occupier of premises, allowing them to be used for the smoking of drugs, and three months for being in possession of cannabis resin; the sentences to run concurrently. The judge also ordered Brian to pay 250 guineas' costs and refused to grant him bail pending appeal. As Brian, stricken, was led away to jail, the court erupted. Journalists mowed down sobbing friends and fans, stumbling stunned from the public gallery to rush off to print the sensational verdict.

Lawyers and psychiatrists, in genuine fear for Brian's actions, went into action. By this time gripping cell bars, white-knuckled Brian looked back at prison officers who took sadistic delight in brandishing barber's shears at him, boasting of how they had been waiting a long time to crop his famous locks. But, after spending a harrowing night in Wormwood Scrubs, Brian was mercifully set free on bail of £750 pending appeal, which had been set for 12 December. Soon, there were street demonstrations against Brian's sentence. One, in particular, led by Mick Jagger's brother Chris Jagger started out peacefully, and ended in ugly confrontation with the police.

In November Judge Leslie Block, who had tried Keith and Mick, overstepped the mark when he addressed a farmer's dinner by making blatantly outrageous references to him having done his best to put away the Stones, supposedly oblivious of the prejudicial effect his outburst could have on Brian's pending appeal. Home Office minister Dick Taverne, one of only two MPs willing to defend the Stones, had something to say to this. He says:

I got into a very public row with Block over that. Earlier in the year I'd already said that the publicity about the charges against the Stones in a preliminary hearing could adversely affect their chances of a fair trial.

Early December saw the disarray continue with the release of *Their Satanic Majesties Request* – at one time *Cosmic Christmas* had been considered as a title – which, just as Brian had predicted, fell on its face. It is best remembered today as an utter catastrophe. Indeed the only praise it attaches relates to a few individual tracks saved by Brian's musicianship. '2000 Light Years from Home' was, many said, single-handedly saved from disaster by Brian's use of the mellotron, investing it with a weird elusive otherworldliness. In the 1970s bands like Emerson, Lake and Palmer would take the concept further, but no one had even thought of this when Brian brought it to the world's attention. Certainly, no matter how sophisticated bands became in the future, none would ever manage to recreate anything like that spiritualism of Brian's mellotron. Depressed or not, he was still leading the field.

This did Brian himself little good, however. Every day was a twenty-four-hour living dread of being imprisoned. He held on, but only just, until the day of his appeal. This time Brian appeared before a panel of four judges, presided over by Lord Parker of Waddington, the Lord Chief Justice. Evidence was again given on Brian's behalf by Drs Henry and Flood, both of whom predicted dire consequences if Brian were sent inside: 'If he is put in jail, it would be disastrous to his health. He would have a complete mental collapse and he couldn't stand the stigma.' They both went on to warn, 'Faced with an intolerable situation, Brian might well make an attempt on his life.'

The court had appointed an independent psychiatrist to examine Brian. Dr Walter Lindsey Neustatter, Senior Physician in Psychological Medicine at the Royal Northern Hospital and Vice-President of the Medica-Legal Society. Dr Neustatter told the court:

He came to my first session dressed in the most extraordinary clothes which one could only describe as flamboyant. I think he wore gold trousers and something which looked like a fur rug. Surprisingly, I found the man inside the clothes quiet and thoughtful with a courteous manner.

Dr Neustatter too confessed to having had difficulty in getting inside the appellant's mind, but he was satisfied that Brian still needed treatment and said that since the appellant had established a good relationship with Dr Flood it would be unfortunate if it could not continue.

The judges were impressed. The nine-month sentence imposed in October was set aside, in favour of a fine of £1000 with three years' probation. Brian was told:

The court has shown a degree of mercy, but you cannot go and boast saying you've been let off. If you commit another offence of any sort you will be brought back and punished afresh. And you know what sort of sentence you will get.

Brian walked out a free man.

The newspapers devoted whole pages to him the following day. Two days later, Brian collapsed and was found unconscious on the floor of his apartment by his chauffeur John Corey. Rushed to St George's Hospital in London's Hyde Park Corner, when he came round he panicked at his surroundings. He trusted no one now and leaping off the bed, insisted on leaving. Less than an hour after admission, against advice he strode out maintaining he was just tired and wanted to go home.

He was, in fact, exhausted. Between 1963 and 1967 Brian had gone on thirty-one tours, a back-breaking round in itself without all the malicious infighting, tension, tussles for supremacy and betrayal. His drug taking and police harassment had thoroughly knocked the stuffing out of him. Emotionally he was drained dry, mentally he was black and blue, and physically the toll on his looks was devastating. Even Alexis Korner who ran across him around this time found it hard to conceal his private shock at the ravages wrought on his young friend.

Yet, according to Janie Perrin, who was closer to Brian than anyone at the time and like a mother to him, as Brian considered his life at the end of the year, he came to the weary conclusion that having gone through every conceivable hell, it could only get better.

NINE

BRAHIM IN JAJOUKA

The very first rock star to have the vision to record ethnic music and see its intrinsic worth, Brian would often say – with perfect frankness – that there were musicians in obscure corners of the world who were playing better than him and would never be heard by a mass audience. He wanted desperately to reach these people, not with any ambition of exploiting them, but rather in the hope of learning from them. With this in mind, Brian decided to return to Marrakesh early in 1968, accompanied by Glyn Johns, to seek out and record the G'naoua.

That same quality of innovation and experiment would show itself when in some Moroccan souk he would suddenly take off at a tangent on the scent of a faintly blowing pipe; and he would end up cross-legged before a street musician watching and listening intently to his playing. Although he couldn't speak the lingo, somehow he always managed to convey his desire to learn. Later, by recording the Master Musicians of Jajouka, he would open up a whole new vista of popular music to the world.

Brian had planned his trip as a positive step to getting back on the relatively straight and narrow, but events still conspired to thwart him.

Before he could even leave London he found himself ensnared in a new set of lurid headlines. Ones – this time – not of his making.

STONE GIRL NAKED IN DRUG DRAMA screamed the damning headline in early 1968. Drug-related anything was the very last label with which Brian needed to be stuck and he was absolutely flabbergasted by what had happened. A former girlfriend of Keith's, model Linda Keith, was a casual acquaintance of Brian's. For reasons best known to herself, Linda Keith went to an apartment which Brian rented for his chauffeur and which she knew Brian was currently using as it was conveniently close to the recording studios. Inside the flat she telephoned her doctor, told him exactly where she was and that she intended to overdose. The doctor promptly tipped off the police who rushed to Chesham Place, broke down the door of the apartment and found her unconscious, in obligatory style, naked and splayed across the bed.

As she was whisked immediately to hospital, the strong winds of scandal had already squalled into a full-scale hurricane by the time Brian blithely walked up to the building, keys in hand, to find it crawling with cops and reporters. He had been working all night and hadn't the least idea of what was going on. Bewildered he announced:

I had been at an all night recording session and when I came back just after twelve, I found the police at the flat. I was absolutely shattered when the landlord of the flat asked the police to have me removed. He said it's because I was trespassing. 'We don't want your kind in this place,' he told me. I explained to him that I rented the flat for my chauffeur and only lived there when I was in town, but he wouldn't listen to me. I've paid six months' rent in advance, but it didn't make a difference. I can't understand it.

Miss Keith made a truly miraculous recovery and was able to sally forth from hospital the very next morning unscathed, while Brian was left buffeting what seemed suspiciously like a manufactured storm, designed not only to rock him, but also to draw unhealthy attention to him. Bad publicity was the last thing Brian wanted to court but since the less he said the better, all he could do was grit his teeth and leave the mess of speculation and London firmly behind him. He took off for Marrakesh with Glyn Johns.

. . .

The G'naoua people are a brotherhood, a religious fraternity originally from the Sudan. Because to Brian black American music originated in Africa, what he had in mind was to tape as much as he could of the G'naoua, then overdub them with a black soul rhythm section and thereby achieve an ethnic as well as a musical statement.

In spite of having buried the hatchet to work together on the score of *A Degree of Murder*, relations between Brian and Glyn were never destined to be any warmer than tepid. Having said this, neither man allowed his personal dislike of the other to blind him to their respective professional expertise. As Glyn admits:

> *For me, Brian as a person was an asshole. But I really respected him as a musician. I went out to Morocco with him and taped the G'naoua. Brian's idea was to take the tapes to New York to use black musicians along with it. It was a clever idea, but in the end nothing came of it.*

The reason for this may or may not lie with the suggestion that a slightly faulty recording machine had been used which picked up an audible hiss on the tape. Of course, had he been so inclined, Brian could undoubtedly have removed the hiss, but in the event he would, in a matter of months, set aside the G'naoua for the Sufi music of Jajouka.

Back at the studio, in any case, his burgeoning interest in Moroccan music was stifled somewhat by the reluctance of the Stones's new producer Jimmy Miller to consider constructively integrating these new and exciting exotic influences, of which Brian was so strongly an advocate, into the Stones's music. Disappointed, Brian tried to compromise by suggesting that if there wasn't scope for its inclusion on the new album, maybe there was a place for it as a separate project? No one, it appears, was particularly interested.

Years later Keith Richards confessed that Brian was always the first to bring in other people's culture and music to the band, to encourage them to experiment. Yet, conversely, Mick Jagger categorically denies that Brian had any exclusivity in his interest in world music. Still, the facts indicate that Brian did take the initiative here and, despite playing the tapes relentlessly to the rest of the band in the hope of persuading them to his way of thinking, he was met – at least to the extent he was searching for – with a closed door. Instead of this sending him into transports of gloom, Brian buried his ideas deep within himself to provide hidden fuel for later projects. The music had stimulated him as nothing else had ever quite done before, and he wasn't about to relinqush that feeling and forget to follow his hunches.

In early 1968, as all this was going on, someone very special to Brian entered his life. Her name was Helen Spittal, a seventeen-year-old college student and from the moment they met their relationship was quite unique. Long inured to fans hanging around for hours longing for just a glimpse of him, when Brian heard from the others that this particular girl had been faithfully perched sentinel outside Olympic studios – three times a week for close on seven months now – determined to meet him, his curiosity was piqued. Especially since it was unflatteringly clear to the other four Stones that no matter how friendly they were to her, it was Brian she was dying to see. Midway through the first week of April she got her wish.

Describing that moment Helen says:

I'd gone straight from college at 6 p.m. as usual to Olympic Sound and waited. Bill, Keith and Mick were all inside and Charlie arrived on his own. He came over to me and put his arm around my shoulders and said, 'It's your lucky night tonight. Brian's coming down.' He just looked at me and smiled as I looked at him in total disbelief. Was I in a tizz after that!

About 8 p.m. a dark blue Rolls-Royce XVH 388 arrived. Anita got out, followed by Suki. And then followed by Brian. I went over to say hello and to see if he'd sign a couple of things for me and I asked him if he'd put 'To Helen' on them. The look and smile I got was as if to say, 'So, you're Helen.' It's difficult to describe exactly how I felt. Relieved, elated, definitely on top of the world. It was so hard to believe. It'd been so long. Yet as we walked over to the studio doors together, it wasn't like it was the first time I was meeting him.

Brian shared that inexplicable feeling. Now – possibly because he had heard so much about her – that he had physically met Helen, he couldn't file her away with his millions of other fans either. And more: some part of him knew that night that she couldn't ever be just another fan to him.

As Brian went back and forth to the studios for *Beggar's Banquet*'s recording sessions, his friendship with Helen Spittal steadily strengthened. Accusations have flown about furiously for years that Brian was utterly incapable of having a platonic relationship with any female; an absurd charge which Helen feels vehemently has been grossly unfair to Brian. She says:

People have such weird and wonderful minds when it comes to Brian. They have said since, was he my boyfriend? That doesn't even bear thinking about. It never crossed my mind, or his. To be honest, I think if anyone had dared to suggest to him that there was anything between us, he would have flattened them.

Although Brian frequently walked about arm in arm with Helen and openly held both of her hands as they talked, his relationship with her was entirely fraternal, even at times avuncular, and was all the warmer for it. He was highly protective of Helen and often came the heavy-handed big brother with her in a way that given the chance he would most likely have been with his real younger sister Barbara. Though he looked forward to meeting Helen outside the studios, he would regularly row with her for her recklessness in crossing the isolated expanse of Barnes Common in south-west London alone, and incessantly kept tabs on whether she was doing her homework properly. Only once did he really fall out with her, and it was such an unpleasant experience that Helen shudders vividly at its memory to this day.

He'd often tell me off about things, usually demanding to know if my parents knew where I was, and such like. But the worst time he had a go at me was one Sunday morning. They had been recording there the previous evening and I'd seen him the night before when we'd chatted a bit before he'd gone in. That morning then I got up at about 5 a.m., walked from my parents' home in Hampton to Twickenham which was about four miles and got the train to Barnes. I walked across Barnes Common and along to Olympic. I knew Brian would still be inside.

Well, Mick came out, followed by Brian arm in arm with Marianne. When Brian saw me he let go of Marianne and just laid into me! 'What the hell are you doing here at this time of day? Have you been here all night?' he thundered at me. 'And just where do your

parents think you are? What must they think of me?' He was so
damned mad! I did manage eventually to answer him that I hadn't
been there all night and that my parents did know that I'd come down
there that morning, but the look he gave me told me never to do it
again. I didn't, I can tell you!

.   .   .

April 1968 fizzled out seeing the Maharishi unmasked as a fraud, his
duped disciples returning forlorn and feeling foolish. And May
brought the release of the Stones's only UK single of the year, 'Jumping
Jack Flash', 'A great song to come back out of the psychedelic era
with,' quote Jagger. Brian, meanwhile, had been having an on-off
affair with Debby Scott, a waitress from Blaise's whom he had met the
previous year. He would ring Debby up and she would instantly jump
to and materialize on his doorstep a taxi ride later. Towards the end of
May, one week after a rather taut and fruitless encounter had resulted
in Debby's flouncing out, Brian once again phoned to ask her over, this
time to his flat in Royal Avenue House, Chelsea.

His nerves were not in good shape. Hungover from the incident
with Linda Keith, he was convinced that the cops, having been
unfairly alerted, were more than ever on his case, spying on his every
move, bugging his phones just waiting to pounce again. It was a very
real and active fear, which produced undiluted but understandable
paranoia. On top of this, to add insult to injury, his self-confidence was
at such a low ebb that he was, for the first time in his life, experiencing
difficulty in making love. His moving morass of inhibitions suffocated
him so badly that when it came to the crunch, he just couldn't face it;
and it was thoroughly demoralizing for him to find himself, even
temporarily, impotent.

Debby arrived, but as time wore on the visit proved no more
successful than the previous week. Upset at Brian's erratic behaviour,
she eventually burst into hysterical tears and, unable to deal with her
tantrum, Brian just wanted her to dress and leave. He rang a friend to
ask her to come over, whose arrival saw the distressed Debby whirl
out. Not more than sixty minutes later Brian, now alone and ferreting
in the fridge for something to eat, was busted for the second time.
Freezing at the thunderous blows raining down on his door, he took

one squint through the security spyhole and then dived for the telephone.

Les Perrin answered his phone at once to hear Brian shout, 'They're comin' in through the windows, Les!' He wasn't entirely exaggerating. A policeman was actually, at that very second, climbing with awkward determination into Brian's flat via its interior rubbish chute. The date was 21 May and no one close to Brian can believe that it was anything but a bad bust, and Les, in BBC Radio 4's *Story of Our Time*, sticks to his guns in his claim that it was dodgy.

I remain convinced of that. I had phoned Brian from Chichester to tell him that a friend of mine had told me that he was going to be busted. He said, 'Well, there's nothing here for them to find.' I said, 'Well, if you have, get rid of it.' He stressed, 'There's nothing here for them to find!'

Brian's father also firmly believes in Brian's innocence. In that same programme he says,

I am absolutely convinced and shall always remain convinced that Brian was unjustly convicted of the second of his drug charges. Brian was innocent of that charge and I base this mainly on the fact that the very night it happened he rang me up in a state of great distress because he was deeply concerned about how his affairs were affecting the family, and he swore to me that he was innocent of it and he hoped I'd always believe him. I promised him on that occasion that I believed him and nothing has ever, or will ever change my mind.

Most damning, however, were the actions of the police once inside Brian's flat. Janie remembers how:

The police broke into his place, came in through the refuse chute. They asked him did he have any balls of wool, skeins of darning wool or something that might contain drugs. Brian was very indignant, very angry even. 'What the hell would I be doing with balls of wool?' he barked.

Just then the police officers searching the other room found what they had come looking for. A lump of hash stuffed – lo and behold! – in a ball of wool. Janie continues, 'Brian just couldn't believe he was being hassled when he was being so careful and not mucking up things after getting back on his feet.'

Later that day Brian was once again wheeled before Great Marlborough Street Court's stipendiary magistrate charged this time with possession of forty-four grains of cannabis resin. He was released on £2000 bail pending trial, once again before Inner London Sessions. Of course, he also faced the aggravated offence of breach of the probation order placed on him on appeal of his first conviction.

Whoever was behind the second bust, it points to a deliberately cruel and callous attempt to crush Brian. He had been trying so hard – staying off drugs and coping with life with a clear head – and was succeeding in putting his house in order: he wanted to rebuild his life. Thrilled with the Stones's new, more earthy single 'Jumping Jack Flash', his attraction to Moroccan music was also very important and sustaining to him. Moreover, although he loathed the regular visits to his smug probation officer, he was sticking to them, and in the studio his contributions to *Beggar's Banquet* were outstanding. The album released at the end of the year would be universally hailed as Brian's 'singular triumph', with critics extolling his remarkable and clever arrangements with the addition of new musical textures with mandolin, marimbas and more. He didn't deserve the knock delivered by his second major brush with the legal establishment.

.   .   .

In May an announcement had been made regarding a Jean-Luc Godard film to be called *One Plus One*. It was to feature the Rolling Stones and their music. As summer got under way, yet another film was announced: *Performance*. It would star Anita and Mick. Keith was now to have a taste of the feelings under which Brian had buckled. It was an erotic film, with the two leads rather realistically throwing themselves into their roles, despite the supposed semi-contempt in which each had previously professed to hold the other. Donald Cammell, who directed the movie with Nic Roeg, once recalled, 'While we were shooting at Lowndes Square Keith hardly ever came near the house. He'd sit outside in the car and send in messages.' Shades of the crippling jealousy which had cut Brian to ribbons little over a year before.

Even though it was suggested that Keith strongly suspected that the love scenes in the film were not being entirely faked, just like Brian before him, he couldn't bring himself to accuse Anita outright. His spleen spilled out, again like Brian, by withdrawing his labour. He was to have been collaborating on the one Jagger/Richard song for the movie, but because of his sick fears he couldn't bring himself to do it.

All those around saw what was happening, and it must have been acidly ironic for Brian to see the same charade being enacted all over again, only this time to someone else. It also must have, at least to some degree, left Keith with a better understanding of the damage that his elopement with Anita had inflicted on Brian.

Perhaps it did. And, perhaps it was indicative of an inner turmoil that he could now relate to Brian's pain, that he was beginning to feel some belated sympathy for his fellow musician and former friend awaiting trial again and on a trumped-up charge, for he offered Brian the chance of relaxing at Redlands in the quiet anonymity of the countryside. Surrounded as he would have been by daily reminders of Anita, it is doubtful whether this would have had a very beneficial effect on Brian, yet he accepted, and for a time stayed there – at the Tudor home complete with mulched moat – with Suki.

This wasn't for very long, though. Brian's eternally itchy feet inevitably caught up with him again. As his plans for the G'naoua tapes had faded into the background, now at the forefront of his thinking was what Brion Gysin had told him about Jajouka.

Approximately two hours' south-west of Tangier, located in the Ahl-Sarif province of Morocco, lie the lower Rif mountains. From the town of Ksar-el-Kebir a road goes to the tiny village of Tattoufte from where, by donkey, civilization is left behind to travel inland up into the mountains to the ancient and remote village of Jajouka.

Brion Gysin had opened the restaurant A Thousand and One Nights within the walls of a beautiful palace in Tangier specifically for the purpose of bringing the Jajoukan musicians to the city to play. Held in the highest esteem by the people of Jajouka, in those days he was the only person permitted to bring strangers to the village. A proud, but warm-hearted people steeped in ritual, the Master Musicians play their Sufi music by appointment to the princes of Morocco and Saudi Arabia. In that summer of 1968 Brion Gysin took Brian to the village at the invitation of Hadj Abdesalam Attar.

Perfectly aware of being extended their highest honour, Brian was overwhelmed. In turn, his arrival among them had a most profound and traumatic effect on the villagers. He was one of the first outsiders ever to go there, and certainly the first person to arrive looking as he did. Abdesalam's son Bachir Attar was just seven years old, a shepherd boy as normal out with his flock that day when his younger brother, Mostapha, came running full tilt, bearing the strangest tale. Bachir remembers, 'When Brian came to my village, it was the first time somebody had come and everybody looked at him because he looked different.'

Dressed in what was normal for Brian, his sensational sweeping Ikat robes, he must have been a truly startling sight indeed. His long, heavy blond hair made an indelible impression on everyone, and on Bachir, in particular. He was the first hippy they had ever seen, and turned Mostapha totally incoherent. Bachir continues:

My little brother, he comes to me and he says, 'Somebody come with big hair in the village!' Well, we don't know about the people with big hair. I said to my brother, 'Keep the sheep here.' I want to run to see this man, to see how he looked. My brother stayed with the sheep and I went back to the village. I ran, and I ran, to see my father and I see the man with big hair. I shake his hand and he looked great!

Greeting his host's eldest son, clasping the tiny hand and kissing his cheek, Brian had no notion of just how dynamic an impact he was having on the lovely bright-eyed boy. Today Bachir openly admits, 'I love him! Blond man with big hair like a hippy!' It was a deep, abiding affection which transcended far beyond the hero-worship of an adoring and impressionable shepherd boy. Abdesalam and all the musicians found Brian to be someone worthy of their respect – something not lightly bestowed. His whole personality, zest, and sheer inquisitiveness about their culture and music, his genuine need to understand them, not to mention his extraordinary ability to pick up one of their ancient instruments and actually be able to play it, earned Brian their everlasting love.

That night they laid on a great dinner for their honoured guest. One goat was killed for the occasion and Bachir, sticking to Brian like gum to a shoe, distinctly remembers when the goat was slaughtered and shish kebabs were proffered, how strongly Brian reacted. 'Brian Jones', he says, 'turned to Brion Gysin and said, "Now I'm eating my liver!"' – meaning he was the blond man, blond like the goat they had just killed: his given name of man like the goat seemed to fit. After the

177

lavish dinner, the musicians then performed part of the sacred ceremony of Boujeloud especially for Brian.

As that night he watched the villagers perform segments of the
night-long ritual of Boujeloud, with headphones clapped to his head
and assisted by sound engineer George Chkiantz, he recorded what
amounted to genuine folklore, all the while its fascinating rhythms
feeding intravenously into his blood, tapping him with insidious
power. 'Brian danced along with the melody of music wildly,' recalls
Bachir, 'crazily, as if in a trance.' Swept away on the hypnotic tide, this
went on for hours throughout the night, well into the following
morning.

Whatever sounds or vibrations Brian heard and felt there, whichever nerves were struck high in the rarefied purity of that stunning
mountain village, only he can know. It was, nevertheless, something of
deep and lasting importance to him, and his fascination with Jajoukan
music was rooted that night. The musicians instinctively knew this. To
every last villager Brian is someone who did a great deal for their village
and their music. 'He is the one,' Bachir emphasizes, 'who brought
beautiful things for Jajouka. We all see him as the one who opened the
door of the music of Jajouka to the world. Meeting Brian Jones
changed my life.' Hearing Bachir's sincerity, it is impossible not to
accept the stark omnipotence of this simple statement.

Brian only went once to Jajouka and spent just that one night
there – yet this was enough. Undrugged, apart from the kif they all
smoked, he was in excellent form. He hadn't been so together for a
long time and both Bachir and Brion Gysin found him a pleasure to be
with. An exchange of souls between him and Jajouka happened that
summer, leaving behind in the village, to this day, a reverence for him
which sits squarely in sainthood and investing in Brian, till his death,
something he had long been pursuing – without quite knowing what it
was.

Brian left the next day for Tangier and wrote then of the Jajoukan
ceremony and its lead singer:

*She and the others are singing not to an audience of mortals but rather
they are chanting an incantation to those of another plane and while
we were recording her she hid her beautiful voice behind the drum she
was playing. It was not for our ears.*

What Brian had planned to do in 1968 by bringing Jajoukan music to the world's attention was to explore, develop and integrate it into the language of the modern masses, to give it the platform it richly deserved and as a consequence to turn the current musical tide which for him was beginning to ebb. Bachir declares:

He was a great musician. The greatest musician in the world I can say. Some day somebody will come to bring out this music of Jajouka to the world and to carve the memories of Brian Jones. Somebody will come. I have a feeling for that.

Still today the children of the village sing his song and when the musicians wish to pay tribute to Brian we sing along too.

That song, sung in Arabic Moghrebi is called 'Brahim', meaning Brian:

When Brahim Jones was with us the people of the
village didn't know what was going on.
When Brahim Jones was with us we were all very
happy.
He recorded our music for the entire world to
hear.
Jajouka has power from the Saint, Sidi Hamid
Sheik is buried there.
Brahim Jones left us, but we will never forget
what he did for us.

Back in London Brian listened to his precious tapes over and over again, playing them forward, backwards. He played them over and over to the rest of the band, determined – despite their continuing apathy – that this was where the future lay. He wasn't wrong. It is worth remembering that twenty years later the ears of the tired music world turned to ethnic music for inspiration, the Stones themselves belatedly realizing that the Master Musicians had a contribution to make after all, when in 1989 'Continental Drift' on the *Steel Wheels* album show cased the musicians. Back in 1968, though, Brian was isolated in his thinking. It wasn't until two years after his death that his work surfaced in the posthumously released album *Brian Jones Presents the Pipes of Pan at Jajouka*.

179

. . .

The Stones's album *Beggar's Banquet* by now was well under way. Abandoning his mellotron and flutes and the beloved Moroccan pipes, Brian returned to pure bottleneck blues guitar with all his passionate elegance, defining as a result the very best tracks on the classic album.

Time, though, was marching on and soon Brian's trial was upon him in June. Appearing before the same Judge Reginald E. Seaton who had sentenced him to nine months the previous year, Brian was extremely nervous. Testimony was heard of how Brian had reacted when the police arrived to turn over his home and a temporary detective told of finding the accused sitting on the floor with the telephone, about to ring his lawyer. When Brian was shown the search-warrant and asked why he had not instantly opened his door his alleged response was, 'You know the scene, man. Why do I always get bugged?'

The circumstances in which the temporary detective who went unaccompanied into a bedroom and apparently discovered the lump of hash in a ball of wool remain, in many minds, wide open to conjecture. And, after all, Brian's only response had been: why? Why was he being persecuted this way? The wool wasn't his. The flat until recently had been occupied by an actress. Brian's contention was that the wool certainly did not belong to him. He didn't darn socks he told the court, in a spark of facetious irritation, and he didn't have a girlfriend who darned socks either.

Brian's highly skilled QC Michael Havers drew shrewd attention to the unprofessional, not to mention dubious, excitement exhibited by the officer who had apparently unearthed the drugs. It was a possibility this could have been construed, as Havers carefully suggested, as being undue excitement on the officer's part. Furthermore, the actress had been checked out in Los Angeles. She agreed that the wool could have belonged to her, but clearly not that it contained any drugs.

Under Les Perrin's guidance, for his appearance on the stand Brian had dressed soberly in a sedate grey pin-stripe suit, white shirt and dark paisley tie. His distinctive blond mane, however, there was no way of toning down and it stood out a mile – almost accusingly – in the drab courtroom. Though Brian was petrified of being found guilty and receiving a prison sentence, which he would undoubtedly be made to serve this time, he kept his head well during cross-examination, the only ragged edges showing in the venomous looks which from time to time would connect between Brian and the prosecutor. For his part, Dr Flood again testified for Brian, maintaining that he firmly believed Brian would run a mile from a reefer. During the proceedings Mick and Keith also arrived in the public gallery, an occasion described as being like an assembly of the Younger Brothers. Certainly their arrival gave the impression, at least publicly, of their support for Brian – albeit silent.

Brian ought never to have been found guilty – even Seaton in his summing up virtually directed the jury to find him not guilty. But there is that something in us that wants to see privileged people punished, a puritanical steak which needs them to suffer for their sins and, nothing daunted, the jury came straight back with a guilty verdict. Brian had just about had it.

Reginald Seaton had appeared uncaring and callous last year in the teeth of appeals for clemency in sentencing Brian to nine months. As he rapped his gavel this time Brian, most of all, expected the worst. Seaton said:

Mr Jones, you have been found guilty. I am going to treat you as I would any other young man before this court. I am going to fine you and will fine you in relation according to your means. £50 with £105 costs.

With fine irony he added:

You will have one week to get up the money. Your probation order will not be changed, but you really must watch your step and stay clear of his stuff.

Reginald Seaton had, it appeared, been utterly disgusted with the jury and their blind determination to find Brian Jones – the Rolling Stone – guilty despite the paucity of hard evidence. One court reporter seasoned in trial coverage admitted that he had never in his career seen a magistrate show such open contempt for a jury.

The judgement was an enormous weight off Brian's mind. Reunited with a tearfully ecstatic Suki, he emerged to his delirious fans grinning wide but inwardly relieved to have it all behind him. Disappearing into the cavernous luxury of his Rolls-Royce, he was smoothly driven away. But the harassment had taken its toll mentally and, though he tried valiantly to shore it up, outwardly at times it was all too apparent. Keith once hit out:

They really roughed him up, man. He wasn't a cat that could stand that kind of shit and they really went for him like when hound dogs smell blood. There's one that'll break if we keep on. And they busted him and busted him. That cat got so paranoid at the end, like they did to Lenny Bruce. The same tactics. Break him down. Maybe with Mick and me they felt, well, they're just old lads.

But it wasn't only the police harassment and pursuant paranoia that was getting to him. His troubles were far too complex to be collapsed into such a neat package. Although he had a steady relationship going with Suki, Brian had never recovered from Anita's desertion. He had really loved her with a desperate destructive love and since losing her he had had many lovers; he had acquired, even allowing for gross exaggeration, quite an extraordinary harem of rainy-day women. But emotionally he was hollow: the groupie girls meant no more to Brian than they did to any other rock star. Females he could command at a crease of his wide graceful mouth were no more than intimate strangers, and Brian was too intelligent not to know that. His trust in women had bottomed out so much that at times he preferred the company of whores. There, the lines were clearly defined. Cynically, he was paying for what he was getting. There was no pretence of affection. Ronni Money agrees:

Yes, he was incredibly vulnerable. I remember he rang me at work one night and it was so sad. He just said, 'Ronni, I'm really lonely. Can you send me a girl?' Well, God, I ask you!! Can you imagine it? There were literally thousands of girls dying to be with him. But it wasn't what it sounded like. He was just so low.

I knew a girl, Dawn, and sent her round. She was there all night and next morning was overcome. She told me, 'He was so sweet and gentle. He didn't want sex. He just wanted to sit and talk. He said he had no one to talk to! He gave me money – a lot of money. At first I wouldn't take it, but he insisted. It was very important to him that I took it somehow.'

His *RSG!* mate Michael Aldred once touched on this.

One begins to doubt whether any relationship is for real. One's own authority is constantly undermined by the fact that one has an image.

182

When somebody comes along instantly like that – prepared to give themselves 100 per cent – it can strike you as superficial and totally dishonest. To be a musician, though, one is always striving for some kind of self-honesty – then I think one is constantly made aware that it's a terrible close thing between reality and illusion, and it becomes so finely edged that one cannot tell the real from the unreal. And I think Brian was seeking honesty from others that probably he couldn't find in the groupies. Although he did have stable relationships. I don't think he was narcissistic but a lot of girls did look like him. I think he was finding he had to rely more and more on himself.

Pat Andrews picks up on this vital vacuum in Brian's life:

By now he was surrounded by people who were with him for all the wrong reasons. They wanted something from him, to bask in his limelight. He was aware of the falseness, I'm sure, and that would've hurt. I know him. He'd have seen through them instantly. But what could he do? That was the life he was in by then.

Pat is adamant that though Brian in one sense was hoist with his own petard, yet the sexual buccaneer, with the legendary reputation as a lover slavishly attached to him, far from reflected the true goals he wanted to score in life. Speaking as the girl who knew first hand, right from the start, of his ruling passion in life she was quite forthright.

The ideal life for Brian always was, and would've remained, to be able to devote all his energies to his music, to be in control of it and where it was going. As for the rest? Well, sex would function as a necessity for him. He would've wanted to have sex without the tangles of a relationship, which was time-consuming for him. And yet make no mistake. At the same time he probably more than anyone I've ever known really needed true feeling and commitment in his life. He needed compassion – very much.

Janie looks further back in Brian's life for the answers.

He was extremely unhappy as a child and growing up. Brian desperately needed to be close to his parents, but it wasn't there. Where were his parents when he needed them? At times when he would phone me, I used to think, why isn't he telling this to his mother or father? Brian really needed love, and not a mamby-pamby love. He needed someone to be firm but loving with him, to listen to him, to feel close to and be real with. Yes, he loved flattery. Adored it. Who doesn't? But it's true. He saw clean through the ones who'd tell him how wonderful he was. That wasn't the love he ached for.

And those self same people, who were busy telling him how marvellous he was, were also busy being really rotten to him behind his back.

Suffocated at every turn, Brian turned his eyes to the country. Cotchford Farm, the former home of A. A. Milne, author of the immortal *Winnie the Pooh* books, was up for sale. Brian went down to see the American couple, the Taylors, who had placed the beautifully secluded estate on the market.

The moment Brian set foot on Cotchford, his heart was lost. Says Suki, 'When we first saw the house we loved it instantly, and Brian bought it literally five minutes later.' Brian had one important proviso. In taking over the house, he stipulated that the purchase was on condition that he managed to inherit the continued employment of a woman who came in daily and carried out whatever work was required in the house: no Mrs Hallett, no deal. Mary Hallett's long service and commitment to Cotchford Farm were invaluable to the smooth-running of the house and happily she agreed to stay; with his terms met, the bargain was closed on 21 November 1968. For the princely sum of £30,000 Brian became the proud owner of Cotchford Farm.

. . .

Beggar's Banquet was released at last on 5 December, after all the delays and disputes with Decca – over the cover design in particular, for which the Stones had wanted a depiction of a graffiti-covered urinal – and to mark its launch the Stones held a beggars' banquet in the Elizabethan Room of the Gore Hotel, in London's Queensgate, complete with serving wenches and a guest list which included a number of other friends from the media. A lively affair to start with, it ended with a custard pie battle in which no one was respected or respectful. Brian caught in a moment of spiteful retaliation, thwacked a pie in Mick's face with what everyone there agreed was just this side of brute force. Relations between Brian and the other four Stones were by this time like petrified wood.

Despite their public conviction that Brian had been framed, Brian still felt that privately the others blamed him for having been busted at all, and a decidedly Arctic atmosphere existed on top of all the other hidden stresses and strains within the band. Despite this permafrost, Brian's work, in particular on slide guitar, has gone down in the annals of pop music as one of the most glorious and mournful sounds in all of rock, perhaps reflecting his isolation and inner unhappiness. Robert Palmer wrote in 1983 in *Rolling Stone*, that Brian's work on *Beggar's Banquet*:

> Did not sound remotely like that of any other musician – black, white, living or dead. In black folk culture slide playing has always spoken volumes. He must have outdone himself on 'No Expectations', because the song's story was his story, the feelings his feelings, as he could never have expressed them himself.

A week later Brian took part in what turned out to be his very last recording with the Stones – never screened at the time – when they shot the *Rock 'n' Roll Circus* over two days at Wembley Studios for Independent Television. Mick, in a ringmaster's outfit, looks decidedly ill at ease with the tiger held at the end of a chain. The audience in fluorescent lime, yellow and orange capes looks lethargically bewildered, obviously exhausted by the 48-hour shoot – while Brian, in a purple velvet jacket and gold trousers with a lamé sash about his waist, is simply flat bored as he glances idly around him during the limp rendition of 'You Can't Always Get What You Want'. Thoughtful and detached, above all, he cannot camouflage the overriding strain etched on his face. He must have been wondering why he was hanging in there at all; close-up shots of him reveal an unnamed, unvoiced, but unmistakably deep hurt.

Other guests musicians noticed this too. Ian Anderson of Jethro Tull, while aware that he had no personal knowledge as such of the set-up, could still detect as a discerning spectator that for Brian the occasion was very far from comfortable. He tells me, 'Brian appeared to me, as an onlooker, somewhat ostracized, both musically and socially, from the rest of the Stones.' Careful to avoid any unfairness to the others, yet Ian opines, 'Doubtless the Stones view that particular period with a mixture of sadness and perhaps guilt.'

It was now an open secret that deep rifts strained the Stones. Says Alexis Korner:

> He [Brian] had lost all contact basically with the band. I can understand both sides of that very well. I think the band tolerated

Brian for a long time. And I think Brian tolerated them for a long time. Because he loved all the success and everything. He really loved that, over enjoyed, over indulged it perhaps. But at the same time he thought he should be playing the blues with a capital T and capital B. And it was a form of treachery to him to be so successful doing this.

Whether it did come down purely, or even mainly, to such an artistic agony of conscience or not, Brian knew deep down he couldn't put off grasping the nettle indefinitely. But, it had been yet another stress-filled year and he was tired of doing battle with everything and everyone. The breather came when they all split to go their separate ways for Christmas. As Mick and Keith took off for Lima in Peru, Brian, taking Suki, headed for Ceylon. While there, he mulled from a happier distance over this dilemma: to exist any longer in a vacuum would destroy him. Rumours talk of a conversation which John Lennon allegedly had with Brian at the Rock 'n' Roll Circus during which Lennon, seeing his friend's plight, had advised him to jump ship and strike out on his own. If true, this must have created an even more intense whirlpool in Brian's already overloaded mind.

In any case the ravine was unbridgable now. Much has been made of Brian's failure to turn up at recording studios and that, when he did, he was less than willing to exert himself. But for Brian his direction was now just too diverse from that which the other band members and entourage were hell-bent on pursuing; to have the necessary impetus to put his back behind music for which he had no feeling was totally beyond him.

Had Brian had the emotional make-up just to get by without any personal goals or ambitions, then his road in life would have been a breeze. But, his calibre of person asked more than this: he was highly talented in his own right – his vision stretching beyond what the Stones had already achieved, to see what they might still be capable of doing. He was as much cursed with the role of being unable to be a passenger, as he had been blessed when the undisputed leader and firmly in the driving seat. Given the frailties of his insecure, sensitive personality, it is hardly surprising that, as long as he did shy away from striking out on his own, he would be hypersensitive about going into the studio with the others. It was there he felt that his presence swung dramatically from being either not wanted, or irritably required. His breaking-point wasn't a million miles down the road.

While in Ceylon, just before the year's end, on a visit to an astrologer said to have worked with Adolf Hitler, Brian supposedly received a bizarre warning: 'Be careful swimming in the coming year. Don't go into water without a friend.' Cotchford Farm, his brand new home, had a beautiful outdoor swimming pool.

TEN

BRIAN JONES QUITS THE STONES

B rian saw in the New Year with Suki in Ceylon and it kicked off to a sour start. Resplendent in a vivid pink suit, psychedelic tie and round tinted specs, he ended up having a right royal falling out with a hotel manager in Kandy who, having taken one look at him, had written him down as a waster. Furiously Brian had lashed out, 'I work for my living. I have money and do not wish to be treated as a second-class citizen!' Being seen as second rate in Ceylon, though, might not be so bad as having a second drug conviction in Britain, to which Brian returned in early January with the hope of having it overturned. Aggrieved at having been charged at all and with two convictions barring his visa requirements to the United States, he was worried that his professional life was now at risk. The appeal, however, was denied.

At the back of Brian's mind throughout the appeal was the thought that, instead of standing in court, he ought to have been 2000 miles away in Jajouka. It was their annual festival which takes place on the Aid el Kebir which follows the moon, when the Rites of Pan are performed. As Bachir Attar explains:

Brian wanted to play the part of Boujeloud. My father said, 'Yes!

Come and dance. Do it.' No one had ever been invited before. But Brian couldn't come.

No one was angry with Brian for not coming. Then Allah took him away. He died before he could really help us.

Tired of the harassment and pressures of city life, Brian moved out of London and took up residence in Cotchford Farm. He had purchased more than a country seat. Chris Barber explains:

I was very much affected when I discovered Brian had bought Pooh Corner. You see, we Englishmen are brought up on Winnie the Pooh and it's a dream of most men to get close to that house. Brian had done it. He'd managed to fulfil a childhood dream to actually own it – something the rest of us could only long for.

Brian did love his new home. Dating from the fifteenth century, its unique character had been moulded largely by A. A. Milne who had converted it from three workers' cottages before adding several sympathetic extensions. The author's wife was responsible for creating the terraced gardens out of what had basically been a hillside meadow, and had planted most of the trees. Brian would wander about his generous gardens, gravitating often to the waist-high sundial with all the Pooh characters meticulously carved around its chunky pedestal. Legend had it that the original manuscripts were buried beneath it and stooping over it, leaning his forearms on the top, Brian would drift off into reverie, cocooned by the resonance of the tale.

Janie knew just how deeply Brian cherished his home:

Yes, he adored the sundial all right, but the thing he was really most proud of was the private lane. There's a private lane beside the house which nobody can come down and this tickled Brian no end that he had this stretch of lane that only he could walk on and where he could be alone. I said to him once you'll go there one day and find it packed with people looking over at you. It was the wrong thing to say! He got quite upset!

His arrival at Cotchford to take up residence there had been cloaked in enormous secrecy. Rumours flew on the farm about the identity of the new owner. Gardener Mick Martin says:

Well, we knew the new owner was coming, but not who he was, and I well remember we hid in the shrubbery to watch the car come down the little hill towards the front of the house. But we were done out! The windows were all darkened and we couldn't see a thing. When he got out, the only way I can describe it is, it was like seeing a teddy bear step out. He was this great big round ball of fur coat and fur hat, and none of us was any the wiser.

Retiring to the potting shed, it was two hours before Shirley Arnold appeared to inform Mick Martin that he now worked for Rolling Stones Incorporated. As Mick confesses:

I must admit when I discovered he was one of the Rolling Stones I was ready to quit on the spot. But I didn't. I went down into the kitchen for the first time to meet him and because I had been in private service all my life, it was always second nature to say, 'Yes, madam' and, 'No, sir.' And so, of course, I went forward and said, 'Pleased to meet you, sir.' Well! Brian absolutely hit the roof. He really was very angry. He said that under no circumstances was I ever to call him sir, that he was Brian and I was Mick.

Suki had moved in with Brian and the new house and her company proved a much needed escape from what was happening in London. In the band trouble was brewing over Allen Klein's gradual move towards the Beatles. Klein, having approached Lennon, had subsequently taken over all EMI's business interests in John. Within days, George and Ringo had followed. Only Paul held out – he wanted to hire New York lawyer and prospective father-in-law Lee Eastman as manager. However, Klein had his way and became their manager. Put out by the associated neglect, the Stones were not pleased by this turn of events.

The filming of Nicolas Roeg's and Donald Cammell's *Performance* too was running into snags and in the end most of it ended up on the cutting-room floor. Jagger had been offered a second film part as Ned Kelly, the nineteenth-century Australian bandit, in the title role of Tony Richardson's production. Marianne Faithfull was to be cast as Kelly's girlfriend, which delighted Mick. What Mick was not pleased about, however, was the fact that, with Brian having bailed out of town into the country, now he had become the target of police harassment. Now he sampled for himself the bitter taste of the persecution with which Brian had had to contend. Any car in which he travelled was fair game to be stopped at a glance with demands for a search. Jagger soon reached the stage of smartly winding up the windows, locking all doors and screeching down the car phone for his lawyer. The cops were out to bust him and Marianne, and it was a salutory lesson indeed to confront personally the malice of the chase and realize how Brian's reactions hadn't deserved to be dismissed as a hopelessly neurotic.

In the midst of all this something else of even greater impact evolved: cash-flow pressures were beginning to nudge the Stones into rolling once more. Their finances had never been straightforward and their astronomical expenditure required constant topping up, which ought to have been a formality, but between one complication and another it wasn't as simple as that. When they received the tempting carrot of £100,000 to play a season at the Las Vegas Hilton, the itch to get back on the road was aggravated a thousand fold.

Faced with their situation, they became determined to tour and the fact that Brian – with two drug convictions – would be automatically denied an entrance visa to the United States was no deterrent. The idea to shelve Brian already in bud soon blossomed now there was a legitimate reason to support the decision. As recording of the new single, 'Honky Tonk Women' went on at Olympic, this was a topic of intense debate. As this cocktail was being shaken, Brian was happily ignorant, rusticating in the country, away from the heat of life. 'At last he was happy and laughing again,' says Suki. 'He had gotten over the drug trials and all the hang-ups he went through. He had really got himself together.' Suki in any event did not reign long at Cotchford, leaving abruptly, by springtime she had moved out.

Yet, life at his retreat was good. For a start it was healthy country living, aeons away from the countless luxurious but impersonal hotel suites. Here, flanked by his devoted dogs, a black and white cocker spaniel called Emily and Luther – after Martin Luther King – a daft lollopping Afghan hound, Brian could roam free in his own grounds without fear of being molested or snapped at from behind every lamppost, even speculate about the enticing prospect of acquiring some horses, to add to the multiplying family of Cotchford cats. Above all he was surrounded by sincere and genuine people who were not demanding or condemning of him, and to whom he was able, and more than eager, to respond.

The hard shell which hid the real Brian began to disintegrate and he became extremely popular with the villagers of nearby Hartfield. He often hung out at the local pub The Hay Waggon where he would shoot pool, knock back a beer and generally pass the time of day with the other customers. Apart from his way-out clothes, he was just another young man drinking at the bar, one who was gradually regaining his looks and beginning to feel the strain drain away at last.

At the farm he enjoyed both the respect and love of his staff. Mary Hallett, in particular, was extremely close to her new hippy boss. Mary had a growing family of her own to see to, but she gave what hours she could spare each day to keeping house for Brian. Mary remembers:

> *Brian was very thoughtful and kind. He would always stop to help me if he saw me moving a heavy piece of furniture and when he went out to buy things for the house, he would call me in to see what he had bought. Once I admired such a lovely little table. At once he said, 'You do like that table, don't you?' I replied, 'Oh, it's beautiful.' 'Then you shall have it,' Brian said, and he gave it to me. It's one of my most treasured possessions.*

Born on Cotchford Farm estate in 1911, Mary moved with her family to a workers' cottage at the end of the lane when a Mr Davies lived in the big house, prior to A. A. Milne. Having worked for the American couple, the Taylors, who took over from Milne, when they prepared to sell up, Mary Hallett, unlike Mick Martin, was gripped with a mixture of edge and excitement when she discovered that the new owner was an infamous rock star. Brian had asked her personally if she would stay on and work for him, before he made a firm commitment to buy Cotchford Farm and so she was privy to his arrival before the other villagers. 'I did wonder what life would be like,' Mary confesses, but the man she found was, in her own words, 'sensitive, lovable and very loyal – much too trusting of people'.

In his first real home Brian enjoyed loafing about, playing his guitar and singing to his heart's content, formulating the many ideas knocking about in his head. He took his responsibilities there seriously too. Says Mick Martin:

> *He talked to me about my wages, and he was obviously willing to give me more, but I said I was quite happy with my money as it was. The only problem I had, which I'd appreciate his help with I told Brian,*

was with transport. And he was very good. He bought me a little Mini van and I had to laugh because he swiped a cap from the Metropolitan Water Board and gave it to me, joking that I could be his chauffeur now.

It was a whole new world to Brian, where things never ceased to amaze him as Mick continues:

He took an active interest in the farm and had definite ideas of what he wanted. But I remember the time he had some new potatoes growing and a late frost was forecast. One Sunday I took my wife and a friend and we covered them with straw. Brian came out and saw us and at first didn't recognize me. He came right up and said sharply that it was a private garden and what was I doing there. Then, when he did recognize me he couldn't get over the fact that somebody was prepared to come out on their day off and do something for nothing. It's just like the first time he saw me carrying logs into the house and he came straight over to me and asked if I minded taking logs in for him. He was a first-class bloke and a super boss.

As the warm weather stole over Britain in 1969 and everyone got set for a sweltering summer, Brian's old enemy reared its head again. Surrounded by acres of fields and flowers, his asthma returned often to plague him quite badly. It hadn't seriously troubled him for years but, just as it had as a child, at times he would be so short of breath that he could scarcely speak. It didn't panic him. He had his respirators, one in every room, as well as the one he always carried with him. But it undoubtedly frustrated him.

This handicap didn't deter him in any way, however, from forging ahead with his plans to organize himself a music room in which to begin to put his ideas into practice. Brian turned the room – which had always been the lounge – into his sound room. Luxuriously carpeted with french windows facing out to the sparkling pool, it had a huge beautiful fireplace where big logs burned and crackled, giving off a woody fragrance. Installing tape decks and equipment, wheeling in his vast array of expensive instruments, he was all set to go.

Falling into something of a pattern, he would usually sleep till mid morning, then hole up for the afternoon in his studio, escaping from time to time into the grounds, deep in thought about how his music was coming along. In the evenings he would normally have guests in, by which time his staff had finished for the day.

193

. . .

Work had lately begun at Cotchford and Brian had been sent Frank Thorogood, an employee of Rolling Stones Incorporated, who had previously carried out renovations for Keith Richards at Redlands. The number of casual labourers, and their exact impact, if any, is unspecified, but certainly their presence had an unsettling effect on everyone. No one appeared either to like or trust them. Staff, friends, even Brian himself, seemed unconscionably edgy of him and the other workmen. Why he let them stay on, even carry on with the work they had been contracted to carry out, was beyond everyone's comprehension – although many people felt that the workmen all considered Brian a soft touch. They would spend more time partying, with drink and women picked up from town, than doing what they were more than generously being paid to do. But, after all, Thorogood and company were working directly for Rolling Stones Incorporated, so perhaps it was not simply up to Brian to fire them, paid as they were by the company and not by Brian himself.

Another reason at least for Brian's lenience may have been that even though he felt that he was being ripped off, at times it gave him, in theory anyway, the comfort of activity around him. He wasn't a man who liked to be entirely alone. But, allowing for these possible explanations, their continued presence is even less acceptable knowing that what little work was carried out, was not done so well. As Janie explains:

> Brian phoned me up another time, upset that the work was going all wrong. He said, 'A beam's fallen down in the kitchen.' I said, 'Well, get them right back this minute to fix it.' But Brian didn't like to. I don't know, he just wasn't the type to demand that they put it right. Now!

And so it went on. No matter how much Brian would moan and groan about them, he wouldn't or couldn't fire them. Brian even allowed Frank Thorogood to live in a flat over the garage at the top of the drive – having been advised by Thorogood that it would be more efficient and convenient for overseeing the work – although Brian was never pleased about that either.

Within himself, however, Brian was very well. Despite the peculiar propensity of the press at the time to perpetuate his image, taken from old photographs, as bloated and bleary eyed, he was not the broken-down wreck as which he was portrayed. True, he had taken a pounding both physically and mentally in the recent past, but rest was what he had needed, and rest was what he had at last allowed himself to take – and it was already more than apparent that he was healing. He still carried more weight than he was comfortable with, but it was coming off slowly and amounted to nothing extraordinary, of which time would have taken care – especially once he got the better of his drinking. Most importantly, however, he was clear of drugs. Indeed not only had he finally kicked the habit, but he had become obsessed – to the point of paranoia – with making sure that no one else took any drugs near him or his home. All of this went hand in hand with his new, calmer outlook on life as a whole. He felt so strongly about it that he asked his gardener if he could come along to the Bible class that he ran for local youngsters. He told Martin:

I'd like to come one Sunday, Mick, to talk to your kids, to tell them that to them it might look like I've got all the money I want, that I can go anywhere and do anything, but my life till now has been rotten. I know it seems to them a world of complete pleasure, but they should know what it's really like.

His mental agility had also returned in copious abundance and he was once more indulging in harmless happy jokes. Mary Hallett vividly recalls one particular prank he pulled on her:

He was a very interesting man to talk to, but, oh, he did like a joke! One day he was alone and at a loss so he asked me to sit and chat with him. During our chat he said, 'Have a drink.' I said, 'Oh, I don't drink.' He said, 'Have a small one.' I said, 'All right. I'll just have a quarter of a glass.' Brian said, 'You never break your promise, do you? If I get a quarter of a glass, you promise to drink it?' I said, 'Yes.' Well! When he brought it, it was a pint glass!

It was such a lovely drink, though, I drank it all. Well, all was well, until I went to stand up when I had no legs! I crawled home, hoping against hope that the neighbours would not see me. Of course Brian was roaring with laughter!

195

What wasn't remotely funny to Brian was the decision he had come to that he was going to put an end to all his swithering. To quit the Stones then and go it alone would have been like crossing a high wire in a gale, but he had never shied away from challenges. He had a group in mind – again his own group – certainly playing what he wanted, but moreover creating a new music of the future. After all, his vision hadn't played him false before. He had suspected for years that moves would start one day to eject him from the band. Brian was no fool; he was well aware that such moves were on going even then. Also, when it came down to it, he was finally through with bashing his head against a brick wall. His friend Phil May looks back at that stubbornness of Brian's:

Foolishly Brian had kept hurling himself on the spikes. I mean it's well nigh impossible if only one of you in any band decides you want to pull in another direction. No back-up means you're isolated. And Brian had been in that position for a very long time. But he would never lie down to it. He kept battering up against it, and kept getting hurt.

Brian did his best thinking on his private lane at Cotchford, and pacing up and down decided he had been hurt – and had hurt himself – enough. For a long time now, he had been immersed in what he personally wanted out of music and the adrenalin flowing through him was at full strength once more, lending him all the old verve and vitality he needed to harness the cauldron of exciting ideas slowly simmering in his studio. He had also contacted Alexis Korner again, with a view to them working together, and so back into his life had walked his oldest and finest friend.

Around the same time too, a new girl entered his life – a Swedish student called Anna Ann Katherine Wohlin, who bore a striking resemblance to Anita Pallenberg – and a sequence of events came to a head. Mick Jagger announced his intention to accept the lead in *Ned Kelly*, the very day he was busted with Marianne Faithfull in their Cheyne Walk flat by the same CID man who had been suffering withdrawal symptoms since losing Brian. Taken to Chelsea Police Station, Mick and Marianne were charged with possession of cannabis and would appear at Great Marlborough Street court. As this was going on, discreet feelers were put out for Brian's replacement and the Stones decided officially to inform Brian of their decision to boot him out of the band he had started. Mick, Keith and a reluctant Charlie went to see Brian to break the news.

It would appear that financial anxiety played a major part in his proposed expulsion. It was the band's belief that they desperately needed to tour for cash and, according to Keith, Brian was too much of a drug casualty and there was just no way they could seriously consider going on the road again with him. That Brian would also be refused a visa to work in America meant that they simply had to ditch him.

Some sense of realization – that were it not for Brian, none of them would be international stars – seems to have stayed their hand a little. A belated sympathetic understanding too from the now personal experience by Mick Jagger of the agonies of police harassment also came to weigh the scales in his favour. But there was never any danger of them not firing Brian, no matter how it was dressed up. They wanted him out. Full stop.

The offer Klein worked out and put on the table was that Brian would be asked to leave primarily so that the Stones could tour America. Some halfcock idea of hoaxing the press and fans that it would be only temporary floated about vaguely, but basically the reason given publicly was that it would allow Brian to concentrate on his solo projects, like the Jajouka album. On top of his share of royalties, a settlement purported to have been in the region of £100,000 would acknowledge the Stones's debt to his musicianship and personality. It must be said that this was an inadequate sum and nowhere near commensurate with the muscle that Brian was within the Stones. The thrust of his vitality and genius had secured them world fame. Still, this was the deal and it was put to Brian.

Tales that Brian waited until the trio had left before breaking down are as exaggerated as the quote from Keith that 'Brian was already effectively dead when he died, because he was already out of the band' was both callous and wildly inaccurate. Brian may have finally severed from the Stones, but he was far from ready to keel over. Years later, Alexis told Brian's son Mark:

Without a doubt your father felt that a great weight had been lifted off his shoulders once he had finally quit the Stones. He knew what he wanted, and that it was no longer with the band. He wanted back to

*R&B. He was writing songs too and working very hard. I was with
him a lot during this time and he was in very fine fettle indeed.*

Ronni too maintains:

*Naw, naw. All this talk about Brian being crushed is a load of shit! I
was in LA by this time, but Brian and I used to ring each other
practically every week all the time he was at Cotchford and the truth
is he was strong. He knew fine he was leaving long before he did. He
often used to say to me, 'They're wanting me out, Ronni.' And he
wasn't being paranoid at all. It was all matter of fact. We used to have
some real long talks and even on the end of the telephone I knew he
really was off drugs. The high he was in was the real him – the way
only Brian could be when he was excited and fired up about something. Believe me, I could tell the difference. He was his old self all
right. I was delighted for him.*

His spirits in fact were excellent all round. Brian called his father
one night late, full of joy urgently inviting them to Cotchford. Says
Lewis:

*Typical of Brian, we had a call in the early hours of the morning, full
of bubbling enthusiasm about the beauties of his house and the
loveliness of the particular summer we were having at that time. And
he said, 'Come down in the morning.' Well, of course, this was easier
said than done. I mean we couldn't come down in the morning, but I
suppose this was about Tuesday. We did in actual fact go down before
the weekend and we spent that weekend with him. We are particularly
glad of course now that we went and were able to go because we spent
an intensely happy weekend with him. Probably the happiest and
closest weekend we'd spent with him since he was a child. And of
course it was in actual fact the last time we ever saw him.*

· · ·

On 7 June 1969 Blind Faith held a huge open-air concert in Hyde Park,
which gave the Stones the idea to stage one of their own. The following
day the announcement broke officially that Brian Jones had quit the
band and the *Daily Sketch* carried the headline: BRIAN JONES QUITS
THE STONES AS GROUP CLASH OVER SONGS. Janie Perrin confirms,
'There were undercurrents, and Mick and Brian did fall out badly,'

but, she maintains, 'It emerged as a mutual arrangement and really it was the best way anyway, because they had grown their separate ways.'

Les released the official statement on Brian's behalf:

Because I no longer see eye to eye with the other Stones over the discs we are cutting, I have a desire to play my own brand of music. We have agreed that an amicable termination of our relationship is the only answer.

The fans were shell-shocked, but not everyone viewed it as a disaster. Linda Lawrence felt, 'When I heard that Brian had quit the Stones I breathed deeply and prayed that this would be a new beginning for us both. Perhaps for the Stones fans all over the world it was a disappointment, but to me it was the most wonderful news.'

But it was a clumsy break and hardly reassuring. It was also a huge step to have taken, which had its immediate repercussions. Janie says:

The day after Brian had quit I got a long telegram from him. It was more like a letter. We were really worried that time. You know, though, he gave instructions that the telegram wasn't to be delivered to me before 9.15 a.m., so as not to wake me. Part of it read:

> I'M VERY UNHAPPY. SO UNHAPPY, I'VE DONE
> THINGS. BUT I'VE SORTED OUT THINGS
> FINANCIALLY AND MORALLY. I'VE DONE THE
> BEST I CAN FOR THE PEOPLE I LOVE. I
> LOVE YOU AND LES VERY MUCH.

I phoned him right away and asked, 'Are you all right?' Brian replied, 'Yes, I am now. I've got it all off my chest.' I asked him what he was going to do that day and he told me he was going to write more music. He was also planning a trip to Morocco again. It was just something he had to get out of his system, that was all. Yes, he was sad. But it was the sadness you feel when a phase, even if it's been a bad one, is over. He had doubts naturally about whether he had done the right thing, breaking from the Stones. But then he was very into his own music and it was reaping results.

Janie has no doubt whatsoever that what Brian had experienced had been no more than a natural wobble in confidence. She is quite adamant that: 'Brian was always ready to go out on his own, definitely. He always felt he could. He just needed somebody to say, "Yes, you can do it."'

Someone whom Brian could trust to do this – whom he felt was always on his side – was Helen Spittal. The following day he called Shirley Arnold at the Stones office and asked her to pass a message to Helen that he would like her to phone him. He had hardly seen Helen since meeting her back in February at the Stones office, when she had presented him with a birthday cake she had baked specially for him. Shirley duly passed on the message when Helen next popped into the office, as she usually did every Wednesday. 'I called Brian that evening,' says Helen, 'and he invited me to come down to spend the day with him and Anna at Cotchford the next day. Thursday the 12th. I can't deny I was nervous about going. Very excited, but nervous. I kept thinking, will I have enough to say to him for a whole day? I needn't have worried. Brian kissed me on the doorstep and with his arm around my shoulders took me straight inside to meet Anna.'

Brian was by now very much at his ease – more calm, confident and positive than Helen had ever seen him. Tactfully, Anna left them alone and taking Helen's hand, Brian slowly walked her proudly around his massive grounds, plucking at the blossoming rhododendrons as he teased and joked with her. 'He was so happy!' Helen recalls. 'He was extremely positive about his own new band and rabbited on about the type of music he would be playing and a lot about Alexis – his help and friendship. He was so fired up, you couldn't help but feel his excitement rub off on you.'

About his quitting the band Helen remembers that he said, 'The Stones don't want me.' I told him he was being daft, but he just looked at me and didn't say anything more about it. Maybe he was trying to get me to delve, maybe then he would have said more. With hindsight I wish I had, but I didn't. But having said that, the beauty of it was not being a Stone wasn't bothering him in the least.' Winding their way back to the house, Brian casually remarked that when he died he wanted to be buried there. Helen says, 'I was horrified. I told him straight not to be so flaming morbid but he laughed and said he didn't mean it like that. He meant it was such a beautiful and peaceful place that he wanted to be there always.'

One thing Helen did notice was the amount Brian drank that day: 'Yes. It was clearly still a problem with him, but it wasn't as if he drank ALL day or anything like that. It's just that he didn't eat. He told me he wanted to lose weight, so he wouldn't eat. I was itching to tell him to cut out the drink and eat sensibly then. But I kept quiet.' For all that Brian was very relaxed. He had no need to put on airs and graces for Helen and was looking rather scruffy in a black and white hooped T-shirt, black and red vertically striped trousers and tatty sandals, as he posed carelessly for her clicking camera – photographs he made her promise she would never publish.

In many ways he had found a sounding-board in his young friend for how he really felt about his life right then. Even his feelings about Anita, though still raw, were much diluted from those dark and desperate ones of 1967. 'He only once went a little sad,' Helen confesses. 'He told me about Anita being pregnant and begged me not to tell anyone. The pain in his eyes was so obvious and then he just went quiet. He really did love her. But he said he didn't hate Keith and that they couldn't help falling in love. But he was hurting beneath it all.'

Though it would have taken an earthquake to blight that special day together, it is worth nothing that Helen did carry away with her two highly disturbing memories. Just like Janie Perrin, Helen completely failed to understand why Brian tolerated Frank Thorogood with whom even she, still so young, couldn't help but sense Brian was distinctly unhappy. Says Helen:

At one point Brian and I were up in his bedroom. He was looking out of the window at Frank swanning about, acting as if he owned the place, and he began talking to me about him, saying that he just wasn't doing anything he was supposed to. I said surely he must have a contract he was tied to and couldn't he get his solicitor to do something about breach of contract to get Frank off the premises. But it was no use. I guess it was for the sake of peace and quiet, but Brian just let things carry on as they were.

The other peculiarity arose when at one point in that hot breeze-less day a taxi driver turned up at the house to deliver some prescription tablets to Brian. 'Brian was most insistent,' Helen rams home, 'that I saw the bottle with him, read the details on the label of what the tablets were, the dosage and everything so that I knew there was nothing untoward about them.'

It appeared to be vital to Brian to prove to Helen – although she had no reason to doubt him – that the only drugs he now consumed were legal and above board. Inescapably there is something very unsettling about the fact that Brian felt he needed a witness – somebody he felt to be on his side – who could speak for the fact that he was only on normal medication. After all, Brian read newspapers too and was well aware that he was being portrayed as still doping himself to the eyeballs. Yet, if anything, his determination to stay clean had intensified and such a portrayal was quite wrong. Only weeks before, when Anna had arrived to stay with him he had personally gone through her luggage to make certain that she had brought nothing with her. Not even so much as an aspirin. On top of that, he was now detached enough to recognize the destructiveness of dope in others. Helen says, 'Earlier, Brian had been talking about the Rock 'n' Roll Circus and how he'd never seen Keith as high on drugs before as he had been that day. And he was worried about it. He was really genuinely concerned about it. From experience I guess, seeing the way Keith could go if he wasn't careful.'

Yet most of their day was idyllic as Brian and Helen wandered about the house and grounds together before drifting out eventually to lie by the pool with Anna, marking time for dinner that evening. Sandwiched between the two girls – head back, eyes closed and fingers laced over his midriff – as Brian listened idly to Anna and Helen talk across him about the Stones free concert in Hyde Park, a mere three weeks away on 5 July, with dry facetiousness he broke in quietly, 'They'd probably charge me to get in.' Yet, whatever Brian's feelings about quitting the Stones, the band's machinery marched on relentlessly without him when the following day – 13 June – Brian's replacement, twenty-year-old Mick Taylor was paraded in all his fresh-faced innocence in public at a park photocall to announce his introduction.

Brian's quitting the Stones was a huge talking point, but his were not the only shifting sands at this time: John Lennon, increasingly distant now from the Beatles, could also have been in line for a walk; the Experience had split up in a headline-hitting dust-up between Hendrix in one corner, and Noel Redding with Mitch Mitchell in the other; Eric Clapton had disbanded Cream; and Brian's mate Graham Nash had quit the Hollies, uniting with Steven Stills and Dave Crosby of the Byrds to form Crosby, Stills & Nash. An entire legion of talent was on the move, or at least open to it.

Back at Cotchford Brian was still firing on all cylinders. On his own, he had a new cutting edge. Though his leanings were a throwback to pure R&B, as musical form he knew it was dead meat. Recently he had been impressed with the swamp rock of Creedence Clearwater Revival and daily blasted the farm with the strains of 'Proud Mary', either from his old record player, or thrashed out on his guitar; his eclectic brain was constantly analysing and on the look-out for new musical influences.

But there were practical matters to organize as well and Brian's thoughts turned to cash flow. He had a lot of overheads to meet with the farm, not to mention keeping up his own lifestyle. But he had also to think of financing his future. The promised settlement from Klein was slow in coming through, which made him edgy; however, just before the end of June he got a telephone call to say that it was on its way. Delighted, Brian flushed out Mary and told her, 'We're all right Mrs Hallett, we're all right. My money is coming from America.' He didn't say more than that, and Mary didn't ask, though it was obviously a great relief to him.

Between bouts of coughing in the humid summer heat, he dissolved back into his cool music room, happy with himself. He had very good reason to be so. Lately he had decided on another course of action which improved his spirits. Finally at the end of his rope with Frank Thorogood and company, Brian had decided to purge Cotchford of all the hangers-on, the impetus for which rests largely with a visit he was anticipating from Janie and Les Perrin, with their daughter Stephanie, that coming weekend.

As Janie explains, 'He'd asked us to come down to see his house and I said yes, I'd love to, but I'm not coming if those cowboys are there. Brian said definitely that he had had enough and was going to clear the place, clear the whole place of everyone for good. "It'll just be you and Les – bring Steph – and Mrs Hallett and me." He said, "I'm going to get rid of this lot. I've made up my mind this time."' Brian was very excited at the prospect of playing host to the Perrins.

He had, however, an even bigger reason to be excited. He was blind with enthusiasm for his work in the studio which had crystallized at last. Janie reveals that: 'Brian had just made a single. This was to be his first record since breaking from the Stones.' She says, 'He'd cut the demo and was really pleased with it. It'd actually just newly gone to press.' Aware of its dynamite potential to set alight the pop world by its ears, full of tense anticipation, Brian rang his father to tell him about it. As far back as 1964 there had been occasional rumblings of a Jones single, worked out with Decca, which had never transpired. This time, though, it was a reality. Having passed Brian's highly critical ear, he and it were ready to go just as dawn broke on the glorious month of July 1969.

ELEVEN

A DEGREE OF MURDER?

Tuesday, 1 July was just another sweltering summer day and for Brian further reason to feel pleased with life. Raring to go, he had much ahead of him. Besides his new single, he had now arranged two further auditions for his new group, this time with Carl Palmer and Vince Crane of Atomic Rooster. Palmer and Crane had contacted him and Brian had expressed his interest by arranging for them to come down to Cotchford on the following Thursday. The weekend to come, of course, was his much awaited visit from the Perrins.

His excitement was dimmed though by the thought of carrying out his vow to give Thorogood and company their marching orders. The decision to sack him hadn't been bravado born of booze; he did want shot of them but he didn't relish doing so. Being in his nature to avoid ugly face-to-face confrontations, the thought of squaring up to possible resistance was daunting and it is likely that the arrival of the latest self-invited lodger stayed his tongue that day.

Her name was Janet Ann Lawson, a State Registered Nurse from Gosport in Hampshire, who had been Frank Thorogood's on-off girlfriend since the previous April. The many claims which would quickly mushroom that she was in any way a nurse to Brian are completely groundless: Brian did not know her. She herself emphasizes in a police statement, 'I would like it to be made clear that I barely knew Brian Jones. I first met him about twelve months ago in Chichester. I next saw him on Tuesday, 1 July when I decided to spend a few days in the country.' She goes on to say that feeling sure Frank would give her houseroom for a few days, she had rung him early on the Monday evening of 30 June and agreed with him to come to Cotchford that night. Frank met her at East Grinstead railway station and drove her straight to his flat above the garage at Cotchford farm.

Brian was thus presented with yet another unfamiliar face when his guests arrived for dinner that following evening. According to Anna, the party comprised only Frank, Janet, herself and Brian; she claims that none of the other workmen or their attendant women was present. They had a meal together and some drinks, then around 9 p.m. it appears that Brian was keen to take a swim. Putting on the powerful floodlights around the pool, he changed and went outside, the other three, preferring to carry on drinking, straggled out to the pool side with their glasses to watch.

For two hours, it is said, Brian swam alone in the pool, decisively and confidently – unimpaired by the brandy he had consumed. There is no suggestion that he drank at all during this time and indeed Janet describes him as 'a good swimmer and acrobatic in the water'. He once, according to Anna, came to the side and asked for his squirter – one of the four Riker medihalers he kept positioned at each corner of the pool – 'but he often used it and I didn't think anything about it,' she maintains. 'He used the inhaler and then went on swimming.' Though Brian had wanted Anna to come into the pool with him she refused, telling him that the water was too cold despite the fact that the temperature was at its regular sizzling 80 °F. Somewhere between 11 p.m. and midnight, Frank and Janet left and returned to the garage flat, while Brian and Anna went off to bed together.

After a muggy airless night, Brian woke next morning to one of the hottest days since records began. The pollen count was extremely high, around the Sussex area in particular, and his asthma immediately began to act up. He was accustomed to coping with attacks, however, and so stayed very quiet, regulating the use of his inhaler and speaking only when he had to do so. Undoubtedly it was not one of his better days. Mary noticed his breathing was very bad that day because of his asthma. She remembers:

> *I didn't see much of Brian that morning, just really the once when he did his best to tell me that he had people arriving who would be staying that night. It was hard to understand what he was saying.*
>
> *That was the last time I saw Brian. I left around 1 p.m., but I never dreamt, that last time we spoke, that anything like that would happen.*

Around the estate, work went on pretty much as normal. As usual, Frank Thorogood made his regular weekly Wednesday pilgrimage to London, and Janet Lawson stayed in the flat alone until his return around 6 p.m. Around lunchtime Tom Keylock telephoned from London to discuss Brian's plans with him for his forthcoming holiday. Then for the whole afternoon he contented himself watching the tennis on television with Anna at his side, and his dogs as ever around his ankles.

As if Tuesday night had been a rehearsal for that evening, the same scenario would unfold as Frank and Janet joined Brian and Anna for drinks and a swim. His guests, whom Brian specifically made a difficult effort, despite choking with asthma, to warn Mary he was expecting, never arrived – in any case they have never been accounted for. It is from early evening onwards that accounts of what happened now begin dramatically to fray. The sequence of events over the next six hours, however, are crucial to what led up to, and ultimately caused, Brian's death. The three statements of Anna Wohlin, Frank Thorogood and Janet Lawson form the nucleus of the only official testimony of events and alone are as reliable as a sieve, rendered even wider gauge when combined with the detailed reports from HM Coroner for East Sussex. There appear to be three distinct divisions of evidence: that which is claimed to have taken place; that which is proven pathologically; and that which could be proven legally.

The evening's activities started about 6.30 p.m. Thorogood told the police that on his return from London then he saw Brian, who was his usual self, watching television. After talking together for a while, Brian supposedly asked him to go into the village to buy some booze. 'I went in a taxi to the Dorset Arms,' he says, 'and bought a bottle of vodka, a bottle of wine Blue Nun, half bottle of brandy and half bottle of whisky. I left the bottles with Brian after having a drink [one] with him.' He had vodka, Brian brandy and Anna wine. 'I left then and went to my flat which is close by,' he adds.

Anna, however, doesn't bear him out. Her version is that she and Brian, after having watched yet more television that evening, had eaten a light snack and, as the time approached 10.15 p.m., were on the point of going to bed. There is no mention of sending Thorogood out for booze, nor even of that single drink, and certainly no alcoholic consumption while they were watching television. She says, 'At about 10.15 p.m. we were going to bed and then Brian suddenly said that he wanted to go for a swim. I wasn't very keen and he went over to Frank's flat and came back with Frank and Janet.' This meant that Brian would have arrived at the garage flat at approximately 10.25 p.m.; a time Janet Lawson independently confirmed to the police, but almost an hour later than that cited by Thorogood.

At 9.30 p.m., when Anna states that she and Brian were still ensconced in watching television, Thorogood maintains that Brian turned up at the flat to invite him and Janet to the house for a drink. 'I think it was nearer 10 p.m.,' he then amends, 'because it was dark and Brian had a torch. Janet and I went with Brian to the farmhouse.' But there is a conflict of statement again here as Thorogood asserts that they all sat and watched *Rowan and Martin's Laugh-In* on the television, which finished that night at 9.50 p.m.

Brian's physical condition on arriving at the garage flat attracts disparate comment, but at least here Anna and Frank came close to tallying. Anna at this point has Brian as cold sober, while according to Frank he had had the one drink roughly two hours earlier – he makes no claim that Brian was in any way drunk when he turned up at the flat. But, Janet Lawson doesn't agree. Describing Brian's intention to rope them into coming to the house she remembers that, 'Brian guided us back to the house with a hand torch. It was clear that he was unsteady on his feet as the light was unreliable. He seemed to be talking quite sensibly, I believe about the drainage system. Nevertheless, it was obvious that he had been drinking.'

Once at the farmhouse and grouped around the dining-room table and the drinks tray, Brian, according to Thorogood, had a second brandy, while he stuck to vodka. Once again Janet says different, maintaining quite specifically that Brian's state was now deteriorating: 'Brian attempted conversation, but it was a little garbled.' This is odd as only minutes before she had sworn he was talking sensibly. 'He excused it', she continues, 'by saying, "I've had my sleepers", or some such phrase. From this I gathered he had taken sleeping pills.' Neither Anna nor Frank back this up and, far more conclusively, the autopsy would reveal Brian had not taken sleeping pills.

Roughly half an hour later – just past 11 p.m. – Brian is said to have been keen to go swimming. Just like the previous night, after putting on the pool floodlights, Brian got changed into his swimming trunks. Only tonight Frank did likewise and Anna also put on her swimsuit. Janet, saying it wasn't a wise thing to do, decided not to join them. Anna went in first, accompanied by Brian's dogs barking at the edge, and swam up and down waiting for Brian to join her. Depending on whose account is believed, Brian was by now either merry and keen on a dip, or downright pie-eyed and determined against any advice to swim. Frank swore in his police statement that 'Brian was staggering but I was not too concerned because I had seen him in a worse condition and he was able to swim safely. He had some difficulty in balancing on the diving board and I helped to steady him. But this was not unusual for him. He went in off the board and I went in the shallow end. He was swimming normally.'

Janet Lawson, however, once again disagrees. 'I saw that Brian had great difficulty in holding his balance on the spring board.' She maintains to the detective sergeant heading the inquiry into Brian's death, Peter Hunter, 'Frank was doing his best to assist him, but not very successfully. Eventually Brian flopped into the water and yet despite his condition seemed to be able to cope and made his strokes to the deep end. His movements were sluggish.' For a relatively short space of time all three – Anna, Brian and Frank – swam in the pool, while Janet, by her own curious admission, felt it necessary to hide herself in the surrounding shrubbery to avoid their repeated calls for her to join them.

In terms of accuracy it is impossible to establish just who did what next, and in particular to ascertain who was first to leave Brian's side. Gradually, over the next ten minutes, though, Anna, Janet and Frank – even Brian's dogs – were to disappear off to the house. None of the three statements confirms the exact sequence, except that the women and the dogs left before Thorogood. According to Anna she got out of the pool because the water was too hot to cool her. With a remarkably symmetry to the previous night, she says Brian came to the side of the pool and asked her for his inhaler. After using it, he carried on swimming as she went indoors. Specifically she states, 'After a while I went up to my room to get dressed, leaving the two men in the water and Janet at the side.'

But Janet unwittingly contradicts Anna's version of events. She claims that 'She [Anna] had been drinking, but appeared capable to care for herself. I felt reasonably assured that they were all able to look after each other. I returned to the music room in the house and played a guitar. I heard Anna return to the house and talk to the dogs as she went upstairs,' meaning she, not Anna, left the pool side first.

Thorogood's version is different again: he maintains that both women left the pool together. Yet, all are agreed at this stage that, with the two women in the house, Thorogood was alone in the pool with Brian.

About ten minutes passed before Janet, who took particular pains to stress throughout the police investigation that as a nurse she had felt it her moral duty to be responsible for the others' welfare, decided she had best check on the pair in the pool. Seeing they were all right, she returned to the music room. She estimated later that Frank was half an hour alone with Brian before tragedy struck.

What happens next – within no more than a handful of minutes – is so chaotically conflicting as to edge on farce. Not one of the three people with Brian that night can corroborate where they were, and why, when Brian died. Nor even remember who first plunged into the pool to pull him out. Anna claims, 'While I was in the house the phone rang. I answered it. It was for me. I heard Frank come in then and he picked up the phone in the kitchen. I told him the call was for me and he put the phone down. Then I heard Janet shout, "Something has happened to Brian!" I rushed out about the same time as Frank. Janet was there and I saw Brian lying on the bottom of the pool.'

There are no details of who had called at such a late hour, or why, but Brian's was an unlisted number and presumably if, as Anna says, she was talking to someone she knew when that panicked shout interrupted them, then her caller would have been aware that something serious had happened, perhaps even been left dangling and anxious on the other end of the line. Yet, there is nothing in the police statements about this and no mention of the caller's identity or indeed any attempt to establish this.

Brian had three phones in his house: one in the music room, and extensions in the kitchen and bedroom. If Janet, as she maintained, was in the music room and that call had been incoming, then it is reasonable to assume she would have heard the phone ring. It is also reasonable to assume that she would have been able to pick up her receiver before Thorogood could have left the pool and walked the thirty-five yards to the house to answer it in the kitchen. Even if she didn't think it her place to answer it, she must have heard it. Yet Janet makes no reference to any incoming call.

She maintains: 'About ten minutes later [after she had checked on them in the pool], Frank returned to the house and asked for a towel. I went to the pool and on the bottom I saw Brian. He was face down in the deep end. He was motionless and I sensed the worst straight away.' Despite being an SRN, Lawson leaves Brian in the water and goes back to the house. 'I shouted under the open window of the bedroom to Anna who was speaking on the telephone. I ran into the house and shouted to Frank. Both joined me.'

The third cog in the wheel, Thorogood, comes up with a completely different version of events altogether. By his own admission, he was alone in the pool with Brian once the women had gone inside. His estimate of how long this was is less than was later established by Janet. He told police: 'After we had been in the pool for about twenty minutes I got out and went into the house for a cigarette, leaving Brian in the pool. I honestly don't remember asking Janet for a towel. I know I got a cigarette and lit it, and when I went back to the pool Anna appeared from the house about the same time. She said to me, "He is laying on the bottom," or something like that. I saw Brian face down in the deep end on the bottom of the pool.'

So Thorogood claims that there was no frantic screech from Janet, no thundering Anna joining him in response to rush outside. He hadn't even left the pool and answered a phone. In fact, he had casually drifted indoors, got a cigarette, lit it and sauntered back outside to be told by Anna – not Janet – that Brian was on the bottom of the pool. It is worth noting here that by Anna's way of it she only knew from Janet's cry that something had happened to Brian, and that she caught up with Frank, equally in the dark, rushing outside to investigate. Yet Frank claims he was calmly on his way back out to the pool, presumably still in his swimming trunks, when Anna dashed towards him from the house, already knowing that Brian was on the bottom of the pool. At this point Thorogood doesn't even mention Janet, or her whereabouts at all. In fact there is not one single common denominator in all three statements, a situation akin to the three descriptions of Brian's rescue from the pool. Who was the first to get him out?

Two of the three witnesses' stories loosely overlap, the third, though, is way off base. Anna says, 'I dived in and got him off the bottom and Frank came in and helped me to pull him out. Janet went to phone for help. Then she came back and said she couldn't get through. I think I must have left the phone off the hook. Then Frank went to phone, and Janet and I applied artificial respiration.' Out of the two women, Lawson was the trained nurse, yet why was it she who did the less vital job of phoning for help?

Janet, as befits her unwitting discord, does not accept this. Her contention is that even as Frank and Anna were hurtling outdoors to join her – alerted by her frantic shrieks – it was she who was already taking action to save Brian. 'I was by then in the water,' she claims, 'but realized I couldn't manage him alone and I shouted to Frank to get into the pool to get Brian out. I returned to the house to use the phone, but I had difficulty as the line was engaged. There were several telephones in the house but I was not sure of the location of them. I returned to the pool to get Frank to use the phone and he and Anna were struggling to get Brian out of the water. I helped and we eventually got him out. He lay on his back and as Frank went to the house to phone, I turned the body over and attempted to pump water out of him.'

The very clear discrepancy in the witnesses' accounts of whether Janet, fully dressed, plunged into the pool or not is particularly glaring. Certainly it is not something one is likely to get wrong. Thorogood, though, loosely squares with Anna. He agrees that 'Anna and I got in the water and after a struggle got him out. His body was limp and as we got him to the side, Janet joined us and helped get him out. Janet said that she had had difficulty with the phone and I went to the house and dialled 999. I returned to the pool and the girls were trying to revive him.' He makes no mention of whether he had had problems too, or of perhaps even discovering that the bedroom receiver was off the hook.

On top of this catalogue of discrepancies, there is one other perhaps not immediately obvious, but nevertheless important, peculiarity: Emily and Luther, Brian's dogs. These same protective dogs were always at his feet and had even been with him at the pool side, until, according to Janet, Anna led them indoors. But what had happened to them? They were not used to being away from Brian for long and it has to be assumed that, with or without Janet's supposed yell on discovering Brian's body, there must have been – at least – a great deal of noisy commotion and alarm. Why didn't the dogs react and hare out to see what was happening to their beloved master? – particularly Luther, as Afghan hounds are notoriously highly strung animals. Since it was never Brian's practice to kennel them, the question of their whereabouts must be raised.

Indeed, a further degree of doubt is interlaced into the fabric of account over whether Brian felt comfortable in Thorogood's company that night. Anna would have it that Brian joked relaxedly with Frank, but Janet, who had only met Brian twice, said in her police statement that she sensed that he seemed anxious about something, to need to keep himself occupied. It seems that deep down Brian was extremely uneasy about Thorogood. Since Monday of that week he had been psyching himself up to getting rid of the workmen by the end of the week. He had been perfectly determined in this, just as he was serious about taking proper command of his life.

Now, tragically, Brian had been cheated of his chance to shed old skins and move his life on. While Anna applied mouth-to-mouth resuscitation, Janet tried external cardiac massage. For fifteen minutes until the ambulance arrived, they say, they tried to elicit some response from Brian. 'I felt Brian's hand grip mine,' claimed Anna, even as it was obvious to Janet that Brian was already gone.

.   .   .

Brian Jones died before July was forty-nine hours old. Already beyond the help of the skilled ambulance crew surrounding his frighteningly unresponsive body, he lay stretched out on his back by the pool as ten minutes into Thursday, 3 July, PC Albert Evans began gathering evidence for the investigation into his grim and untimely death. Rumours of foul play would become rife; wild imagination sewn into sordid speculation, letting loose theory upon jacked-up theory, many accusing the police of a massive cover-up.

However, it now emerges that – far from being guilty of any attempt at concealment – at least one of the officers involved in the investigation of Brian's death was in fact deeply unhappy about its outcome. With clear justification it was impossible instantly to buy the three main statements given that night – each of which conflicts seriously, down to the most minor detail, with each other. The charge of manslaughter would be mentioned, against one individual, who was in particular possibly culpable in the eyes of the law. Nothing fitted. Certainly the tragedy was unexpected and there was no inevitability about Brian's death.

Although the date is given officially as 3 July, the estimated time of death, according to the pathologist, is somewhere between 11.30 p.m. and midnight on the 2nd. Certainly the ambulance crew had already taken over in the presence of Dr R. Evans from Hartfield, before PC Albert Evans – no relation – arrived on the scene at 12.10 a.m. on Thursday, 3 July. It was after this, in the presence of PC Evans, that the doctor pronounced life extinct in Brian and arrangements were made to have his body removed to Sussex's Queen Victoria Hospital in East Grinstead, where he was formally identified to Dr Albert Sachs, the pathologist who would conduct the post-mortem in the presence of the Criminal Investigation Department.

There have been many claims that a time lapse, amounting to as much as two hours, occurred before the authorities arrived on the scene. This claim was soon complicated when, not long afterwards, the *Express* newspaper revealed that police waited vigil by the bedside of a woman patient critically ill in Chichester Hospital. The *Express* item records that 'New evidence on the circumstances surrounding the death of Rolling Stone Brian Jones is being studied by the Director of Public Prosecutions.' It also said that a report was being compiled by detectives in Chichester and continues:

Detectives are anxious to find out from Mrs Joan Fitzsimmons, a local taxi driver, who she drove on the night Jones died, 3 July. The police information is a result of 'several interviews' with men, all acquaintances of Mrs Fitzsimmons and who talked with her after the death of Jones.

If a time lapse did occur, the inference is that this was to allow time to ferry people from the scene before the authorities swarmed in. All attempts to run down the whereabouts or fate of that taxi driver have drawn a blank, but the guests whom Brian had expected that night spring obviously to mind. Yet Anna at no time in her deposition appears to have been aware of any imminent arrivals.

Leaving aside the mystery of the time lapse, once the authorities had arrived, the serious business of investigation soon began. As Brian was a world-famous rock star it was foreseen that his sudden death would attract massive media coverage and so the men assigned to head the inquiry were experienced police officers, Detective Chief Inspector Robert Marshall and Detective Sergeant Peter Hunter.

During his life Brian's relationship with the police had always been notoriously negative and it was now more vital than ever that open minds were kept all round. A very thorough investigation began at once, starting with Brian's three companions that night, all of whom were immediately separated and interviewed at various locations including Cotchford Farm and East Grinstead police station. Given the circumstances of his death, the possibility of foul play had to be uppermost in any efficient detective's mind and, furthermore, no comfort was to be drawn later from the results of the autopsy which was currently under way.

One member of Brian's staff interviewed by the police, and to a certain extent taken into their confidence, is 100 per cent adamant that the police steadfastly refused to swallow the version of events given to them. He says:

The police sergeant in charge told me very definitely that he was deeply, deeply unhappy with the whole situation. He said they were trying very hard to bring a charge of manslaughter.

They couldn't prove murder. But manslaughter. That's what they were after and they poked and poked about for a long time.

215

In British law the definition of manslaughter is: 'The unlawful killing of one human being by another, without malice aforethought.' Malice aforethought is the state which carries the intent with which an unlawful killing is effected; which state must be proved for the crime to constitute murder. Anxieties could only be severely sharpened when the results of the post-mortem carried out that same day came to hand. The pathology report submitted by Dr Albert Sachs, together with the biochemist's report independently carried out by the Royal Sussex Hospital in Brighton, and HM Coroner Dr Sommerville's conclusions on the case make devastating reading. They completely discredit all the claims salient to Brian's condition, and thus annihilate all the main theories about how he died.

After his death it was widely believed that Brian had had some sort of asthma attack in the water, failed to reach the edge of the pool for his inhaler and drowned. And this is easily inflated into the balloon of fact by the irrefutable truth that Brian, with a life history of the disease, had been suffering badly from asthma that day. Contrary to popular belief, however, Brian did not have an asthma attack. According to Sachs,

In an asthmatic attack the bronchi are in spasm. This would tend to seal the lining tissue and prevent the entry of water while the spasm lasted. The viscid adherent mucus in the bronchi which is present in an asthmatic attack was not found. As the interval between his last being seen alive and found in the bottom of the pool face downwards was only five minutes, I feel it is unlikely that he had an attack of asthma at the time of death.

In layman's terms, if Brian had been choking furiously for air, as the result of an asthma attack, it would have been impossible for him to drown. Add this to the fact that Brian was well used to coping with attacks in water – had even experienced attacks while swimming in the sea as a child – was no more than feet away from any one of four inhalers, or for that matter from a side on to which to cling, and the recipe is hardly one for death by drowning. Besides, if he were drowning this way, he would have been making one hell of a racket coughing and splashing about, yet there is no mention of anyone hearing him struggle or indeed of any music playing which might have covered his shouts.

The possibility that Brian died from overusing his inhaler to give him a kick is also categorically ruled out. While there have been cases of deaths following excessive use, there was no sign of inhaler abuse in Brian's body at all. Furthermore, he did not die unexpectedly of natural causes, or from a condition relating to any previous drug abuse or illness of any kind. The reports of his physical state of health have been studied independently by expert medical opinion and Brian was not in any condition suddenly to die.

Far and away the most disturbing truth relating to Brian's death, emerges, however, from the detailed biochemist's report. The favoured belief that Brian was full of dope and booze is a grave distortion of the facts. Brian's blood barbiturate was nil. His blood alcohol was 140 mgs per cent, that is equivalent to $3^1/_2$ pints of beer. Yes, Brian would have been arrested for drinking and driving over the legal limit but, taking into account the important factor that he had been a heavy drinker for a number of years already – which affects the amount a person can consume without it necessarily impairing them – he was, in the words of a doctor consulted, 'definitely nowhere near paralytic'.

Brian was also subjected to thin-layer chromotography, a technique designed minutely to separate and analyse the body's components, and which failed to reveal the presence of any amphetamine, methedrine, morphine, methadone or isoprenaline. What it did reveal, however, is far more alarming: two dense spots, one yellow-orange in colour and one purple which were not able to be identified. Brian's urine revealed an amphetamine-like – not amphetamine, and the distinction is important – substance 1720 mgs per cent, nearly nine times the normal level. The report records that 'These figures suggest ingestion of a fairly large quantity of a drug.'

According to Anna, Brian only drank brandy. Before Brian was officially pronounced dead, PC Evans had gone into the house and immediately confiscated a half bottle of brandy, four-fifths consumed, and had it taken away for analysis, together with a bottle of vodka two-thirds consumed and a half bottle of whisky half consumed. No analysis report, however, accompanied the inquest papers received, nor does it appear that any used glasses were confiscated for analysis.

It is perfectly possible – even easy – to argue that Brian took the drug of his own volition. After all it had become almost a national pastime myopically to see Brian Jones as a self-destructive neurotic pathetically dependent on drink and drugs. But, on close investigation, this doesn't wash. It is true that Brian still had to come to grips with the amount he drank, but from all accounts he was definitely getting there. He was also completely clean of drugs, extremely anxious that no one took them near either him or his home and, indeed, when it came to the pills his doctor had legitimately prescribed him Anna says, 'He didn't like taking them. He was afraid of drugs.' There were also no drugs confiscated from his house when it was searched later. Nor, significantly, were there any drugs in his system, bar that one.

Which brings back the question of what actually happened that night? If Brian were staggering about on the diving board, then it wasn't booze; rather it was from the swift overpowering effects of having recently received one large dose of a drug. It is impossible to establish whether the drug alone would have killed him, but what it would have done was to make him dangerously malleable. On examination Brian bore no internal injuries, no evidence of violence. Under normal circumstances if there had been a struggle, assault, or tussle of some sort, his body would have shown tell-tale contusions and bruises. None was found. Brian was a powerfully built man and, with his senses about him, without doubt would have been capable of formidable resistance.

The theory of Brian simply 'falling asleep in the bath' also arises. Particularly since, after Anna's complaint the night before of the water being cold, Brian had accommodatingly turned up the thermostat to a steaming 90 °F. Certain recent drownings have revealed that warmth combined with excessive drink and drugs accelerates coma and death. But this suggestion rebounds into fiction by knowing it was established pathologically that Brian wasn't so drunk as to be unable to climb out of his own pool. Faced with all this, and three severely conflicting statements, there was no way it could remotely be rubber-stamped 'accidental drowning'. Brian did drown: the frothy fluid around his nostrils, together with the voluminous haemorrhaged state of his lungs which had 'pit on pressure' were fully consistent with this. The big mystery remains how and why? There is still an elusive quality surrounding Brian's death which is as infuriating as it is fascinating, with the endless connotations involved.

. . .

Running parallel to all the ugly conjecture around Brian's death was its shocking reality. His parents, the first to be informed by the authorities, were naturally grief-stricken and shattered. They saw no rhyme or reason to their son's death. In his own brief statement to police Lewis's utter confusion is evident as he says, 'When my wife and I stayed the weekend at his home at that time he was very fit and well. The last time I spoke to him on the telephone he was full of beans.' Just weeks before Brian had proudly propelled his parents around his beloved home. Now, at 5 a.m. on Thursday, 3 July, in a hospital mortuary, Lewis faced the horrendous heartbreak of formally identifying his son's body.

Already numb with horror were his staff, who had awoken to the terrible news. As Mary says, 'In the night, I was aware there were strange noises. I got up and went out into the lane. There, all I could see were flashing lights and police with walkie-talkies everywhere. It was no business of mine so I went back to bed. But next morning I went down and there were all these reporters and photographers.' She goes on, 'The workmen told me what had happened and that I was not to answer any questions.' So great was the shock to Mary's system that to this day all she can recall was mechanically making the place tidy, while all around her people rushed to and fro. 'To be honest,' she confesses, 'I was so bewildered I just wanted to go home, to get away from it all.'

Already well away from it all were the Stones. They were busy recording at Olympic and accounts vary over when they first heard that Brian had died. Said to be stunned, somehow they still managed to carry on recording for some hours before congregating later that morning with the staff at the Stones's office. Some speak of Charlie continually crying, and of a generally dazed disorientation. Yet, peculiarly, it was business as usual, even to the extent of going ahead with their recording that evening's spot on *Top of the Pops*. The priority of plugging their latest single 'Honky Tonk Women' clearly remained unchanged. It was released on 11 July, the day after Brian's funeral had taken place.

It is extremely hard to conceive of the degree of detachment required to allow all this to continue. To many people it was unnaturally remote behaviour, and the decision, also quickly announced, to go ahead with Saturday's open-air gig in Hyde Park came as an even greater surprise. Termed a tribute to Brian, that is not how some closest to Brian saw it.

Pat struggling to cope with her devastation – after having been told the news of Brian's death by a next-door neighbour who had heard it announced on the early morning radio news – personally held the view that the real reason for the band's apparently callous desire to carry on as normal, as if nothing had happened, concerned something very different.

Poor Brian had only been dead two days, he hadn't been laid to rest and his inquest was coming on the Monday. Yet still the Stones – the band Brian had created – could go on up there and perform in public as if nothing had happened! I feel it was vital to them as a band that they shouldn't be seen as being in any danger of disintegrating.

While the press and media had a field day reporting his death, Thursday and Friday blurred into each other as the entire world reeled at the finality: Brian Jones was really dead. Family, friends and fans keened with immeasurable sorrow, as did fellow musicians, many of whom found themselves icily sobered. Seen at face value, Brian had become rock music's very first casualty of riotous decadence. Mick Avory of the Kinks speaks for many of his contemporaries when he says, 'Their reaction was the same as mine. It made them realize it could happen to them if they didn't ease up.'

When Saturday dawned it was to yet more blistering sunshine as the unrelenting heatwave continued, drawing over one quarter of a million people to London's Hyde Park for what was loosely being termed the Stones's come-back concert. Beaded and bangled, the crowd brought joss-sticks and flowers to the world's biggest ever wake. Over 400 fainted in the midday sun, several waded knee-deep in the Serpentine to try and cool off, while others, irrespective of their sex, took MC Sam Cutler's advice to whip of their vests and put them over their heads. With the eyes of the world's media trained on them, the atmosphere was tight as the Stones arrived under heavy guard, their armoured truck complete with swatting outriders cutting a slow swathe into the private enclosure.

The massive stage supported on scaffolding and festooned with giant plastic palm trees began filling up even as it was announced that the Stones were on. In a frilly white knee-length dress over trousers, Jagger led the other four on stage, making an instant appeal for hush. 'Cool it and listen,' he ordered. 'I want to say something for Brian.' As a canopy of quiet descended, he read two verses from Shelley's 'Adonais', before thousands of white butterflies were released from cardboard boxes into the air as the Stones plunged into their first number 'Lemon Squeezer'.

The seventy-five minute act was atrocious and the video makes painful watching. With the exceptional heat, the amplifiers kept going wrong and guitars just got more and more out of tune. A highly emotional event for tens of thousands there, it was heightened further by the gigantic blow-up of Brian's face hoist high above the set. It was also abundantly clear, despite rehearsals, that this was the group's first live performance for over two years. Into the bargain, it was the worst possible baptism for Micky Taylor. He had never met Brian, but was acutely aware that comparisons were inevitable. Visibly uncomfortable, hiding behind his wavy hair he overconcentrated chord by chord and, although understandably nervous, in lilac velvet tunic he stuck out as a bland and unlikely replacement for his dynamic predecessor.

Such concerns, however, were far from people's minds. Still racked with grief, that day Alexis Korner was there only in body. So steeped had he been with Brian – recently acting as his rehearsal manager for his new band – that accepting his death was just impossible. He once said, 'What do you say when a concert turns into your friend's funeral? I suppose you say it was a good funeral.'

But the unfillable void that was Brian's absence had further reaching implications than this. There were those who had already come to their own conclusions. Noel Redding confesses, 'For me it was over. I made a note in my dairy in fact which I've still got today. It reads, "There ain't no Rolling Stones without Brian Jones!"'

The Stones of course would go on, now for over two decades, but many believe more on the strength of their inimitable sixties reputation, than as a continuing, truly subversive force in music. Some twenty years later, looking back, despite an initial three-year burst of creativity culminating in the 1972 album *Exile on Main Street*, it would become apparent that the progressive and experimental genius, which Brian Jones brought in aces to the Stones, was lost for ever. As rock critic Robert Sandall puts it, 'Yes, I would say there is a broad consensus among those who really know the score that the Stones definitely ossified after Brian's death.'

. . .

In more ways than one Brian's death marked the end of an era and the dawning of a new one. The once rebellious group Brian had too efficiently personified suddenly had a whole new look. After the Hyde Park concert their much maligned fans also stunned the authorities. Instead of rampaging over the city afterwards, they actually cleaned up fifteen tons of debris before dispersing, thus considerably lightening the load of the brush sweepers filtering into the park the following daybreak.

It was the next day too that Mick again appeared to act disrespectfully to Brian's memory, by jetting straight off to Australia to take up his film role as Ned Kelly. He was said to have been under severe contractual pressure to do so. Hours later on Monday, 7 July in East Grinstead, the formal inquest into Brian's death opened before Dr Angus Christopher Sommerville. Anna Wohlin, Janet Lawson and Frank Thorogood were all called to give the coroner their version of what was termed 'a drunken late-night swim which ended in death'. As agog journalists packed the sombre magistrates' court Dr Albert Sachs delivered his findings and, after due consideration, Brian was deemed to have drowned, swimming while under the influence of alcohol and drugs. The coroner's verdict on Brian, formally designated 'Entertainer of Cotchford Farm, Hartfield' came down as death by misadventure.

The tragic circumstances surrounding Brian's death ought never to have been collapsed into that single inadequate word. Misadventure means 'accidental death not due to crime or negligence', a state which had not yet satisfactorily been determined. It does not, however, necessarily follow that the findings of a coroner's inquest are materially brought into account when a decision is being made about whether or not to institute criminal proceedings. The fact that misadventure had been recorded did not mean that criminal proceedings were no longer a possibility.

The funeral was set for that Thursday, 10 July, in his home town of Cheltenham. Although a great many close friends, including Alexis Korner, Les and Janie Perrin, John Appleby, Pat Andrew's father, Suki Potier and Linda Lawrence with Julian, joined his family, only two members of the Stones turned up: Bill Wyman and Charlie Watts. With Mick Jagger in Australia, Keith Richards, according to Bill Wyman, was working in the studio. It was, however, a massive funeral. Bill once recalled:

> When we drove through Cheltenham all the streets were packed with people. I've never seen anything like it. It was like a coronation or something. And all his family and relations were all like tranquillized and everything and everybody was cryin' and upset. There were thousands of fans everywhere.

At 1.30 p.m. Canon Hugh Evans Hopkins conducted the twenty-minute service in St Mary's Church, leading the congregation in the hymn 'The King of Love My Shepherd Is'. Speaking first of Brian as the lively blond choir boy he had once been, he went on:

> He was a rebel. He had little patience with authority, convention and tradition. In this he was typical of many of his generation who have come to see in the Rolling Stones an expression of their whole attitude to life. Much that this ancient church has stood for for 900 years seems totally irrelevant to them and yet it is not humbug to come today to offer our prayers on this tragic occasion.

The rector also invoked prayers for Marianne Faithfull of whom news had just come through that she was fighting for her life in an Australian hospital following a drug overdose. Then the cortège of five hearses, four of them laden with flowers, and eight limousines made the mile-long journey to Priors Road, where hundreds more tear-streaked fans crammed the cemetery for a glimpse of the glinting bronze casket crowned in wreaths. As Brian's body passed through the cemetery gates, a constable on duty smartly saluted, an action which choked Charlie Watts as he followed in one of the cars behind. For hours, long after the burial, devoted fans sat cross-legged and bowed at the stark graveside, lost in meditative prayers for their dead idol – reluctant to let him go.

But, even in death Brian had been made to suffer for his cardinal sin of having flouted convention. Father John Heidt, the present rector of Cheltenham's St Philip and St James's explains, 'You see Brian ought to have been buried with us, but my precedessor would not allow it because of the rumour going about at the time of possible suicide.' Canon Hopkins himself refers to Lewis and Louise Jones, even at their darkest hour, having asked him with 'understandable diffidence' whether he would permit their son a Christian burial from the parish church. All of this because Brian had been an unsavoury Rolling Stone.

.   .   .

What was about to take place later that day, however, was infinitely more unsavoury. Among those in church that afternoon had been some of the workmen. They ought to have had no more to do with Cotchford since Brian's death, but, in fact, they returned late that afternoon from Cheltenham to take over his home – on whose authority, it is still unclear.

Although no one was individually identified, a group of them conducted themselves with the shameful irreverence and distaste. One estate worker was livid:

> They went to his funeral, then came straight back to the house bringing their women with them. They drank, laughed and joked crudely and cavorted about. They even took their women into Brian's bed! It really turned me over.
>
> I was out in the grounds and they hadn't even bothered to close the curtains. You just couldn't help but see them in there, in Brian's bed. It was utterly appalling.

Later, lorries arrived and, as one person watched unseen, possessions from all over the house, including the contents of Brian's sound room – with the exception of only one or two of his treasured musical instruments – were methodically loaded.

> Anything of value was being carted out and packed into the backs of vans. And I'll tell you more than that. You used to have to go up to Brian sometimes when he was in bed, because he often slept till noon.

By his bed there was always piles of money, just lying there – tall piles.
If I wanted something, I'd explain to Brian and he would stretch out
and peel off notes and give them to me. All I can tell you is when the
police searched the house they couldn't find a single note. Not one.
Now this had been a regular thing – piles of money by his bed.

The looting wasn't done yet. Sometime soon after that a bonfire
was then set ablaze in the garden. This time gardener Mick Martin
explains:

A group of men were burning an enormous amount of stuff. I know,
because I had a very nice little Bible and they'd flung that on too.
Well, I wasn't having that and went immediately and got it out. But,
yes, they were burning Brian's things – his clothes, shirts and what
have you. I don't know on whose sayso, but they cleared no end of stuff
out of his house and burned the lot.

There is an offensive viciousness to this behaviour, almost like dancing
on Brian's grave.

By now the police investigations were one week old. At that time, in
1969, before the introduction of the Crown Prosecution Services, the
burden lay with the Sussex CID to decide whether or not a criminal act
had been committed. It was always open to them, of course, to refer the
case to the Director of Public Prosecutions, whose task it is to consider, on
the strength of ingathered evidence, whether or not to recommend
criminal proceedings for help in any decision. But despite specific
reference in that *Express* newspaper article to 'new evidence on the
circumstances surrounding the death of Rolling Stone Brian Jones' being
studied by the Director of Public Prosecutions, the matter, according to
R. M. Hipgrave, currently Superintendent of Sussex Police at East
Grinstead, was never referred. Though the investigation continued for
some time, in the end the final decision was taken by Sussex CID alone.
And what was their decision? That, officially, nothing they found
warranted criminal proceedings against any one person.

It is extremely difficult, almost impossible, to understand this
decision in the face of not only the deep reservations privately expressed
by one senior investigating officer on the case, but also the minefield of
inconsistencies which dogged the whole affair. And this puzzle has been
made no easier to solve by its direct conflict with an even higher authority.

HM Coroner for East Sussex David Wadman clearly stated that

Brian's death was investigated by the Home Office in addition to the Sussex police. He warned, though, of any intention to pursue this: 'I am bound to say that I think it is extremely unlikely that you'll obtain any further information. I'm sure they would regard the results of their investigation as confidential.' In fact the Home Office reaction went even further. Strangely they denied any knowledge of having carried out an investigation. A spokesman said, 'We do not have any information touching Mr Jones's death.'

The new probe, which threatened only months later that same year, involving Jean Fitzsimmons, the taxi driver under intensive care, also took a dive. It had arisen as the result of a man having been arrested for an offence at Chichester. Because he claimed to have knowledge of suspicious circumstances relating to Brian's death, DCI Marshall visited him in Lewes Prison, but came to the conclusion that his claims could not be substantiated. This proved just one more dead end to add to all the rest.

AFTERWORD

A s the tangled web of disbelief and unease enmeshed itself around the circumstances of Brian's death, this proved disturbing for everyone, not least his parents. But, Lewis Jones, in an interview after his death, said: 'One must always look for some sign of a silver lining in whatever cloud one is presented with. And one of these silver linings has been the enormous affection in which Brian was held, not only in this country, but throughout the world.' Proof of that undying love would, and still does, manifest itself time and again.

The fate of Brian's single – recorded in that long hot summer just before he died – remains a mystery. Janie Perrin, who held the original demo for years, has it no longer, yet graphically relayed Brian's electrifying enthusiasm for it. Knowing the oft-proved strength and perspicacity of that enthusiasm all too well, Lewis Jones hoped the single would be released posthumously, as a fitting tribute to his talented son, and indeed lost no time in enquiring into the possibility, literally – to the consternation of a few at his timing – straight after Brian's funeral. Sadly, though, his plans came to nought. No Brian Jones single has ever seen the light of day and, extraordinarily, the sheer existence of that precious demo has never been mentioned publicly in the ensuing years.

Brian Jones is survived by three sons – one of whom was adopted and of whom, sadly, little is known. The other two, Julian Mark Andrews and Julian Brian Jones, tell their story here as a fitting tribute to their father.

. . .

For anyone who has ever known Brian, meeting Julian Mark Andrews would be a heart-stopping experience: he is his father incarnate. Not only facially, he has with no contrivance also inherited Brian's characteristics, mannerisms and voice inflections, even subtle expressions down to the tiniest nuance. 'I must confess, it is kind of intriguing,' he remarks with the care he applies to almost everything he says. 'I met Alexis years ago and he was so stunned he spent the whole night just staring at me.'

That sort of reaction is something Mark has become well used to over the years. Yet to look at him and see only a clone of his famous dad would be quite unforgivable. At twenty-nine he has very much an assertive identity of his own, is his own man with his own ambitions in life. Highly intelligent, sensitive and with an ingrained grace as natural as his innate respect for women, he radiates charisma without even trying.

There is also though, for all his magnetic personality, such a tangible wariness in him that despite his impeccable manners one is warned at once that nothing immediately reveals itself with him. For example, it would be hard to imagine Mark raising his voice in anger – a more subtle and effective means of expression would be more his style. His cutting wit hides an infectiously teasing warmth and as he allows himself gradually to unwind, the occasional glimpse he permits of his innermost feelings is enticing.

Today Mark is successful in his chosen field, working for a multinational corporation. 'I've had quite a few different jobs,' he recalls. 'Because I dropped out of university, I didn't get my degree and although I later got my HNC, it's not looked on as the same.' Forever seeking a compromise of earn-and-learn, at one point as an Educational Scientific Technician, he discovered a natural flair for teaching but strongly resisted all suggestion to pursue that profession. 'It's too insular for me,' he confesses.

Mark is very much a studier of life and taps very quickly into the politics of his surroundings. He also has an incredible abundance of energy and is altogether very physical. In his spare time a normal week consists of aerobics, weight training – his first love – jogging, badminton and martial arts. A karate and Tae Kwon-do expert, he is closing in rapidly on his black belt: 'Partly it's self defence, but mostly it's to be physically and mentally fit. Prancing about doing eighty great kicks into thin air to perfection is fine, but I prefer a moving target to connect with.'

It is not the aggression which appeals to him, it is rather pitting himself against himself, to know when he has fought, even if he's lost, that he utilized his skills to their fullest. The all brawn and no brain tag attached to martial arts is something he distances himself from completely. 'I hate machoism. I prefer the company of women to be honest. I'm more relaxed with them. Possibly with not having dad around I hadn't that male dominating figure thing in my life. Whatever, I enjoy the company of females.'

That casual mention of dad is deeply deceiving. Mark is a great conversationalist and will spiritedly debate anything. But without doubt his rawest subject is his father. He knows he is inextricably linked to Brian and accepts the fact, but it is understandably a source of both deep pride and pain for him.

All his life he has come up the hard way. Not only because he has never known the cushion of the financial security which ought to have been his. But worse, he has born the burden of fame without the attendant compensation of all the benefits that this provides. From junior school through adolescence into his working life he has fought with petty jealousy and edged hostility from those who are somehow intimidated by who his father was. And perhaps the ugliest of all – insincerity. Myths also accrete around him. 'I'm expected to hop about in my helicopter, or roll up in the old Silver Shadow. Do you know I was once a pathologist?' he drily cracked with reference to a newspaper article. 'I told the guy I liked *Quincy*!'

This wariness of insincerity has even invaded his private life. Although newly married, he admits to having had to be wary of women. 'There was once this young lady at a party,' he gives as an example, 'whom all the guys were after. When it came to my turn to

229

chat her up she wasn't having me either. Well, I shrugged and went back to the bar. Then my cousin whispered in her ear that she'd just spurned Brian Jones's son. God! Did she make a beeline for me! I was pinned flat to the bar! I don't know quite what she hoped for, but her sudden fierce interest had nothing to do with Mark Andrews. So I guess that was a turning point.' Over the years he has cultivated a shrewd blend of attractive cynicism and a dangerous awareness of people and their ploys. He has been caught off guard. He has certainly been betrayed. But it would take a fool to underestimate him.

Intense ambivalence only begins to explain all the opposites going on inside Mark over Brian. He never has gone about telling people who is father was and not because he isn't proud of Brian. He is. Deeply. But these feelings which he bottles up inside naturally are extremely intricate. In more surface matters he can directly associate with his father, like their mutual dislike of cliques and regimentation. 'I'm not all dad, I'm half of him. But in lots of ways I know how he felt about things. Genetically I'm similar, yet dissimilar. Possibly I'm more confident than dad was.' Musically too Mark though he has very catholic taste will admit, 'I do love R&B which is going back to dad, of course. I love Muddy Waters, Jimmy Reed, etc. I didn't have the chance to learn an instrument, but the saxophone is my favourite. Again because dad's first move was to the sax.'

And yet there is an anti-reaction; a need to stay separate. 'It gives me a thrill and a buzz to know he's my dad. I'd be lying to you to say otherwise. And yet there's this other part of me that turns away and I don't want to know. I want to be me for myself. I can't remember dad at all. The first time I heard him speak was on an old *Ready Steady Go!* clip and when I watch him on TV I have these feelings, sort of a twin syndrome thing. On the one hand he's the dad I never had, so I have this sense of loss. I try not to let it rule my life, but I do feel it. But I love being his son. Sometimes inwardly I feel it sets me apart. Then on the other hand, there I am a son of this famous man but there are all these problems. It carries aggravation which I've had to cope with all my life. It's fame without the positive benefits like obviously money, but also influence and opportunity. So I have a combination of feelings there.'

It doesn't come easy to Mark to reveal so much of himself, and his vulnerability is tempered always with a protective matter of factness.

But the one area he has no hesitation in coming hard down on is Brian's musicianship. 'Without offspring's pride, I rate him very high. When you think of what he did achieve, can you imagine what he'd be doing now? He was a multi-instrumentalist. I mean people like Clapton are good lead guitarists. But dad was a musician!'

It has hurt, angered and often amused Mark to read some of the nonsense written about his father. He has had to adopt a defensive mechanism to enable him to cope. He knows Brian wasn't perfect. He can also see the biggest rub in many minds about him. Being brutally frank Mark explains, 'Why Brian is often classed as a bastard is this. He made his hobby, his life. It was his passion and he was successful at it. People don't like that. It aggravates them. If you make a career out of your love it's too single-minded and when they don't share your passion, they feel left out.'

Naturally Mark has mixed feelings about what happened to Brian within the Stones. He concedes they were all young at the time, but still think they could've handled his dad better. 'When he wasn't able to look after himself, I can't understand why they didn't help him. They say the band is a family. So how can it be like a marriage when you stand by and watch your partner dissolve away and do nothing.'

As for the events leading up to Brian's death, he is even more confused. 'Alexis told me all about dad then, about how hard he was working and how well he was. So I have never accepted the image people have portrayed of him.' Neither does Mark believe that enough was done about it. Mixed up too in all the unsatisfactory mess there is a feeling that in some way Brian's death provided a need for the Stones. 'It almost provided a gem in a way. Today the Stones are still going on the strength of their sixties image. But that's my dad's image. I mean they draw on his imagery. And dad exerted an incredible influence over people.'

Mark's feelings over Brian are diverse. He feels hurt for Brian, yet has been hurt by him too. 'I know sometimes I come across as being callous, but I'm not. Yet, yes, there is a form of bitterness there. At times I feel what happened to him didn't just affect his life. Of course it affected him worst. But it also affected my mum's and mine.' He goes on, 'I don't dwell on it, but there is this – what could've been. Dad did have paternal feelings. He was getting older too and more settled. If he'd lived, given the chance, maybe I'd have gotten to know him.'

Of ambitions Mark was enthusiastic: 'I'd love to travel, learn foreign languages. I'd love to do my degree of course and I'm also into charity work. Basically I just want to try to enjoy life.' With his raw appetite for life anything is possible. But one thing is certain. Were Brian alive today, he would be proud to be Mark's father.

.   .   .

The first major achievement in interviewing Julian Brian Jones is first to catch him, then somehow manage to hold him long enough to talk! An incredibly restless young man, he loves the outdoors particularly the Californian mountains which right now suits him down to the ground. 'I've just bought a piece of land and am busy building a house on it,' he says straight off in a kind of breathless inquisitive tone as he temporarily parks himself down. 'I've no electricity yet, but, hey, I've got a generator.'

That sort of enthusiastic optimism characterizes Julian. At twenty-six he is brimful of confidence, yet charmingly devoid of an ounce of arrogance with it. Warm, approachable and vibrantly alive, there is also an attractively subtle air of challenge about him which invests you with a feeling that, given reason, he could be quite formidable. He is also so disarmingly frank that his first assault on your senses is a lasting one.

As physically fit as he is mentally sharp, everything about Julian's looks is captivating. The immediate strength inherent in his chiselled jawline is quickly compensated by a pair of penetrating eyes, and from time to time an engaging smile will run across an elusively familiar mouth. But his overriding impact has to be his complete openness about his father. His pride in being Brian's son is immeasurable. There is no messing with Julian. 'I'm very proud of my father,' he announces. 'I love him deeply.' As Julian talks easily then of Brian the soft timbre of his only slightly accented voice could lull one into believing he has somehow absorbed his father's persona but this would be quite wrong. For Julian emerges very much as an individual in his own right.

He has a healthy lust for life and is very much wrapped up in the myriad things going on. 'I turn a buck where I can to make ends meet,' he says candidly. 'I work in the studio when I can, help Don [Donovan, his stepfather] if he needs me. I paint people's houses and things like that. Just now my house takes up a lot of my time trying to knock it into shape.'

Mention of the studio produces a definite shift up in gear. Music is very much his driving force. Having bided his time, now he is posed on the threshold of launching his career. 'I've got an album coming out soon,' he reveals with obvious anticipation. Julian performs with an eight-piece reggae band and thrives on the gathering experience. So far he hasn't explored whether he's inherited his father's famous talent. Quite rightly, he makes no attempt to excuse that either. 'No, I don't actually play an instrument,' he says, 'although I have a go at drums. I've got rhythm so I'm told and I love beating into the bongos. But I sing and throw myself about. I enjoy that.'

Having said that, clearly already his forte lies in writing songs. 'I've written a few songs, a couple of them for Brian. One's called "Heavy Inside" which is all about dad and my feelings on the way he's been treated.' The perfectionist in him wasn't quite ready to class it as a finished article yet, but the lyrics are both hardhitting and poignantly tender.

For as long as Julian can remember he has lived in the States, paying frequent visits to his maternal grandparents in England's Windsor. Because his mum Linda fell for and married singer/ songwriter Donovan when he was quite young there is a tendency to feel somehow that he has had it easy. But it wouldn't be true. Certainly theirs is an extremely tight-knit loving family, with Donovan having been a devoted dad to him. No restrictions have ever hampered Julian's always evident even stronger allegiance to his natural father, nor even his remarkably familiar streak of obstinate independence. But still there have been pressures along the way. 'Yes, there have been some hard times in the past,' he confesses, 'but you know, you get over those and move on.'

Julian has also had his share of deeply personal disappointments to cope with. Though it doesn't come easily, he tries hard to attach a generous philosophical approach to the horrendous abuse that he's had to stand by and see heaped on his father over the years. 'I'm not saying it hasn't hurt, because it has. But then what can you do? Life's hard.'

Beneath the surface, however, at times an involuntary vulnerability does escape. An attempt he once made to try and make contact with his other set of grandparents was deliberately denied him by an officious secretary who refused on pain of losing her job to divulge the Jones's address. 'God, I wasn't after Brian's money,' says Julian cut to the quick. 'All I wanted was to have the chance of saying, "Hi, how're you doin'?" to dad's mum and dad before they passed on. They're my blood relations after all.'

Neither is Julian finding it increasingly easy to look with any tolerance any longer at the trials his father faced within the Stones. At fourteen he met the other members of his dad's band for the first time when he had gone along to see a concert. 'Charlie invited me backstage,' he explains. 'It was all very exciting, of course, and Mick certainly was the nicest to me, sort of paternal. They asked if I'd like to go with them on to their next gig at Oakland, which I did. Now, when I go to see them, it's different. I feel, I dunno, a coldness from them. I mean they're civil and that, but definitely cold. And for me? Well, in these past couple of years especially I know I'm changing. I can't help myself.'

Julian would be the first to admit that he harbours barefaced protectiveness and can show plain aggression if he feels Brian is threatened. But it doesn't blinker him. Quite simply he knows what a musical genius his father was and the more mature he has become, grimly the less he appreciates how matters transpired for Brian in the last few years of his life.

Yet for all this his sensitivity is never very far from grasp. 'I remember meeting dad once when I was very little,' he says urgently. 'I was frightened and crying and dad picked me up high in his arms. I can always remember his face as he hugged me close. Sometimes if I need to, I shut my eyes and I can bring that moment back. It helps.'

Nothing helps in the bitter frustration Julian struggles with over his father's death. Direct and quite ruthless, his feelings could do him violence if he let them. Too many questions have plagued him for too long which only leads him deeper into a quagmire the more he tries to work them out. Offsetting these negative feelings he also believes just as strongly that his dad's death has wrongly eclipsed his whole life. 'It's not that it doesn't matter that dad's dead. Far from it. And it isn't helped any by the pall of guilt which seems spread around. But he's gone and it should be his life and all he achieved that should be remembered for his sake.'

In part Julian's answer to that is to have already kicked around in the studio with a few of the Stones's early numbers like 'Not Fade Away' and 'It's All Over Now'. 'They turned out not bad,' he almost sounds surprised. 'What I'm definitely going to do though is put music to some of dad's writings. Over the years folk have passed on to Don some poems and songs that Dad wrote, and Don's given them to me. One poem written for mum in particular I'd like to set to music, so I'll work on that.'

One other area which more than vaguely attracts Julian is acting. As a five year old he starred in a sci-fi movie *Saturation 70*, filmed as it happens not too distant from where he is now putting down roots, and the experience has whetted his appetite for the challenge. 'Oh yes, I'd love another crack at acting. It was so much fun.'

Julian then is a quite extraordinary mix. He is both distinct yet indistinct from Brian. Quite separately he leads an exhilarating, active and full life of his own, yet willingly threaded always with reminders of being his father's son. Just as his past is inexorably linked, so too is his future. His forthcoming album will be bound to be greeted as the launch of Brian Jones's son on the music scene – yet in style, heart and content it is entirely his individual achievement. The juggling act can never have been easy but he seems to have the balance uniquely right.

INDEX